BEYOND BEEF

The Rise and Fall of the Cattle Culture

Jeremy Rifkin

A PLUME BOOK

PLUME
Published by the Penguin Group
Penguin Books USA Inc., 375 Hudson Street,
New York, New York 10014, U.S.A.
Penguin Books Ltd, 27 Wrights Lane, London W8 5TZ, England
Penguin Books Australia Ltd, Ringwood, Victoria, Australia
Penguin Books Canada Ltd, 10 Alcorn Avenue,
Toronto, Ontario, Canada M4V 3B2
Penguin Books (N.Z.) Ltd, 182–190 Wairau Road,
Auckland 10, New Zealand

Penguin Books Ltd, Registered Offices:
Harmondsworth, Middlesex, England

Published by Plume, an imprint of New American Library, a division
of Penguin Books USA Inc. Previously published in a Dutton edition.

First Plume Printing, March, 1993
20 19 18 17 16 15 14 13 12 11

 REGISTERED TRADEMARK—MARCA REGISTRADA

LIBRARY OF CONGRESS CATALOGING-IN-PUBLICATION DATA
Rifkin, Jeremy.
    Beyond beef : the rise and fall of the cattle culture / Jeremy
Rifkin.
        p.   cm.
    Includes bibliographical references and index.
    ISBN 0-452-26952-0
    1. Beef cattle. 2. Cattle. 3. Beef industry. 4. Beef. 5. Beef industry
—Environmental aspects. 6. Cattle trade—West (U.S.)—History.
7. Beef—Social aspects. 8. Food habits. I. Title.
[SF207.R54   1993]
394.1'2—dc20   92-38422
                                                                    CIP

Printed in the United States of America
Original hardcover designed by Eve Kirch.

BOOKS ARE AVAILABLE AT QUANTITY DISCOUNTS WHEN USED TO PROMOTE
PRODUCTS OR SERVICES. FOR INFORMATION PLEASE WRITE TO PREMIUM MARKET-
ING DIVISION, PENGUIN BOOKS USA INC., 375 HUDSON STREET, NEW YORK,
NEW YORK 10014.

JEREMY RIFKIN is an author, activist, and philosopher who is best known for his environmental work and his critique of modern technologies, including genetic engineering. His books include *Biosphere Politics*, *Algeny*, *Time Wars*, and *Entropy*. President of the Greenhouse Crisis Foundation and of the Foundation on Economic Trends, he lives in Washington, D.C.

ALSO BY JEREMY RIFKIN

Common Sense II

Own Your Own Job

Who Should Play God (with Ted Howard)

The North Will Rise Again (with Randy Barber)

The Emerging Order

Entropy (with Ted Howard)

Algeny

Declaration of a Heretic

Time Wars

The Green Lifestyle Handbook (editor)

Biosphere Politics

Voting Green (with Carol Grunewald Rifkin)

Carol,
my love and a friend of animals

ACKNOWLEDGMENTS

I would like to give special thanks to Erik Jansson, the research director for the *Beyond Beef* book. His firsthand knowledge of the cattle and beef industry has been invaluable in the preparation of the manuscript. I would also like to thank several other people for their contribution to the research and preparation of *Beyond Beef*: Anna Awimbo, Ruth Vander-Lugt, Clara Mack, Carolyn Bennett, Beulah Bethea, Helen Mathis, and Jennifer Beck.

I would also like to thank Tom Devine and the Government Accountability Project for their assistance, as well as Andrew Kimbrell for his many helpful editorial suggestions.

Throughout this project my agent, Jim Stein, and editor, Rachel Klayman, have been particularly supportive. Their personal commitment to the issue and to my work is greatly appreciated.

Finally, I would like to thank my wife Carol Grunewald Rifkin for helping me to understand the issues and concerns that have found their way into the book. Many of the ideas that have been incorporated into *Beyond Beef* are a result of countless conversations over the past few years on the cattle and beef issues. Carol's long-standing personal and professional commitment to animal rights has helped inspire this effort. Her depth of knowledge and sensitivity to the issues surrounding the cattle and beef culture have shaped much of my own thinking, and I am grateful for her help throughout the process.

CONTENTS

Part Two—How the West Was Won

Part Three—The Industrialization of Beef

Part Four—Feeding Cattle and Starving People

Part Five—Cattle and the Global Environmental Crisis

Part Six—The Consciousness of Beef-Eating Cultures

Introduction

There are currently 1.28 billion cattle populating the earth.[1] They graze on nearly 24 percent of the landmass of the planet and consume enough grain to feed hundreds of millions of people.[2] Their combined weight exceeds that of the human population on earth.

The ever-increasing cattle population is wreaking havoc on the earth's ecosystems, destroying habitats on six continents. Cattle raising is a primary factor in the destruction of the world's remaining tropical rain forests. Millions of acres of ancient forest in Central and South America are being felled and cleared to make room for pastureland to graze cattle. Cattle herding is responsible for much of the spreading desertification in the sub-Sahara of Africa and the western rangeland of the United States and Australia. The overgrazing of semiarid and arid lands has left parched and barren deserts on four continents. Organic runoff from feedlots is now a major source of organic pollution in our nation's groundwater. Cattle are also a major cause of global warming. They emit methane, a potent global warming gas, blocking heat from escaping the earth's atmosphere.

Cattle and other livestock consume over 70 percent of all the grain produced in the United States. Today, about one-third of the world's total grain harvest is fed to cattle and other livestock while as many as a billion people suffer from chronic hunger and malnutrition.[3] In developing nations, millions of peasants are being forced off their ancestral lands to make room for the conversion of farmland from subsistence food grain production to commercial feed grain production.

While millions of human beings go hungry for lack of adequate grain, millions more in the industrial world die from diseases caused by an excess of grain-fed animal flesh, and especially beef, in their diets. Americans, Europeans, and increasingly the Japanese are gorging on grain-fed beef and dying from the "diseases of affluence"—heart attacks, strokes and cancer.

The devastating environmental, economic, and human toll of maintaining a worldwide cattle complex is little discussed in public policy circles. Most people are largely unaware of the wide-ranging effects cattle are having on the ecosystems of the planet and the fortunes of civilization. Yet, cattle production and beef consumption now rank among the gravest threats to the future well-being of the earth and its human population.

Beyond Beef is the story of a unique relationship forged between human beings and cattle over the millennia of history. We have prayed to these animals, sacrificed them to the gods, and used them to provide food, clothing, shelter, traction, and fuel. They have enriched our spiritual lives and fed our appetites. We have elevated them to divine status, yoked them to the plow to turn the soil, milked them to provide nourishment for our young, and eaten them to gain strength and energy.

Much of the religious and secular life of Western civilization has been erected on the broad shoulders of these powerful ungulates. In early recorded history, human beings prayed to bull gods and cow goddesses. They were the progenitors of creation. They represented generativeness, virility, and fertility. Cattle also represented wealth. The word "cattle" is derived from the words "chattel" and "capital." Cattle are the oldest form of mobile wealth and have been used as a medium of exchange throughout much of Western culture. The devolution of cattle from the status of a divinity to the status of currency and commodities serves as a historical mirror to our own changing relationship to nature. The cow has been a useful projection and metaphor for defining our sense of self in the world as well as a utility for fashioning the world around us.

The human-bovine relationship has come together at various times and in various places to form "cattle complexes," elaborate cultural networks that have helped shape the environmental, economic, and political dynamics of whole societies. While the Indian and African cattle complexes are well known and well explored, little attention has been paid to the great European and American cattle complexes and the pivotal role they played in determining the shape and direction of Western history. These great cattle complexes are responsible, in part, for the mushrooming environmental and economic crises now facing the planet and human civilization. If we are to gain a better understanding of the effects that cattle grazing and beef eating are having on our lives, and the life of the planet, we need to trace the history of the great cattle complexes of Western civilization, examining the myriad ways they have influenced our world view and our world.

In *Beyond Beef*, we will examine the human-bovine relationship throughout history, from the first archaeological records dating back to the Lascaux caves to the assassination of Chico Mendez in the Amazonian rain forests. Parts One through Three will be given over to an exploration of the historical role of cattle in Western civilization. These sections will examine the world's great cattle complexes, beginning with the palace abattoirs of ancient Sumer and ending with the automated factory feedlots on the Iowa plains. Of particular interest will be the forging of the Euro-American cattle complex in the nineteenth century and the "world steer" cattle complex in the present century, and the unique constellation of cultural and historical forces that gave rise to the modern beef culture.

In Part Four, "Feeding Cows and Starving People," we will examine the human impact of the modern cattle complex and the world beef culture. We will look at the new artificial protein ladder that has been erected in this century, with grain-fed beef ensconced on top. The transfer of the world's grain production from food to feed is among the most significant changes in the redistribution of wealth in the whole of recorded history. Its human effects and economic consequences will be examined with an eye toward understanding the enormity of the human tragedy currently unfolding.

In Part Five, "Cattle and the Global Environmental Crisis," we will look at the range of environmental threats that have been created, in part, by the modern cattle complex. These threats differ significantly from the environmental problems of the past. The new threats are global in scale and are beginning to affect the entire biosphere and the very biochemistry of the planet. For a public used to thinking of environmental threats exclusively in terms of automobile exhaust, factory effluents, and toxic and radioactive materials, the magnitude of the environmental destruction caused by modern cattle production will likely come as a shock. Still, the ecological devastation created by the burgeoning world cattle population exceeds many of the other more visible sources of environmental harm.

In Part Six, "The Consciousness of Beef-Eating Cultures," we will examine the psychology of cattle complexes and the politics of beef eating in Western society. Ancient beef-eating myths and dietary practices have been used throughout history to maintain male dominance and establish gender and class hierarchies. In the modern age, beef eating has been used as a tool to forge national identity, advance colonial policies, and even promote racial theory. The role of beef eating in establishing cultural values and creating social boundaries will be explored, as will the role of the cattle complex in shaping the American frontier mentality. In the last part of this section we will analyze the role of the modern cattle complex in the emergence of the suburban highway culture. We will examine the sociology of the hamburger—a uniquely American phenomenon—and assess the moral and ethical implications that flow from the deconstruction of modern meat.

The book concludes with a plea to humanity to move beyond the beef culture in the twenty-first century. Dismantling the global cattle complex and significantly reducing the consumption of beef is an essential task of the coming decades if we are to have any hope of restoring our planet to health and feeding a growing human population.

The elimination of beef from the human diet signals an anthropological turning point in the history of human consciousness. By moving beyond the beef culture we forge a new covenant for humanity, one based on protecting the health of the biosphere, providing sustenance for our fellow human beings, and caring for the welfare of the other creatures with whom we share the earth. I have written this book in the hope that it will contribute to moving our society beyond beef.

Part One

CATTLE AND THE MAKING OF WESTERN CIVILIZATION

1

Sacrifice to Slaughter

Several millennia before the birth of Christ a powerful king emerged among the peoples of the Nile river. Narmer-Menes united Upper and Lower Egypt into a single kingdom, creating the first great empire in Western history. Although he is remembered by historians for his extraordinary military accomplishments, Narmer-Menes's spiritual achievements were no less significant. The new king introduced bull worship throughout his kingdom, creating the first universal religion.

According to legend, the bull god Apis was conceived by a special cow who had been impregnated by a ray of moonlight.[1] The young bull god was elevated to the spiritual throne of the new Egyptian empire, and from this vaunted position he ruled over the heavens and the affairs of society.

The bull god represented great strength and virility and the masculine passion for war and subjugation—an appropriate symbol for the age of conquest. Narmer-Menes ruled over Egypt by the grace of the new bull god. The king, in turn, was worshiped by the people as a bull god, as were all of his successors in the great dynastic reigns of the Egyptian empire. The kings were called "mighty bulls" and "bulls of the heavens." A thousand years after the reign of Narmer-Menes, kings of the eighteenth and nineteenth dynasties were de-

scribed in court chronicles as great bull gods who destroyed their
enemies with their powerful hoofs and gored them with their sharp
horns.[2]

The great bull god Apis shared the heavens with the cow goddess
Hathor. It was believed that Hathor gave birth to the sun itself.
Hathor represented fertility and nurture, the fecundity of the cosmos.
The sky was conceived as a giant cow whose legs extend to the four
corners of the earth and who is held up by other gods.[3] The queens
of ancient Egypt were all viewed as cow goddesses and worshiped
by the people.

Apis symbolized the vigor of youth and everlasting life and was
embodied in a real-life bull kept in sanctuary and attended to by the
priests. At the end of the old year the Apis bull was slaughtered in
an elaborate ritual; his flesh was consumed by the king in an effort
to incorporate the animal's fierce strength, majestic power, and virility into his being so that he might enjoy immortality. The ritual
slaughter of the Apis bull was a time for renewal, for resurrecting
the personal and political fortunes of the kingdom. It marked the
end of the old year and the beginning of the new.

The impending death of the Apis bull sent the priests to scour
the realm for a successor. When a new bull was located, its owner
was handsomely rewarded and the priests immediately placed the
animal in seclusion. For forty days and nights the bull was kept
hidden away. Naked women were paraded in front of the animal to
incite the god and secure the fertility of both the women and land
of Egypt.[4] At the end of the period of seclusion the bull was transported to the holy city of Memphis in a sacred barge inside a golden
cabin. Upon arrival, the Apis bull was enthroned in the great temple
of Ptah, where he occupied a suite of special rooms equipped with
elaborate sleeping quarters. The Apis bull was served special foods
and given holy water from the sacred wells of Egypt. Cows were
kept in adjoining rooms to serve as concubines.

On holy days the bull was adorned with religious garments and
paraded before the people in extravagant processionals. The birthday
of the Apis god was preceded by a week of joyous feasting.

The Apis god was imbued with great powers, among which was
the ability to predict the future. The animal's every movement and
even its demeanor were viewed as signs or omens. The privileged

often paid to spend a night in the temple near the Apis bull so that their dreams could be interpreted with the help of the bull's gestures. It is said that the bellowing of the Apis bull foretold the invasion of Egypt by the armies of Augustus.

After the ritual slaughter and eating of the Apis bull its remains were mummified and buried in a special chamber entombed inside a grand sarcophagus weighing over fifty tons.[5]

Humanity's relationship to cattle has radically changed since the days of Narmer-Menes. Today, the birth of calves begins with "teaser bulls," also called "sidewinders." These animals are used to identify cows in estrus (heat). A teaser bull has undergone a surgical operation that reroutes his penis so that it comes out through his side.[6] The bull becomes aroused in the presence of cows in heat and attempts to mount the females. Because his erect penis is off to the side, he can't penetrate the cow's vagina, but he does leave a colored dye on her rump from a marker that's been hung around his chin. Ranchers use the marker to identify the cows in heat so they can be sequestered and artificially inseminated.

More recently, a new generation of estrus-synchronizing drugs has been developed and commercially marketed, allowing cattlemen to dispense with teaser bulls.[7] The drugs are injected into all of the cows in a herd at the same time so that they will all come into heat simultaneously. The Upjohn Company touts the efficiency and predictability of its own estrus-synchronizing drug with the advertising slogan "You call the shots."[8] By synchronizing the estrus cycles of an entire herd, commercial ranchers can plan ahead, picking the ideal time of the year for the calving season.

After birth, young male calves are castrated to make them more "docile" and to improve the quality of the beef. There are several methods of castration. In one procedure, the scrotum is grasped and stretched out tightly, a knife is stuck up through the scrotum and then used to cut open the sac, and each testicle is pulled out with the long cord attached. In another procedure, a device called an emasculator is used to crush the cord.

To ensure that the animals will not injure one another, they are dehorned with a chemical paste that burns out the roots of their horns. Some ranchers prefer to wait until the calves are older and then use an electronic dehorner with a cupped attachment that cauterizes the horn tissue. With older steers, saws are also used to cut off the horns and the roots, without the use of anesthetics.

Calves enjoy a short reprieve and are allowed to run with their mothers for six to eleven months on the open range before being transported to the giant mechanized feedlots where they are fattened up and readied for slaughter. There are some 42,000 feedlots in thirteen major cattle-feeding states. The 200 largest lots feed nearly half the cattle in the United States.[9] The feedlot is generally a fenced-in area with a concrete feed trough along one side. In some of the larger feedlots, thousands of cattle are lined up side by side in cramped quarters.

In order to obtain the optimum weight gain in the minimum time, feedlot managers administer a panoply of pharmaceuticals to the cattle, including growth-stimulating hormones and feed additives. Anabolic steroids, in the form of small time-release pellets, are implanted in the animals' ears. The hormones slowly seep into the bloodstream, increasing hormone levels by two to five times.[10] Cattle are given estradiol, testosterone, and progesterone.[11] The hormones stimulate the cells to synthesize additional protein, adding muscle and fat tissue more rapidly. Anabolic steroids improve weight gain by 5 to 20 percent, feed efficiency by 5 to 12 percent, and lean meat growth by 15 to 25 percent.[12] Over 95 percent of all feedlot-raised cattle in the United States are currently being administered growth-promoting hormones.[13]

In the past, managers used to add massive doses of antibiotics to the cattle feed to promote growth and fight diseases that run rampant through the animals' cramped, contaminated pens and feedlots. In 1988, over 15 million pounds of antibiotics were used as feed additives for livestock in the United States.[14] While the cattle industry claims that it has discontinued the widespread use of antibiotics in cattle feed, antibiotics are still being given to dairy cows, which make up nearly 15 percent of all beef consumed in the United States.[15] Antibiotic residues often show up in the meat people consume, making the human population increasingly vulnerable to more virulent strains of disease-causing bacteria.

Castrated, drugged, and docile, cattle spend long hours at the feed troughs consuming corn, sorghum, other grains, and an array of exotic feeds. The feed is saturated with herbicides. Today 80 percent of all the herbicides used in the United States are sprayed on corn and soybeans, which are used primarily as feed for cattle and other livestock.[16] When consumed by the animals, the pesticides accumulate in their bodies. The pesticides are then passed along to the consumer in the finished cuts of beef. Beef ranks second only to tomatoes as the food posing the greatest cancer risk due to pesticide contamination, according to the National Research Council of the National Academy of Sciences.[17] Beef is the most dangerous food in herbicide contamination and ranks third in insecticide contamination. The NRC estimates that beef pesticide contamination represents about 11 percent of the total cancer risk from pesticides of all foods on the market today.[18]

Some feedlots have begun research trials adding cardboard, newspaper, and sawdust to the feeding programs to reduce costs. Other factory farms scrape up the manure from chicken houses and pigpens, adding it directly to cattle feed. Cement dust may become a particularly attractive feed supplement in the future, according to the United States Department of Agriculture, because it produces a 30 percent faster weight gain than cattle on only regular feed.[19] Food and Drug Administration (FDA) officials say that it's not uncommon for some feedlot operators to mix industrial sewage and oils into the feed to reduce costs and fatten animals more quickly.

At Kansas State University, scientists have experimented with plastic feed, small pellets containing 80 to 90 percent ethylene and 10 to 20 percent propylene, as an artificial form of cheap roughage to feed cattle.[20] Researchers point to the extra savings of using the new plastic feed at slaughter time when upward of "20 pounds of the stuff from each cow's rumen can be recovered, melt[ed] down and recycle[d] into new pellets."[21] The new plastic pellets are much cheaper than hay and can provide roughage requirements at a significant savings.[22]

Every aspect of the steers' environment is closely monitored, controlled, and regulated on the feedlot to optimize weight gain. Even flies can be a source of annoyance, disturbing the cattle and keeping them from eating; cattle can lose up to half a pound a day fending off swarms of flies.[23] Flies also spread diseases, including pinkeye and infectious bovine rhinotraceitis. Highly toxic insecticides are sprayed from high-pressure nozzles atop tractors that drive along access roads next to feedlots "fogging the pens and sometimes the animals inside with a cloud of poison." In the biggest feedlots, where 50,000 head or more are sequestered, managers sometimes turn to aerial spraying. Crop-dusting aircraft fly back and forth over cattle pens and spray feedlots with insecticides, drenching the facilities with toxic rain.[24]

After being fattened to their "ideal" weight of 1,100 pounds, the mature steers are herded into giant truck trailers, where they are cramped together without room to move. Because the journey to the slaughterhouse is often a rough and brutal one, animals frequently fall and are trampled upon inside the trucks, suffering broken legs or pelvises. Unable to rise, these animals are known as "downers."

The cattle are transported for hours or days along interstate highways without rest or nourishment and frequently without water. At the end of their journey, intact animals are deposited in a holding pen at the giant slaughterhouse complex. Downers, however, must wait hours to be unloaded. Although downed animals are frequently in severe pain, they are rarely euthanized or anesthetized, as that would translate into a lost carcass and additional expenses. Often spread-eagled on the floor of the trailers, unable to stand or walk, these hapless animals are chained by their broken legs and dragged from the truck onto the loading ramp to await their turn for slaughter. Animals who die en route are thrown into a heap on the "dead pile."

Some of the more modern plants, like the Holcomb, Kansas, plant of Iowa Beef, take up fourteen acres or more.[25] The steers enter the slaughterhouse single-file. Immediately upon entry they are stunned by a pneumatic gun. As each animals sinks to its knees a worker quickly hooks a chain onto a rear hoof, and the animal is mechanically hoisted from the platform and hung upside down over the slaughterhouse floor. Men in blood-soaked gowns, handling long knives, slit each steer's throat, thrusting the blade deep into the larynx for a second or two, then quickly withdrawing the knife, severing the jugular vein and carotid artery in the process. Blood spurts out over the workstation, splattering the workers and equipment. A journalist describes the scene:

> The kill floor looks like a red sea. . . . warm blood bubbles and coagulates in an ankle deep pool. The smell sears the nostrils. Men stand in gore. . . . each night the gooey mess is wiped away. . . .[26]

The dead animal moves along the main disassembly line. At the next workstation the animal is skinned. The hide is cut open at the midline of the stomach and a skinning machine strips the animal of its hide, leaving the skin in one piece. The carcass is decapitated, the tongue is split and removed, and both head and tongue are impaled on hooks attached to the disassembly line chain. The carcass is then gutted. The liver, heart, intestines, and other organs are removed. After the viscera are removed, the body is hurried along to the next station, where the carcass is cut down the center of the backbone with motorized saws and the tail is pulled off the animal. The split carcass is hosed down with warm water, wrapped in cloth, and sent to a meat cooler for twenty-four hours. The next day workers use power saws to cut the carcass into recognizable cuts—steaks, chuck, ribs, brisket. The cuts are tossed onto conveyor belts, each manned by thirty to forty boners and trimmers, who cut off and box the final products. The neatly trimmed, vacuum-packed cuts of beef are then shipped off to supermarkets across the country, where they are displayed along brightly lit meat counters.

2

Gods and Goddesses

Animals, in myth and legend, in folklore and science, have been our most reliable teaching aides. They have served as metaphor and very often as scapegoat. The evolution of human consciousness is inseparable from our changing relationship to the other animals. In an otherwise barren universe, living nature has served as a giant mirror that we have come to rely on to know ourselves. We have, to a great extent, fashioned our sense of self over the millennia by way of the other animals. The rich diversity of animal life on earth provides a constant reference point for our own species. Their movement, behavior, interactions, and idiosyncrasies are continually being observed and manipulated, and in the process we find out about ourselves. We human beings have a long history of projecting our own needs, anxieties, and aspirations onto the rest of the animal kingdom. In a very real sense, we have created ourselves in nature's image, even as we have attempted to re-create nature in our own.

Of the millions of animals that live and interact with us here on earth, one species in particular has played a unique and central role in the human odyssey. The bull and the cow, of the bovine species, have traveled with us from the very beginning of our sojourn. Their fate and ours have been intertwined in a myriad of ways and at every critical juncture of human history. We have seen ourselves in them and we have used them to create our culture. Western civilization has been built, in part, on the back of the bull and the cow.

The bull has always reminded us of our maleness—he represents generativeness, ferocious power, domination, and protection. He is the most territorial of beasts, passionate and aggressive, the embodiment of fertilizing power. The bull is pure unrestrained energy. A formidable force, he is fearless, unreconcilable, and purposeful.

The cow is one of the most gentle and sublime of creatures, the embodiment of patience. Her enlarged udders are available for all the world to suckle. She is nurturer and nourishment, the giver of life. She is self-contained, peaceful, a serene image, grounded and tranquil. The cow is purity, and represents the forces of benevolence and good in the world.

Our present-day cattle descended from two wild ancestors, the giant aurochs of western Asia, North Africa, and Europe and the smaller highland shorthorns. The auroch, the ancestor of most of today's breeds, was an imposing creature, measuring up to seven feet at the shoulder and sporting imposing lyre-shaped horns.[1]

Cattle figure more prominently than any other image in the pictorial representations that are our first historical record. The paintings in the Lascaux caves in France and other rock drawings scattered throughout Europe and the Middle East depict images of the giant aurochs either running wild over the grasslands or downed and wounded, pierced with arrows and spears.[2]

Much of humankind's early consciousness was directed to the bovine. Primitive ritual, including the ceremonial reenactment of the bovine hunt, became commonplace. Incantations, dances, mythmaking, all helped Paleolithic man and woman capture both the spirit of the bovine and the animals' physical being. Our ancestors worshiped the maleness and femaleness of these creatures and attempted to incorporate their spirit by consuming their flesh.

Our relationship to the cow has been both sacred and secular, spiritual and utilitarian. In their relationship to the bovine, Paleolithic man and woman may have sensed the possibilities of their own unfolding. The bull and the cow represented the light and shadows of human existence, the juxtaposition of energy and matter, virility and fertility, the death force, rebirth and renewal—themes that would lift human beings' gaze to the heavens in search of their place in the cosmic scheme.

At the same time, human beings' relationship to the bovine was a very practical affair. These great animals of the field were a source of meat. Their bones were fashioned into fishhooks, harpoons, and spears. Their hides were tanned and made into tents, boats, and clothing. Cattle have long been regarded as the most useful of animals.

Cattle were first domesticated in Mesopotamia and were used primarily as a sacrificial animal in religious ceremonies. The Sumerian people worshiped the bull god Enlil, god of the storm, and his spouse the lunar cow goddess Ninlil. When the lifegiving floodwaters of the Tigris and the Euphrates overflowed each year, fertilizing the soil, it was believed to be the result of the union of these two great divinities.

The horns of the bovine were said to resemble the lunar crescent and were believed, by a society that worshiped the lunar cow goddess, to hold magical power. Interestingly, cattle were the first animals to be yoked and used as a form of traction. In Mesopotamia, ropes were tied directly to the horns of the cattle—because of their magical value—and attached to sleighs and wagons used in religious processions.[3] Later, priests ran the newly domesticated bovines through their fields, believing that their godlike fertilizing power would ensure a bountiful crop. Long after the ox-driven plow had been used to till the soil, popular lore continued to credit the magical qualities of the animal's horns with the success of the yearly harvest. An ancient hymn pays homage to the bovine: "The great bull, the supreme bull which treads the holy pasture . . . planting corn and making the fields luxuriant."[4]

The ox-driven plow ranks as the first great power-driven tool of Western history. The fact that this most utilitarian use of animals is shrouded in religious significance bears witness to the labyrinthine nature of the cattle complex and the ancient dichotomy between human beings' two natures: one sacred and lofty, and directed to the heavens; the other carnal and earthly, and directed to the turning over of the soil.

Today, we think of cattle in terms of steak and hamburger, milk and cheese, and by-products ranging from gelatin to finely tanned Italian purses and wallets. Our sense of the animal reflects the utilitarian sensibilities of the time. It might come as a surprise to many, then, that much of the religious experience of the West, from before recorded history until well into the Christian era, was dominated by bull gods and cow goddesses, the cult of the bovine. Indeed, even Judeo-Christian liturgy was affected by the great cattle cults, a fact long overlooked by cultural historians.

In his book *The Horn and the Sword*, Jack Randolph Conrad traces the influence of the Middle Eastern cattle cults in the centuries before the birth of Christ. From Egypt, says Conrad, the cattle cults spread south along the Nile into North Africa, extending eventually into all of East Africa and as far south as present-day Zimbabwe and South Africa, where they remain, to this day, the spiritual and secular center of tribal life. Among the Banyankole tribe in Africa, when the king dies, his body is bathed in cow milk and then laid to rest inside the hide of a freshly killed cow. When the young men of the Masai tribe are circumcised they are asked to demonstrate their courage and manhood by seizing hold of the horns of a bull. In the Dinka wedding ceremony, the "bridegroom smears his wife's breasts and shoulders with the stomach contents of a bull he has just killed" to ensure her fertility. After the birth of each child, its head, neck, and chest are "smeared with the blood of a freshly killed bull whose flesh has been eaten by the family."[5] The Zulus wash their newborn with cow dung and present the infant with a necklace made from the hair of the cow's tail.

In the pre-Christian era, bovine cults were popular in the northern Mediterranean in the region that comprises present-day Jordan, Syria, Lebanon, and Israel. In the land of the Hittites, the wild bull was the supreme god that ruled over the rain, thunder, and lightning. The Hittite weather god took on various names—Teshub, Adad, Ramman, and Sandas. In Palestine the bull god was known as Baal, the "bellowing or roaring one." He was both the storm god and the god of fertility. The bull god of the Mediterranean was accompanied by a cow goddess, Astarte. Together, they ruled over the whole of creation.

The seafaring Phoenicians spread the cult of Baal to their far-flung colonies reaching west and north into Greece, Italy, and Spain. The bovine influence was so great among the Phoenicians that they made the first symbol of their alphabet, the letter A, in the image of a bull's head.

Even the early Hebrews worshiped the bull, sometimes referring to the animal as the "bull of Jacob." Conrad argues that later translations of the Old Testament often used the word "mighty one" to substitute for earlier usage of the word "bull."

After the exodus from Egypt, the Hebrews were still heavily influenced by the bovine cult and were even admonished by Moses upon his descent from Mount Sinai for continuing to worship the golden calf. In the Book of Numbers the Hebrews allude to the bull god who delivered them from the Pharaoh and led them to the promised land: "God who brought them out of Egypt is the horns of a wild ox for them."[6] Many later historical references picture Moses as an incarnation of the Hebrew bull god. Michelangelo's statue of Moses, in the Church of San Pietro in Vincoli in Rome, depicts the Hebrew liberator as horned. After settling in Canaan, the once nomadic Hebrews fused their worship of Yahweh with the popular cults of Baal. As they made the transition from a nomadic warrior people to agriculturalists, their bovine worship shifted from an image of the bull as strength to one of virility.

Conrad points to the increased intermingling of Hebrew religious practices and the bull-worshiping cults of the Canaanite people. During the reign of Solomon, the sacred Temple was adorned with bronze bulls and sculptures of horned men.

In the western Mediterranean, on the island of Crete, the ancient Minoan civilization worshiped a bull god whom they identified with the sun. The Minoans minted special coins with the image of a bull surrounded by rays of light stamped on them. At the palace of Minos the king often dressed up as a bull and the queen as a cow. They performed ritual dances, some of which ended in symbolic intercourse, designed to bring fertility to the land and a rich harvest. At the palace at Knossos the walls were covered with frescos of giant aurochs.

Cretan warriors wore horned helmets into battle to strengthen their resolve. Specially trained athletes appeared in the arena with the bulls. When the animal charged, the athlete would grasp his horns, allowing the animal's mighty thrust upward to catapult him into the air, where he would perform a forward somersault and land with his feet on the back quarter of the bull. These sacred athletic feats were performed in front of large crowds of spectators in the hope that a portion of the animals' strength and power might be transferred to men. In other public ceremonies the bull would be killed, its flesh eaten raw, to incorporate the beast's godly qualities of virility and strength into the human body.

In Crete, as in Sumer, Egypt, and other bovine cultures, the bull god was sacrificed so that people could live. The death of the bull released his "spirit." Eating the flesh ensured that the spirit lived on in human beings.

The divine bull also figured prominently in Greek society. Dionysus, the god of life and fertility, was referred to as the "Bull horned" and the "Son of a Cow."[7] The Greeks worshiped the bull as an embodiment of god. In the Dionysian ritual, devotees stole into the mountains at night, symbolically shedding the restraints of civilization. The celebrants, wearing the horns of bulls, danced faster and faster, whipping themselves up into a frenzy. In the midst of such wild physical abandon, a young bull was paraded into their midst. Falling upon him with bare hands, they ripped the young animal apart, tearing into its flesh, drenching their hands and bodies in its blood. They ate the bull's flesh, still hot and raw, while shrieking and leaping into the air until the first glimpse of the sunrise. They believed that in consuming the bull they became like the gods. They and their land were blessed and sanctified in the blood of the bovine.

The Italians take their very name from the word "Italia," meaning land of cattle. When the people of the peninsula massed to resist the encroachment of Rome, they fought under the protection of the bovine cult, and like others in other lands, they wore horns of bulls into battle. Archaeologists have discovered coins of the period depicting the Italian bull god Mars, the god of battle, alongside a fierce bull that had "gored and hurled to the ground the she-wolf of Rome."[8]

By the middle of the first century B.C. the bovine cult even found its way to Rome. The Mithra cult was an amalgam of various bull-worshiping religions centered in the Middle East, North Africa, and as far away as Asia Minor. Mithra was originally an ancient Aryan divinity, the god of light. Early on, the sun god fused with the popular bovine cults of the day. Mithra was often referred to as "the lord of the wide pastures." He was the giver of life, "the lord of fecundity." Wise and pure, this "lord of light and goodness" battled the dark forces of evil. By the end of the second century, Mithraism was declared an official religion of Rome and was far more popular than the young Christian cult of the time. The bovine cult permeated virtually every aspect of Roman life. When a young couple exchanged wedding vows at the altar the bride would declare, "Where thou art the bull I am the cow."[9]

The great Mithraic myth of the ritual slaying of the bull was particularly attractive to the soldiers of the Roman legions, who spread it throughout the empire. According to the myth, Mithra received the divine order to slay the bull god. After numerous failures he succeeded. The death of the great god beast is followed by a host of miracles:

> From the bull's body sprang all the plants and herbs that men now find useful. From the spinal cord sprang wheat, the staff of man's life, from the blood came the grape vine and wine, the sacred joy of life.[10]

The force of evil, resentful of man's newly secured bounty, sent his demons to attack the corpse. But as legend has it, their assault on the dead bull's genitals led to still another miracle. The bull's seed was released, gathered up by the moon, and from it sprang all the "useful" animals on earth, whereupon the soul of the bull god ascended back into heaven, where he became the guardian of herds.

Disciples of the Mithraic faith were baptized into the cult on special holy days. Worshipers lined up inside a pit under a bull. The priest then reenacted the Mithraic myth, ending in the slaughter of the animal. The novices lifted their heads up toward the dying bull, letting the hot blood pour out into their mouths and over their bodies. After being purified in holy blood, they were each given a small portion of seed from the bull's testicles to eat, ensuring their immortality on judgment day when "the holy bull of bulls would come to earth and Mithra would bring all men to life."[11]

The Mithraic religion shared many features with Christianity, making the two powerful competitors. Both cults believed in the duality of good and evil. Both believed in heaven and hell and everlasting salvation for those baptized in the faith. The Mithraic cult might have triumphed over Christianity had the Emperor Constantine not converted to the faith. Still, Christian clerics felt compelled to expropriate many of the Mithraic rituals in order to gain a popular following. Conrad points out that Christianity borrowed the sin-cleansing blood bath from the Mithraic cult, substituting the blood of the dying Christ for the blood of the bull. The Christian religion also took over the Mithraic holy day, December 25, which celebrated the birth of the sun, and made it the birthdate of Christ.

In a final *coup de grâce*, the new Christian cultists transformed the Mithraic bull god into the new symbol of darkness. The god of its adversary became the devil incarnate. At the Council of Toledo in A.D. 447, the church published the first official description of the devil. According to the prelates he is

a large black monstrous apparition with horns on his head, cloven hoofs—or one cloven hoof—ass's ears, hair, claws, fiery eyes, terrible teeth, an immense phallus, and a sulphurous smell.[12]

3

Neolithic Cowboys

While much is known about the cattle cults in the Middle East, North Africa, and ancient Europe, far less anthropological attention has been given to a second locus of bovine influence that emerged independently, thousands of miles to the north on the vast grasslands of the Eurasian steppes, an area bounded by eastern Europe and the Ukraine in the west and Mongolia and Manchuria in the east. The nomadic herdsmen of the steppes survived by conquest and confiscation. They were highly mobile, warriorlike, and expansionist in outlook. They followed the grasslands south into India, east into China proper, north into the Baltic Peninsula and Scandinavia, and west into the Spanish Peninsula and British Isles.

They were the great invaders, the feared horsemen from the north, who drove great herds of cattle into Europe in successive waves, trampling and subduing the small peaceful Neolithic village communities of the ancient world. Their gods were weather gods, quick and ruthless as the nomadic herdsmen, and able to protect the semiwild horsemen of the steppes in their forays into distant lands. Their divinities stood in sharp contrast to the bovine gods of the Middle East, North Africa, and Europe, who ruled largely over grain cultures and were worshiped as much for their generative qualities as for their warrior attributes.

The gods of the herdsmen guaranteed military victory and booty. The gods of the cultivators guaranteed the spring flood and fall harvest. The gods of the nomads were mobile and quixotic. The gods of the agriculturalists were more sedentary and predictable, like the changing seasons.

Much of Western history is an account of the ongoing struggle between two groupings, one herdsmen, the other agriculturalist, the first depending on grass, the second on grain. Both paid homage to the bovine, although each ascribed different attributes to the creature. These two distinct traditions often interacted, each tempering the worldview of the other. Their relationship has been stormy, scarred by confrontation and capitulation.

The clash between the nomadic herdsmen and the tillers of soil began some 6,000 years ago when the horsemen of the Eurasian steppes first encountered the Neolithic farmers of Europe.

European culture dates back well before the fifth millennium B.C. Village communities and small townships peppered the continent from the Aegean and the Mediterranean, up through Italy and central Europe, along the Danube River Basin, and up into the eastern Balkans. Primarily agriculturalists, with some small-scale herding, these early European people seemed to live a relatively peaceful existence. According to Marija Gimbutas, their societies were egalitarian and matrilinear, and there is little, if any, evidence that they had military fortifications and weapons.[1]

The European village communities were well versed in the art of copper making. Craft technology was advanced, and the archaeological treasures of the period reveal a highly artistic culture. Paintings on vases, pottery, and figurines were mature in conception and sophisticated in execution. Evidence suggests a high degree of interest in ornaments, mostly of a religious nature. Rudimentary script can be seen on miniature vessels as well as on dishes and cups, suggesting that writing in ancient Europe predates Sumerian script by some 2,000 years.[2]

Beginning around 4400 B.C., Europe was rocked by a wave of invasions from the east. Nomadic horsemen of the Eurasian steppes swept into southern and eastern Europe, destroying the tranquil agricultural life that had flourished for several thousand years. The invaders, known as the Kurgan people, are believed to have descended from a stock of earlier mixed agriculturalists who farmed and herded along the periphery of the Eurasian steppes in the region of the Ukraine.[3] As these people exhausted the land with primitive and ineffective grazing techniques, they were forced to move their small domestic herds to more marginal land to the east, where they continued to farm and herd. Their eastward movement was stymied for a time at the foot of the Ural Mountains. On the other side of the great Russian mountain chain lay the plains of the Eurasian steppes, a vast ocean of virgin grass, seemingly inaccessible to human exploitation.[4]

The domestication of the horse changed the situation, opening up the grasslands of Eurasia to bovine pastoralism. The introduction of herding into the Eurasian grasslands marked the beginning of a 6,000-year journey of pastoral conquest and domination that has now extended to the rangelands of the American west, the tropical forests of Central and South America, and the arid plains of the Australian outback.

The Kurgan people were the first to breed horses that could carry human mounts. These first horsemen of the plains proved a formidable force in human history. The horse gave the Kurgan people great mobility. From atop their mounts they could manage large herds of cattle over vast regions. With the help of the horse, the Kurgans conquered the Eurasian steppes, creating the first great nomadic cattle empire in world history. The horse also gave the Kurgans a powerful military advantage, which enabled them to overrun much of the Eurasian landmass in the ensuing centuries.

Periodic droughts on the Eurasian grasslands forced the Kurgans westward into Europe and southward into India and Iran in search of grazing land. The first wave of invasions into southern and eastern Europe, between 4400 and 4300 B.C., was followed by a second wave of assaults on central Europe between 3400 and 3200 B.C. and a third penetration into western Europe and Scandinavia between 3000 and 2800 B.C.[5] The "battle-ax" cultures of the east were the first great frontier cultures of the western world.[6] Like the cowboys of nineteenth-century America, their military superiority lay in the mounted steed, their wealth was measured in cattle, and their territory was the arid grassland of the temperate zone.

By the first century A.D., waves of nomadic invasions had spread the Kurgan influence throughout much of Europe as well as India and Persia and as far east as China. Although the cattle culture never gained a permanent foothold in China, Kurgan invasions were often marginally effective at exacting tribute and securing temporary gains. In the twelfth and thirteenth centuries, Genghis Khan and his grandson and heir, Kublai, overran much of China for a time, pushing the Sung dynasty to the city of Hangchow, where it capitulated to the Mongol hordes.[7]

The Kurgan influence transformed Europe over a 3,000-year period of invasion and conquest. The people of the Eurasian steppes brought the mounted horse and cattle culture to Europe. They also brought the ideology and weapons of war. The archaeological record is a grim testimonial to the impact of the Kurgan invasions. It shows an abrupt end to a highly advanced and peaceful farming culture.[8] Battle-axes and daggers supplanted figurines and painted pottery beginning in the fourth millennium B.C. By the time the Huns swept over Rome and north into the heart of France and western Europe under Attila in the fifth century A.D., Europe had already been transformed by centuries of terror.[9]

The people of the steppes left no impressive physical monuments, no great works of art, no written language describing their deeds and exploits. Perhaps that's why their influence on Western civilization has been virtually ignored, until recently, by historians, who prefer to dwell on the cultural legacy stretching from ancient Sumer to imperial Rome.[10]

While the Kurgan people introduced large-scale herding and superior military technology into Europe, they also introduced very different concepts of security—concepts that would lead Europeans to become the great colonizers of the earth in the modern era. The Kurgans measured security in terms of speed and mobility. In this sense, they differed fundamentally from the grain-producing empires of the Middle East and North Africa and the small village-based agricultural societies of ancient Europe.

In agricultural societies, security is found in a deep sense of belonging to the land. The ground is hallowed, a sacred dwelling place protected by the gods and watched over by one's ancestors. The ground brings responsibilities. It binds each generation into a sacred web of obligations and commitments. In an agricultural society, to belong is to be attached to the land, the changing seasons, and the age-old cycle of birth, growth, death, and regeneration.

The Kurgans had no allegiance to place. The land was something to capture, possess, and exploit. It had strategic and economic value, but no sacred or intrinsic value. Their sense of being was internalized, bound up in their weapons and cattle, the things they could take with them. The nomadic people of the steppes brought a new consciousness with them: fiercely independent, militaristic, detached from the land, acquisitive, and utilitarian. Over time, their worldview and their bloodlines melded with the peoples they subdued, creating a unique mix of European sensibilities and Eurasian restiveness.

If Kurgan consciousness helped prepare the psychological ground for the modern era, it was Kurgan cattle that helped prepare the economic ground for modern capitalism and the colonial era in world history. The very word "cattle" comes from the same etymological root as the word "capital." In many European languages, the word "cattle" was synonymous with the words "chattel" and "capital."[11] Cattle meant property. Wilfred Funk, in his book *Word Origins and Their Romantic Stories*, points out that a chattel mortgage was long considered a cattle mortgage and up until the sixteenth century the English people spoke of "goods and Cattals" rather than "goods and chattels."[12] The Spanish word for cattle, *ganado*, meant property or *ganaderia*.[13] Even the Latin word for money, *pecunia*, comes from the word *pecus*, meaning cattle.[14]

Cattle was one of the first forms of movable wealth, an asset that could be used as a standard medium of exchange between people and cultures. Both the grain-producing empires of the Middle East and North Africa and the Mediterranean maritime powers traded in cattle. In ancient Greece, families often gave their female children cattle-derived names to emphasize their "worth" and to attract male suitors. Polyboia means "worth many cows," Euboia means "rich in cows," and Phereboia means "bringing in many cows."[15]

Although cattle were regarded as a form of capital by the Romans as well as the Huns, it was the Eurasian herdsmen who became the first real protocapitalists, transforming cattle into a vast store of mobile wealth that could be used to exert power over both people and territory.

The emergence of the great Western cattle cultures and the emergence of world capitalism are inseparable, each feeding the appetites of the other. To better understand how cattle lost their divine stature in world history, eventually being reduced to the role of productive capital, it is necessary to peer below the surface of Kurgan culture and examine the complex social structure of these nomadic people. It is in the rich tapestry of Kurgan social relationships that the seeds of a new world order were first sown.

4

Gifts and Capital

The Kurgan culture and its many offshoots were organized into social hierarchies with three distinct classes. Priests were at the apex of the social pyramid, with a warrior class below the priests and commoners at the bottom of the pyramid. In his book *Priests, Warriors, and Cattle*, Bruce Lincoln examines the complex interrelationship between priests and warriors in the Kurgan cattle complex.

The priests' primary role was to offer sacrifices to the Kurgan gods, in the form of cattle, in order to win their favor and ensure the health and well-being of the community. In the Indo-Iranian sect, two gods ruled supreme in the heavens: Mitra, the god that joined human beings together, and Varuna, the god of magic and cosmic law. A pantheon of six or seven minor gods also existed in the Indo-Iranian cosmos. The most frequent request of the gods was for more men and more cattle.[1]

In virtually all of the Indo-European sects of Kurgan ancestry—Indian, Iranian, Germanic, Norse, Roman, Greek, and Russian—the priestly role revolved around the continued ritualistic reenactment of the myth of the first sacrifice. According to the ancient myth, the first priest, Manu, sacrifices the first king, Yemo, along with the first bovine. From the body of the slain primordial ox, all of the animal and vegetable species are created.

The constant ritual reenactment of this myth, in which a bovine was sacrificed each time, allowed the Kurgans to re-create the world over and over again, symbolically providing a never-ending cornucopia of earthly riches for the Kurgan people. By offering up bovine sacrifices to the gods, the Kurgans ensured for themselves gifts in return from the gods: more cattle and more men.[2]

The warrior class had its own warrior gods, who also lived in the heavens but below the high gods of the priestly caste. They were generally associated with the weather: storms, lightning, and thunder. Among the Indo-Iranians, Indra, the bull god, ruled supreme among the war gods. Indra protected the warriors, providing them with strength and valor so that they could subdue their enemies in battle and secure booty. Wealth was accumulated by plundering other peoples and their lands and was considered a gift of Indra and the war gods.[3]

The primary responsibility of the warrior class was to wage war and expropriate cattle. In Sanskrit the very term "battle"—*gavisti*—means "desire for cattle," and a successful warlord was often referred to as Gopa, "lord of cattle."[4]

Like the priests, the warrior class reenacted its own first myth, the tale of the first cattle raid. According to this ancient Indo-European tale, the hero, Trito, aided by the war god, Indra, slays a three-headed serpent and takes his cattle from him. The confiscation of the cattle, however, is justified as an act of retribution, as the serpent had stolen the cattle himself. The cattle-raiding myth was enacted over and over again through the centuries, offering cosmic justification for stealing cattle from the aboriginal populations of Europe, Persia, and India. During the initiation rites, young warriors were made to drink sauma, an intoxicant, and to eat meat to gain strength over their enemies. All of the Kurgan cattle raids took on a ritual character. The warriors were assisted by special priests in reenacting the myth of the cattle raid in preparation for the raid itself.

Over the centuries, says Lincoln, the priestly caste and the warrior class came into continual conflict in Kurgan sects. For the priests, cattle took on importance as a sacrificial animal, a gift to appease the gods. Although the warriors were expected to steal cattle, to provide both a sacrificial gift to the gods and a stock of wealth for the community, the second objective often overshadowed the first. The warriors began to view their booty more as valuable assets, capital that could be used to amass both power and privilege.[5]

The growing schism between priests and warriors over the proper use of cattle reflects the epic struggle throughout Western history between the sacred and the secular. The priests remained attached to the ancient economics of indebtedness and gift-giving. They viewed their health, wealth, and well-being as gifts bestowed by the gods. They were beholden to forces beyond their control, always at the mercy of divine authority, existing as a mere dependent clause in the cosmic script. The warriors, on the other hand, became increasingly emboldened. Flushed with victory, hardened by millennia of warfare and raids, they came to see themselves more as independent actors, forces to be reckoned with in their own right. Their cattle were a testimonial to their power. Cattle became their capital, and they, in turn, became protocapitalists.

A radical new form of economics was being readied for the world stage, one based on ruthless acquisition and later justified by naked self-interest. In the process, the bovine metamorphosed into a new creature. The sacred notion of divinely inspired generativeness, embodied in the bovine, was replaced with the secular notion of wealth-generating economic productivity. The cow, once a god, was slowly transformed into a commodity. The transformation in the human-bovine relationship took place over 4,000 to 5,000 years, reflecting the slow change in European consciousness from the sacred to the secular.

Everywhere the steppe people migrated, the cattle cultures fundamentally altered the psychological and physical landscape. In a few instances, the influence of the Kurgan invasions was so pronounced that it continued to affect the sociology and politics of specific cultures until well into the modern era. Nowhere was this more true than in India, Spain, and the British Isles, where the Indo-Iranian and Celtic descendants of the Kurgans played a major role in defining national character. In each of these cultures, unique ecological restraints and historical opportunities spawned very different cattle complexes and very different approaches to the modern era. In India the cattle complex helped create a static social order. In Spain and Britain the cattle complex helped ignite the fires of colonial expansion, propelling Europe into the New World.

Understanding the role the cattle complex played in these three very different societies is essential in coming to grips with the devastating impact that cattle grazing and beef eating is having on the human population and the world environment in the last decade of the twentieth century.

5

Holy Cow

Descendants of the Aryan nomads from the Eurasian steppes invaded the subcontinent of India around 1750 B.C., decimating the Indus civilization.[1] In search of grass, they found an ideal ecological niche in the fertile Indus valley. They brought with them cattle, horses, weapons—and their gods.

The Aryan nomads worshiped Indra, the bull god of thunderstorms.[2] As we have already learned, Indra was a mighty bull whose strength and virility was tested time and again in mythical clashes with various monsters who stole his cattle. Each time he triumphed and celebrated his victory by fertilizing the ground with rain, which in turn impregnated his herds of cows.

Like their ancestors from the Eurasian steppes, the Aryan people were beef eaters. The Aryan warlords were able to secure the allegiance and goodwill of the aboriginal population of India by the lavish distribution of beef during ceremonial rituals and other sacred occasions. After 600 B.C., the Aryan overlords and their Brahman priests found it increasingly difficult to supply an adequate amount of beef both to meet their own gluttonous appetites and to appease the local populations under their rule. The result, says anthropologist Marvin Harris, was that the Brahmans ate beef while the people went without, forcing a crisis of governance.[3]

At the root of the Indian beef crisis was a combination of intense population pressure against a depleted soil base and dwindling natural resources—a problem that has been repeated over and over again wherever the cattle complex has emerged. When the herdsmen first arrived in India, the population density was low and land was plentiful. Much of the Gangetic plain was still forested. By 300 B.C., however, the region had become the most populous in the world, with between 50 and 100 million people.[4] The forests had been denuded and much of the land eroded to the point of exhaustion. With increased population pressure, farms became smaller and less able to spare precious land for grazing animals. Much of the pastureland was converted to raising wheat, millet, lentils, and peas to feed a growing population.[5] To survive, however, farmers required at least two oxen for plowing the fields and at least one cow to breed replacements and provide milk. The peasant population could not afford to eat their only source of power. Without the ox it was virtually impossible to plow the hardened soils of northern India. Without the cow they would have no way of providing a new generation of bovines to work the fields.

While the poor teetered between survival and famine, the victims of periodic floods and droughts, the Brahman caste and the Vedic chieftains continued to slaughter the cattle of India, consuming enormous amounts of beef and, in the process, further exhausting the food chain of the giant subcontinent.

Angry, the peasants lashed out, demanding equity and admonishing their rulers for their callous disregard. The rulers of India turned a deaf ear. It was then, says Harris, that the people turned to a new religious sect, the Buddhists, who condemned the taking of any animal life. The Buddhist religion was a welcome tonic. It spoke directly to the plight of the poor, condemning ostentatious shows of wealth and preaching the saving grace of abstinence and voluntary poverty. For the peasants the new religion offered the hope of salvation tinged with a strong dose of retributive justice.[6]

Since the Buddhists condemned all killing, including ritual slaughter, it put them directly at odds with their Brahman masters. The slaying of animals and the eating of beef were condemned by a growing number of peasants who could no longer afford to kill their own cattle for consumption. They were resentful of the wanton privilege being exercised by their beef-eating overlords, who continued to confiscate cattle from the peasants for their sumptuous feasts. Legend has it that when a Buddhist reminded a Brahman that eating meat from a sacred cow would displease the gods, who had imbued the animal with "cosmic power," the priest replied, "That may very well be, but I shall eat of it nevertheless if the flesh be tender."[7]

The Buddhists struggled with Hindu Brahmans for the allegiance of the Indian masses for nine centuries.[8] The Hindus eventually prevailed, but not before adopting many of the Buddhist practices into their own doctrine. Most important of all, the Hindu religion reversed its position on animal sacrifice and condemned the ritual slaughter of cattle. The new doctrine of *ahimsa* championed nonviolence and the sacredness of life.[9] This was, indeed, a significant gesture for a religion whose leaders descended from cattle-raiding warriors of the steppes. It ought to be noted that even the Vedic word for "war" meant "desire for cows."[10]

Rewriting their own history and religious tenets, the Hindus argued that the gods did not really eat meat and that the ritual meat eating described in holy texts like the *Rig Veda* was meant to be metaphorical. Milk was substituted for meat in Hindu rituals and became the primary source of protein for the formerly meat-eating Brahman caste. The Hindus went even further, encouraging the worship of cows, something the Buddhists did not do.

Today the cattle complex conditions every aspect of Hindu daily life. At present there are nearly 200 million cows in India, many roaming freely throughout the streets and villages.[11] All are the subject of veneration. The Hindus believe that everything that comes from the cow is sacred because the cow is the mother of life.[12] Gandhi called the cow "a mother to millions of Indians."[13]

Harris describes some of the countless Hindu religious practices involving the sacred bovine:

The priests make a holy "nectar" composed of milk, curds, butter, urine and dung which they sprinkle or daub on statues and worshippers. They light the temples with lamps that burn ghee, clarified cow's butter. And they bathe temple statues daily with fresh cow's milk. At festivals commemorating Krishna's role as protector of cattle, priests mould the god's likeness out of cattle dung, pour milk over the navel, and crawl around it on the temple floor. . . . At

other festivals people kneel in the dust raised by passing cattle and
daub their foreheads with the fresh droppings.[14]

The cattle complex permeates even the most mundane aspects of
daily life. Village doctors collect dust from the hoofprints of cattle
and use them to concoct medical remedies. Hindus carry jugs filled
with *gomutra*, cow urine, which is considered a sacred fluid and is
used to bathe sick children.[15] The government maintains old-age
homes for over half a million cows that are too frail or ill to roam
the streets.[16] The animals are housed, fed, and cared for at government expense. When foreigners have questioned the costs involved
in managing nursing homes for cows throughout India, the Hindu
retort is equally incredulous: "Will you then send your mother to a
slaughterhouse when she gets old?"[17]

Hindu wall calendars are adorned with cow pinups. The most
popular is the female/cow chimera: a beautiful young woman with
the body of a plump white cow.[18]

Killing a cow is considered among the most heinous of crimes.
Until recently, cow killing was punishable by death in Kashmir. The
penalty has since been reduced to life imprisonment.[19] If a cow is
killed inadvertently, the guilty party is made to shave his head and
is then confined for one month to a cow pasture, where he is covered
with the skin of the animal he killed. Each day of his confinement,
he must follow in the footsteps of the cows and swallow the dust
kicked up by their hoofs.[20]

It is no wonder that cow killing is treated so seriously. The Hindus
believe that inside each cow live 330 million gods and goddesses.
Whoever kills a bovine, according to Hindu doctrine, will fall back
through eighty-six transmigrations and end up at the lowest rung
on the ladder of incarnation as a devil.[21]

Since Hindus live alongside Muslims and other religious groups
that do not share their reverence for the bovine, open hostilities and
"cow riots" break out periodically, resulting in the loss of human
life. In 1966, cow riots left eight dead and forty-eight injured on the
steps of the Indian House of Parliament.[22]

In India, the cow is much more than an object of worship. To a
great extent, the very survival of the Indian population depends on
the contribution of this most useful of animals. The cows provide
most of India's dairy requirements. The ox provides traction for 60

million small farmers whose land feeds 80 percent of the Indian population.[23] Indian cattle excrete 700 million tons of manure annually, half of which is used as fertilizer to maintain the soil. The rest is burned to provide heat for cooking. Harris has estimated that cattle dung provides Indian housewives with the thermal equivalent of "27 million tons of kerosene, 35 million tons of coal, or 68 million tons of wood." Cow dung is even mixed with water and used as a paste to make household flooring. Each day small children all over India follow the family cow around on her daily rounds collecting her valuable excrement for a variety of household uses.[24]

Cattle hides are used in the Indian leather industry, which is the largest in the world. Even the carcasses of ancient cows are sold to slaughterhouses and used as a source of meat for Muslims, Christians, and others whose religious practices do not include prohibitions on eating beef.[25]

Although cattle are the mainstay for much of the economic life of the peasantry, they do not compete with the human population for the arable land, as many in the west have supposed. In one study it was found that less than 20 percent of the cattle diet in West Bengal is composed of foodstuffs edible by humans.[26] Cattle live primarily off household garbage, chaff, stalks, and leaves. They are also fed oil cakes made of cottonseed, soybean, and coconut residues that are inedible by humans.[27]

The cattle complex that emerged in India managed to strengthen both the sacred and the profane aspects of human beings' relationship to the bovine. Only in East Africa, among the many cattle-herding tribes, has a similar balance of sacred and secular been struck over the centuries. In India, 700 million people, one out of every eight people on the planet, live for and through the bovine.[28] Their historical experience with cattle is unique among the Aryan tribes who spread their influence from the Eurasian steppes through the whole of Indo-Europe. Mohandas Gandhi perhaps best captured the essence of the Indian relationship to cattle:

The most characteristic feature of Hinduism is the reverence with which it treats the cow. To protect the cow seems to be one of the most admirable manifestations of human progress. To me, the cow is the embodiment of the whole infra-human world; she enables the believer to grasp his unity with all that lives. It seems to me as self-evident truth that the cow is a natural choice as a symbol of that unity. . . . The cow is a poem of compassion. . . . To protect her is to protect all the dumb creatures of God's creation.[29]

Still Gandhi was not unmindful of the great usefulness of the cow to the well-being of the Indian people. He once remarked: "The cow was, in India, the best companion. She was the giver of plenty. Not only did she give milk but she made agriculture possible."[30]

While India continued to revere the cow over the centuries, even as its people used the animal to survive and prosper, a very different arrangement was struck throughout much of Europe proper. In central and western Europe, the Aryan descendants of the steppe people were forced to tread a very different path in their relationship to the bovine, a far more secular course that would lead to world colonization and exploitation of peoples and lands on several continents.

6

Matadors and Machismo

Today, when we think of the bull, we are likely to think of Spain—the pageantry and cruelty of the bullfight and the machismo of the matador. The bovine has helped define the image of the Spanish people as it has the image of the Indian people—but in the case of the Iberian Peninsula it is the masculine image of the bull that haunts its history, whereas in India it is the feminine image of the cow that has come to define the national character.

Cattle flourished on Spanish grazing land, making the country an important port of call for traders and an attractive prize for a long succession of cattle-raiding cultures. The Phoenicians established trading posts at Cádiz and Málaga, bringing their cattle gods with them. Traders from the Middle East introduced the cult of Baal to the Iberian Peninsula. The Greeks also came to Spain in search of cattle. The Greek myth of the Tenth Labor of Hercules recounts the tale of a legendary hero who is sent to Spain to steal the best red cattle and bring them back to Greece for sacrificial use. The Spanish cattle were sacrificed to the cow goddess Hera, wife of the bull god Zeus.

The influence of Phoenician, Cretan, and Greek traders was significant, but limited primarily to the coastal regions of Iberia. Then in 400 B.C. the Celtic nomads descended into Spain, overwhelming the whole of the Iberian peninsula. The Celts brought with them a fierce warrior bull cult. The new bovine gods melded with the earlier bull god influences of the Mediterranean and the Near East, creating a uniquely Iberian cattle complex. The Roman invasion brought the Mithraic bull religion to the peninsula, adding still another layer to the many bull cult influences that were slowly forming the Spanish character.[1]

Of the many anthropological markers of the bull cult era in western history, none remains more vivid and vital than the Spanish bullfight. It has survived the centuries, despite repeated attempts by the church and the crown to loosen its hold over the Spanish people. The church has felt particularly threatened by the ritual, continually worrying that its pagan influence over the people would undermine church authority. Still, the bullfight has prevailed. Its appeal may be attributable to the hybrid nature of the Spanish cattle cult. A strong mix of Mithraic blood sacrifices and Celtic bravado fused in the Spanish bullring.

Sacrificial acts, which had been the centerpiece of early bullfighting ceremonies in Crete, had been progressively overshadowed in the Roman corridas by the display of human prowess.[2] By the time the Roman and Celtic influences finally melded in the bull rings of Spain, a new man–bull relationship had emerged. The Spanish matador maintained his warrior status but cast off his remaining sacred garb. The bull was no longer to be served up to the gods, but to man himself. In the Spanish bull ring, bovine sacrifices, which had long been used to curry favor with the gods, gave way to a symbolic battle between man and nature, captured in the life-death struggle between the matador and the bull. Centuries before Melville's Captain Ahab battled with the great white whale, Spanish matadors were already apprenticing for man's new role on the world scene, facing down the "forces of nature" in dusty arenas in scores of small village towns on the Iberian Peninsula.

Spanish explorers transported the ancient Iberian cattle complex to the shores of America in the sixteenth century. The Spanish conquerors of the New World bore a striking resemblance to the fierce nomadic tribesmen of the Eurasian steppes who had set out to conquer Europe over 5,000 years earlier. From the very beginning of the modern colonial era, cattle played a prominent role in the confiscation of new lands and the subjugation of native people, just as it had earlier when the nomadic herdsmen ran roughshod over the European landmass.

"Carnivorous Europe" had long depended on a steady supply of spices from the east to mask the flavor of spoiled meat.[3] Often spices such as pepper, ginger root, cloves, mace, nutmeg, and coriander were added to meat "to cover up the incipient decay."[4]

Interest in finding a new maritime route to the spice islands of the East was spurred by the commercial dealings of the Ottoman Turks, whose territory stood between Europe and the Orient. In the fifteenth century, the Turks began to exert mounting pressure on the overland spice trade, significantly raising export taxes on cargo shipped from the eastern Mediterranean to the main European port of Venice. At one point the price of spices jumped by 800 percent or more.[5] Even at the new exorbitant prices, Europeans were willing and able to pay, anxious to secure spices for their growing meat addiction.

Meat consumption, and especially beef consumption, rose significantly in the early fifteenth century in Europe. The black plague had reduced the human population of Europe. In the aftermath, the living conditions of peasants and craft workers improved for a short while as landlords and merchants were forced to raise wages to meet the needs of a scarce labor force.[6] Much of the increase in wages went to the increased consumption of meat.[7] Historian Fernand Braudel characterizes the period as "a riot of meat" consumption. In France, he says, "Meat in all its forms, boiled or roasted . . . was served in a pyramid on immense dishes called mets." In Germany, reports Braudel, public ordinances issued in 1482 mandated that all craftsmen receive two dishes of meat at their noon meal. In Alsace, peasants were guaranteed two pieces of beef each day. Germany and Italy were awash in shipments of half-wild cattle from the pasturelands of Poland, Hungary, and the Balkan countries in the sixteenth century.[8]

Increased population pressures led to the deterioration of pastureland after the mid-sixteenth century, forcing many European peasants and craft workers to adopt a largely vegetarian diet. It is perhaps no mere coincidence that by the middle of the seventeenth century, the number of meatless days had increased to nearly half the days of the year on the Catholic calendar in England and France.[9]

Beef remained scarce until well into the nineteenth century, when improvements in transatlantic travel and modern canning and refrigeration processes opened the way for the shipment of massive amounts of North and South American beef to Europe at prices the new factory workers and middle class could afford.

During the critical period of the late fifteenth and early sixteenth centuries, however, when meat consumption was still increasing and the cost of spices still rising, interest in securing a new sea route to the spice islands became a favorite topic of conversation among aspiring merchants and explorers anxious to find a way around the extortionist policies of the Turkish middlemen.

Among the hopeful was a young Genoese, Christopher Columbus. By happenstance, Columbus came upon a book written by Marco Polo, the Venetian explorer who recounted his fabulous journey back from the Orient via the spice islands. Polo, who became a millionaire from the voyage, wrote of the "great abundance of ginger, galingale, spikenard, and many other kinds of spices."[10] Columbus was enthralled by Polo's account. He left his name on the flyleaf of Polo's book.

Determined to reach the spice islands of the East, Columbus finally persuaded Queen Isabella of Spain to bankroll an expedition. He discovered not the spice islands but the Caribbean. In three successive voyages back to the Americas he continued to believe that he had in fact journeyed by sea to India. He even called the natives "Indians," hoping against hope that he had indeed found the much-sought-after short cut to the Orient.[11]

Although Columbus failed in his mission to secure a new route to the spice islands of the East, he inadvertently stumbled upon a discovery of far greater significance: virgin forests and plains and vast grasslands covering two new continents. In search of spices to enhance the taste of beef, Columbus found new pastureland for grazing cattle. Today, half a millennium later, vast tracts of North, Central, and South America are devoted to raising over 400 million head of cattle to meet the demands of the wealthy beef-eating populations in western Europe, the United States, and Japan.[12]

Columbus was the first to introduce cattle to the New World. On January 2, 1494, the explorer set anchor near Cap-Haïtien, Haiti, on his second voyage to the Americas. He unloaded "twenty-four stallions, ten mares, and an unknown number of cattle." As historian Daniel Dary writes, "They and their progeny were destined to change the face of the New World and bring about a revolution comparable in impact to the industrial revolution nearly three centuries later."[13]

7

Cattlizing the Americas

Conquistadores and Spanish priests were determined to create a new Spain on American shores. To accomplish their objective, they set about the task of fertilizing the New World with Spanish longhorn cattle, hoping to establish an Iberian cattle complex in the Americas. Conditions at home spurred the process along. Spain was facing a crisis in its stockraising by the sixteenth century. The Iberian Peninsula was overgrazed. Forests had been cut down to make room for additional pastureland. Still, the increased demand for beef, tallow, and hides put additional pressure on Spanish soil, resulting in massive desertification.[1] The serendipitous confluence of depleted Spanish grazing land and virgin grasslands in the Americas proved irresistible.

The tough, highly mobile longhorn cattle of Spain were ideally suited for the wilderness conditions of the New World. Spanish galleons began unloading their bovine cargo throughout the West Indies—in Puerto Rico, Jamaica, and Cuba and on other islands. The cattle population was allowed to run wild, and within a matter of years it began to outstrip the human population on the islands.[2]

In the 1500s, Gregario de Villalobos led a Spanish expedition onto the Mexican mainland, near present-day Tampico, bringing with him several head of cattle. Within a year, Villalobos became lieutenant governor of New Spain, and from his governmental headquarters in Vera Cruz he began coordinating "the arrival of Spanish settlers, supplies, and an increasing number of horses and cattle."[3]

In that same year, Hernando Cortés's horsemen defeated the Aztecs and captured what is now Mexico City. Montezuma's legions were awed by men mounted on horses, which they called "big dogs."[4] Many Indians believed the charging cavalry were human-animal chimeras, and they cowered before the invading armies. Behind the advancing armies came the cattle, first in a trickle, then in wave after wave. The area from Veracruz to Mexico City provided ideal grazing land for Spanish longhorns. The animals prospered in their new habitat, reproducing faster than in their native Spain. A Franciscan priest, Alonso Ponce, wrote of the success of the bovine transplantation: "They reproduce as in Castile, only more easily, because the land is temperate and there are no wolves or other animals to destroy them as in Spain."[5]

Cortés divided up the defeated Indian population of New Spain, placing the natives under the control of individual Spaniards, each of whom was granted an encomienda, or land trust. Cortés claimed 23,000 Indians for his own encomienda.[6] The Indians were converted to the faith, clothed, and indentured, providing a cheap and abundant labor force for the conquering Spanish.

Worried about the growing concentration of power in the hands of Cortés and his men, and anxious not to lose control over New Spain, the Spanish crown issued a series of decrees designed to weaken the power of the encomienda. Among other things, the Spanish government granted the Indian population the right to create small farms and use common grazing lands around Indian villages. Disputes between Spanish ranchers and local Indian populations erupted in the ensuing decades, as cattlemen allowed their herds to trample on Indian farmland in defiance of official decrees.[7]

Eventually, cattle became so numerous in and around Mexico City that the Spanish were unable to attend them alone. Up until the 1540s, Indians were forbidden to own or ride horses, for fear they would become expert equestrians and mobilize an effective challenge to Spanish rule. Commercial interest, however, soon overcame military precautions. Spanish priests were the first to see the advantage of "converting" the Indians into mounted horsemen. The church needed men to watch over their own herds, which they had established at each new mission. They taught the Indians how to ride, making them the first cowboys of the Americas.

These native cowboys adopted the Spanish sombrero and sported neck bandannas, leather jackets, and chaps. Although leather boots were rare and expensive, being a mark of status worn by wealthy Spaniards, the "vaqueros" were allowed to own iron spurs, which they strapped over their bare ankles. The rotating sharp-pointed disks often measured eight inches or more in diameter.

The wearing of spurs had been a sign of high rank in Europe and was first practiced by the mounted horsemen of the Eurasian steppes three thousand years earlier. Spurs were generally awarded to men of valor, singling them out for special attention. In the New World, the spur became a badge of distinction for the vaqueros, making the early Indian cowboys, and later blacks, mestizos, mulattos, and poor whites, a semiprivileged group among the working poor, distinguished by their mounts and their iron footgear.[8]

The discovery of silver at Zacatecas in 1546 and the silver rush that followed greatly increased the demand for beef and leather and for vaqueros to watch over the burgeoning herds. Beef prices skyrocketed in the mining camps, a pattern that was to be repeated in the North American west three centuries later in the wake of the gold rush in California. Cattle provided not only beef for the miners, but tallow for candles to light the shafts and hides for pouches to transport the silver ore from the mines to the smelters. Cow leather was also used to fashion saddles, water bags, cowboy jackets and chaps, and countless other accouterments.[9] Fortunes were made in cattle in the sixteenth century, and a new cattle aristocracy emerged, whose wealth and power dictated the terms of Mexican politics for the next four centuries.

In 1598, a rich silver mine owner, Juan de Õnate, received permission from the Spanish crown to colonize the upper Rio Grande. He led an expedition of 400 men and their families into what is now north-central New Mexico. Õnate also brought with him over 7,000 head of cattle, seeding the southwest with the European bovine.[10]

One hundred years later, the Spanish headed north to what is now eastern Texas, bringing supplies adequate to establish a mission outpost. The leader of the expedition, Captain Alonso de León, was called the Johnny Appleseed of cattle by later western historians. Returning home to Mexico, after establishing a mission on the San

Pedro Creek, north of present-day Weches, Texas, he left "a bull and a cow, a stallion and a mare" at each of the river crossings. By the first decade of the eighteenth century, wild cattle were roaming the Texas prairies. Historian Herbert H. Bancroft estimated the cattle population of Texas to be in excess of 100,000 head by 1780.[11]

The seeding of cattle in North America owes as much to the enterprising skills of Catholic priests as to the bravado of military commanders and the wiles of powerful Spanish ranchers. In Arizona, Father Eusebio Francisco Kino, an experienced rancher, introduced cattle raising among the Indian population in the valleys south of the Gila River in 1687. According to historian Herbert E. Bolton, Father Kino "was easily the cattle king of his day and region." Within fifteen years he established the beginning of ranching in the valleys of the Santa Cruz, the San Pedro, and the Sonoita. "The stockraising industry of nearly twenty places on the modern map owes its beginnings on a considerable scale to this indefatigible man."[12]

In what would be Texas, New Mexico, and Arizona, mission priests converted Indians and bred cows, Christianizing and cattlizing. Their influence was perhaps most felt in California, where Franciscan priests established a succession of missions reaching from San Diego to San Francisco.[13] The California climate and topography was well suited for cattle. Writing in 1770, Fray Juan Crespi gave an account of the new land on the first Spanish expedition into the region: "The country is delightful for it is covered with beautiful grass which affords excellent pasture for the animals."[14]

Indians were converted to Christianity, then transformed into cowboys to attend the growing herds of mission cattle. The crown encouraged the enterprising Franciscan priests, granting them exclusive title over ever larger tracts of California land, in hopes of "civilizing" the western coast of North America for Spain. By 1834, nearly 31,000 mission vaqueros were tending up to 400,000 cattle and 62,000 horses.[15]

After Mexico declared its independence from Spain in 1821, the new government began to look askance at the tremendous wealth and power amassed by the Franciscan cattle barons in California. In 1834, the new government ordered the secularization of the missions. The priests responded by ordering the mass slaughter of their herds and the sale of their hides.[16] Although the decision greatly reduced the cattle population of California, it left a skilled labor force of

Indian vaqueros to provide a cheap labor pool for Spanish ranchers and, later, Anglo cattlemen.

The Spanish seeded other regions of the Americas with cattle as well. Ponce de León introduced cattle into Florida in 1521. Hernando de Soto followed de León in 1539, introducing hundreds of horses and cows onto the semiarid grasslands of Florida. As in the southwest, missions were established, first in St. Augustine, later in Tallahassee, and cattle were raised for local consumption.[17]

Jesuit priests followed Spanish armies into South America in the 1530s, establishing missions in Argentina, Paraguay, and Brazil. They brought their cattle with them. Many of the missions were looted and destroyed by bandits, the cattle left to scatter into the wild. A hundred years later, feral cattle had taken over much of the rich grassland of Latin America.[18] Cattle were so numerous on the pampas that their meat was virtually valueless.[19] Whole herds were slaughtered en masse, in wild cattle-hunting expeditions. As in the North American buffalo hunts a century later, the animals were skinned for their hides and tallow, the meat left to rot in the sun. In Montevideo, according to one account, carcasses littered the ground for a two-mile stretch outside of the city. In seventeenth-century Brazil, cattle were said to be as thick as locusts along the San Francisco River. João Capistrano de Abreu called the period "the era of leather" because people ate beef three times a day. Beef carcasses were often hung out on corral fence posts to dry. People would cut off a slab of beef whenever they were hungry, choosing only the best cuts, leaving the rest to rot. The population of Caracas consumed 50 percent more beef than Paris at that time even though it had only one-tenth the population.[20] One seventeenth-century traveler wrote of what he found in Argentina:

> All the wealth of these inhabitants consists in their animals, which multiply so prodigiously that the plains are covered with them . . . in such numbers that were it not for the dogs that devoured the calves . . . they would devastate the country.[21]

Cattle swarmed over the continent, filling and altering every available ecological niche. By the 1870s there were over 13 million cattle grazing on the Argentine pampas alone. Ranchers became rich exporting hides to Europe.

Salted beef and jerky were also exported in ever greater volume to fill the increasing demand for beef among the working classes of Europe. The jerky was little more than "slices of cows . . . dried in the sun." The pieces of beef were so hard, said one observer, "that one cannot chew them without beating them thoroughly with a piece of wood, from which they do not greatly differ, nor digest them without a strong purgative."[22]

Still, Europeans were clamoring for "fresh" beef, their own pasturelands having been overgrazed long ago or converted to cereal production to feed hungry industrial laborers and the urban poor. The solution to their problem came in 1878. The first refrigerated steamer, the *Frigorifique*, set out from Argentina on its maiden voyage to Le Havre, France, packed with fresh beef. The meat was kept at a constant temperature of 17 degrees Fahrenheit by an ammonia-compression machine. The ship docked at Le Havre with 5,500 frozen carcasses, creating a sensation in food history. Guests at the Grand Hotel in Paris dined on the fresh beef of the pampas, and South America became the new grazing land of Europe.[23]

Cattle, chattel, and capital went hand in hand during the colonization of the Americas. Conquistadores, missionaries, and later wealthy landed aristocrats colonized the new lands with cattle. Indian and African slaves, and later poor European immigrants, were put to work tending herds on both continents. The Americas, from the southwestern region of what is currently the United States to the boot of Chile, were awash in cows and New World serfs. The new herdsmen went by different names in different countries: in Chile, the *hauso*; in Argentina, the *gaucho*; in Venezuela, the *llanero*; in Mexico, the *vaquero*—all were part of a new indentured class of migratory laborers, poorly paid, mercilessly exploited, whose only distinction lay in their mounted steeds. Uneducated and landless, these seasonal workers so glorified in literature were the henchmen and handymen of the rich—their cattle warriors on the plains of the New World. They helped secure the fortunes of both the Spanish crown and the new landed gentry in the Americas.

Today, the ruling class of much of Central and South America descends from families who colonized the New World with cattle. In Chile a ranching elite gained control over much of the Chilean countryside during the eighteenth century. By the latter part of the nineteenth century, the cattle oligarchy of Chile owned giant cattle ranches and some managed herds of 20,000 or more. Through their powerful agricultural society, they dominated much of the political life of the nation. By 1924, less than 3 percent of the ranchers in the central valley of Chile controlled 80 percent of the agricultural lands.[24]

Uruguay followed a similar pattern. Spanish colonial policies encouraged concentration of power. Large tracts of grazing land were given over to a few families who ruled over the country in much the same manner as the landed aristocracy in Spain. The cattle barons banded together, forming the Uruguayan Rural Association, a powerful stockmen's club that managed the economic and political fortunes of the nation with an iron hand.[25]

In Argentina, the landed gentry formed their own trade associations, the Argentine Rural Society and the Jockey Club. After the defeat of the pampas Indians in 1879–80, Argentina's cattle barons moved to consolidate their control over the remaining grasslands on the great South American plains.[26]

In Venezuela, the cattle barons were able to establish their hegemony by the mid-eighteenth century. In 1750, thirty ranching families controlled much of the Venezuelan grasslands.[27]

The cattle barons of the Spanish-American grasslands were not unlike the pastoral warlords who overran the forests, plains, and villages of Europe several millennia ago. Throughout Central and South America they established a hierarchical herding culture, steeped in violence and subjugation and maintained by ruthless exploitation of native peoples and lands.

8

British Beefeaters

Three centuries after the Spanish first colonized the New World with cattle, the English launched their own cattle invasion of the American plains. The counting houses of Fleet Street and Glasgow usurped vast stretches of North American grassland in the 1880s, making much of the country west of the Mississippi a pastureland for British cattle. The true story of how the American west was won has never been told. It is a story of financial manipulation, land grabs, and under-the-table dealings, orchestrated from the clubs, counting houses, and country homes of the British aristocracy. The British played a major role in colonizing the American west. While American frontiersmen and cowboys cleared the way for westward expansion, it was the English business class that provided much of the financial muscle to turn an outback into the richest and most profitable pastureland in the world.

To understand how the British came to play such a pivotal role in the taming of the frontier and the shaping of post–Civil War America, it is necessary to step back and examine the unique history of the English cattle complex—a history punctuated by the continual conquest and confiscation of other lands and the subjugation of other peoples to provide the British with an ever-expanding supply of beef.

The English were the great beef eaters of Europe. Their Celtic ancestors established a cattle culture on the British Isles before the time of Christ. The Romans brought their own cattle culture with them in A.D. 43, when they invaded the isles. Roman husbandry dominated the lowlands while the Celtic cattle cultures continued to maintain a foothold in the north and west in Ireland and Scotland.[1]

Beef was the preferred ration of the Roman army in England, and the increasing demand provided the native population with a ready market for their cattle.[2] Even after the Roman withdrawal from the British Isles, cattle remained the dominant form of wealth and beef eating remained the centerpiece of the British diet.

While Europe was known as the carnivorous continent, the island people of Britain consumed far more beef than their continental neighbors. Their craving for beef was deeply rooted in Celtic tradition, which reveled in the hunt, the slaughter of animals, and lavish meat orgies. That tradition continued among the feudal nobility and later among the landed gentry. When James I hunted stags, he would personally cut their throats, then "daub the faces of his courtiers with blood, which they were not permitted to wash off." It was also customary "for ladies and women of quality, after the hunting of deer, to stand by until they are ripped up that they might wash their hands in the blood supposing it will make them white."[3]

Although the sacred aspects of animal slaughter had long since been eliminated from English consciousness, the presumed "power" of meat, and especially beef, remained fixed in British thinking, especially among the nobility. The consumption of large quantities of beef was believed to ensure greater strength and virility. On the eve of the American Revolution, when Britain was effectively extending its military reach to virtually every continent on earth, an Englishman wrote, "You find more courage among men who eat their fill of flesh than among those who make shift with lighter foods."[4]

In medieval England, the nobility spent personal fortunes and countless time and energy preparing elaborate meat-eating feasts in an effort to outdo one another. Among the wealthy, food and its preparation became the primary means of expressing rank and privilege. It has been said that in England "the poor ate to live, while in too many cases, the rich lived to eat."[5] The competition among the nobility became so intense and relentless that King Edward II was forced to issue a decree in 1283 to restrain "the outrageous and excessive multitude of meats and dishes which the great men of the kingdom used in their castles, and by persons of inferior rank imitating their example beyond what their stations required."[6] The king's edict limited the number of meat courses permissible at a given setting, a decision of great consequence, since a man's political clout depended in no small part on his ability to attract powerful supporters to his table.

Meat was used as a political and social tool at each lord's table to clearly delineate the appropriate rank and status of the invited guests. The high table was always served first, followed by the next table of rank, and so on. The best cuts of meat were alloted to those first served. The less desirable cuts were distributed down the line. When venison was served, the entrails or "umbles" of the deer were always distributed last to the guests of least distinction, thus giving rise to the popular expression "to eat humble pie."[7]

The gluttony of the British feudal lords and landed gentry is legend. Even as late as the Victorian era the aristocracy and upper classes engaged in an orgy of meat consumption. Novelist J. B. Priestley remarked: "Not since imperial Rome can there have been so many signposts to gluttony."[8] In the country homes of the landed gentry, each day would be given over to grand hunting parties, elaborate food preparation, and ostentatious meals fussed over and attended to by numerous butchers, cooks, butlers, and scullery maids.

While the rich wallowed in beef, the poor were virtually excluded from a beef-centered diet until well into the last quarter of the nineteenth century, having to settle instead for what the English called the "white meats"—cheese, milk, butter, and other dairy products. In between the rich and the poor, a growing working class and an increasingly prosperous and powerful bourgeois class emerged in the early modern era, aspiring to the beef-eating ways of the nobility. On the eve of the industrial revolution, England was already the beef-eating capital of the world. By 1726 some 100,000 head of cattle were slaughtered annually in the London market alone. It was said that Londoners "eateth more good beef . . . in one month than all of Spain, Italy, and parts of France in a whole year." British seamen of the eighteenth century were each provided with a staggering 208 pounds of beef a year, in the belief that a concentrated red meat diet would give them a decisive edge over their adversaries.[9]

A Swedish visitor to England in 1798 wrote, "I do not believe that any Englishman who is his own master has ever eaten a dinner without meat."[10] So beef-driven was England that it became the first nation in the world to identify with a beef symbol. From the outset of the colonial era, the "roast beef" became synonymous with the well-fed British aristocracy and middle class.

Englishmen were known for their skill in preparing beef, which was generally spit-roasted. One foreign observer wryly quipped that "Englishmen understand almost better than any other people the art of properly roasting a large cut of meat, which is not to be wondered at because the art of cooking as practiced by most Englishmen does not extend much beyond roast beef and plum pudding."[11]

Britain's attachment to beef became an obsession in the early modern era, influencing much of the direction of its colonial policies. The growing demand for beef among the British aristocracy, the emerging bourgeois class, and the military forced the British government to search for new pastureland in the seventeenth century. Scotland and Ireland became the first colonial grazing lands, followed in the nineteenth century by the North American plains, the Argentine pampas, the Australian outback, and the grasslands of New Zealand.

9

Let Them Eat Potatoes

The Celtic grazing lands of Scotland and Ireland had been used to pasture cows for centuries. The British colonized the Scots and the Irish, transforming much of their countryside into an extended grazing land to raise cattle for a hungry consumer market at home.

By the mid-eighteenth century, British demand for wool to feed the growing textile market put increasing pressure on Scottish pastureland.[1] Sheep raising began to compete with cattle raising, and both animals vied with the native human population for arable land. Many rural Scots were thrown off their land to make room for cattle raising and sheep rearing. Landless and penniless, thousands of Scottish farmers were forced to migrate to the lowlands on the coast in search of unskilled jobs in the emerging industrial factories.

Ireland, which had been under English domination since the twelfth century, was already the major source of cheap salted beef for British colonies in the Caribbean by the seventeenth century. One observer wrote in 1689 that "the islands and plantations of America are, in a manner, wholly sustained by the vast quantities of beef . . . and other provisions of the product of Ireland."[2] By the late 1700s, the Irish beef trade, like the Scottish, was redirected toward the domestic market in England.

The British enclosure movement had displaced thousands of rural English families, creating a cheap new labor pool to fill the unskilled jobs in the industrial factories of London, Leeds, Manchester, and Bristol. Shortages of foodstuffs and rising prices were fueling discontent among the new working class and middle class of the cities, threatening open rebellion. British officials and entrepreneurs quieted the masses with Scottish and Irish beef. Historians of the period point out that were it not for the Celtic pasturelands of Scotland and Ireland, it might well have proved impossible to quell the growing unrest of the British working class during the critical decades of British industrial expansion. Historian Eric Ross says that the hunger for cheap beef "lay behind England's impulse to procure Scottish and Irish meat and in the end, to base their own industrial growth on the relegation of these peripheral regions to an ancilliary role as pastoralist food reserves." By 1850, says Ross, "Much of the meat in London's market was imported from England's Celtic fringe."[3] Even today, 140 years later, Scotland and Ireland remain largely a grazing land for the British beef market.

The British taste for beef had a devastating impact on the impoverished and disenfranchised people of Scotland and Ireland. Of the two Celtic colonies, Ireland fared worse. Pushed off the best pastureland and forced to farm smaller plots of marginal land, the Irish turned to the potato, a crop that could be grown abundantly in less favorable soil. Eventually, cows took over much of Ireland, leaving the native population virtually dependent on the potato for survival. In 1846, a blight devastated the Irish potato crop, causing mass starvation and death. Many of those who survived picked up their few remaining belongings and set sail across the Atlantic to the shores of the New World.

The Irish food crisis only served to help the British. English bankers seized control of abandoned pockets of Irish land, turning agricultural fields to cow pastures and greatly increasing the flow of beef to English cities. Between 1846 and 1874 the number of cattle exported from Ireland to England more than doubled, from 202,000 to 558,000 head. By 1880, Ireland had been virtually transformed into a giant cattle pasture to accommodate the English palate. The statistics were staggering. Over "50.2 percent of the entire surface of the country and two-thirds of its wealth were devoted to the raising of cattle." A decade later, over 65 percent of Ireland's meat production was being shipped to England. Irish meat accounted for 30 percent of the domestic consumption of meat in England.[4]

While Scotland and Ireland were able, for a time, to provide for the growing demand for beef in England, even their rich pastures became strained beyond carrying capacity and were unable to keep pace with the near-insatiable British appetite. The English soon turned their gaze west once again, this time across the Atlantic to the great plains of North America, where a vast sea of grassland lay in wait ready to feed the cattle that would, in turn, feed the beef cravings of Englishmen and the rest of carnivorous Europe.

It was on the plains of Texas, Kansas, Nebraska, the Dakotas, Wyoming, and Colorado that British bankers met up with the Spanish cattle culture. In the years following the American Civil War, Texas ranchers had driven their Spanish longhorn herds up past the rail links of Abilene, Kansas, into the rich grasslands of the prairies, there to be grazed and fattened before their final shipment east to the slaughterhouses of Chicago. The Spanish longhorn was a wiry animal. Tough, resilient, and able to withstand the extremes of Texas summers and Dakota winters, the longhorn was an ideal creature for the climate and topography of North America. Its carcass, however, was far too tough and lean to suit the increasingly discriminating tastes of the British gentry and middle class, who had become accustomed to beef marbled with fat.

The British taste for fatty beef brought together two great agricultural traditions for the first time in history: the grain-producing culture whose roots date back to the first great cereal civilizations of North Africa and the Middle East, and the great bovine herdsmen whose line of descent dates back to the horse-mounted nomads of the Eurasian steppes. The two great agricultural systems linked up on the western plains of the United States where the rolling grasslands of the prairies met the flat agricultural lands of the midwest. It was here that a historic bargain was struck between British bankers and American cattlemen that changed the course of history and altered the dietary regime of much of the human population in the twentieth century. Spanish cattle, descendants of the horned aurochs of the Iberian Peninsula, would be transported from the western plains to the midwestern farm belt, where they would be fattened up on a rich diet of corn until their flesh was marbled with specks of fat.

Beef would then be transported by rail and steamer to English ports and finally to the dining tables of the beef-eating people of the British Isles and Europe.

Today, in the United States, over 70 percent of the grain produced by the agricultural sector is fed to livestock, primarily cattle.[5] Worldwide, one-third of the planet's production of grain is being fed to cattle and other livestock.[6] The convergence of grass and grain, herding and agriculture into a single cattle complex has had a major impact on modern society and the ecology of the twentieth century.

The transfer of much of the world's grain production from man to beast might never have come to pass were it not for the peculiar shift in British appetites from lean to fatty beef in the early nineteenth century.

The story of how the British became addicted to fatty beef is surely one of the more bizarre episodes in the history of the European cattle cultures. It deserves to be examined, since it has had such a profound effect on the settling of the American west and the global agricultural policies of the current century.

10

Corpulent Cows and Opulent Englishmen

The British landed gentry first took a liking to fat-laced beef in the last decade of the eighteenth century. In the year 1800, the British publicized their newfound love of fatted cattle with a nationwide tour of the celebrated Durham Ox, a giant bovine marbled with fat and weighing in at nearly 3,000 pounds. The legendary creature was housed in a specially designed carriage and with appropriate British pomp and circumstance was paraded through the cities and villages of England and Scotland for six years; eager spectators paid a handsome admission fee to gaze on its massive bulk. In 1802 some 2,000 people paid half a guinea for an engraving of the squarish roan-colored beast.

The Durham Ox captured the public imagination. In the land of John Bull and roast beef, this giant bovine seemed an appropriate symbol of the new British self-image. The English had extended their reach and power around the world in the eighteenth century. By the beginning of the nineteenth century the Union Jack flew high in countries on every continent. While the new British opulence was expressed in a myriad of ways, none proved more revealing than the new pastime of the landed gentry, the raising of prize cattle.

Although the landed gentry had long taken an interest in cattle, they had left questions of rearing to their herdsmen and peasants.

Suddenly, and rather unexpectedly, the landlords themselves turned to stock breeding with a zeal that at first surprised their fellow countrymen. Stock-breeding associations were chartered, their ranks filled with the names of Britain's most distinguished families. The most famous of these was the Smithfield Club, which held its first public show in 1799. In subsequent years the Smithfield Club stock show became a social event of immense importance, drawing the cream of British nobility and even the royal family.[1]

Wealthy breeders dedicated themselves to the task of rearing massive bovines for show at the various fairs. These portly beasts were paraded before their equally portly British masters at select agricultural gatherings, providing a kind of bovine testimonial to the opulence of the English aristocracy. Historian Harriet Ritvo observes that "in toasting their noble animals, the elite livestock fanciers were celebrating themselves."[2] The ruling class of England, still somewhat uncomfortable with its new position as empire builder, busied itself with creating lines of shorthorn cattle that could embody their new sense of self in the world. Their preoccupation with the hobby reached absurd heights by the nineteenth century. Such magazines as the *Quarterly Review of Agriculture* described the prize-winning animals in amorous language that might have brought a whimsical smile to more than a few common yeomen:

> Irresistibly attractive . . . the exquisitely symmetrical form of the body . . . bedecked with the skin of the richest hues . . . ornamented with a small . . . head [and] prominent mildly beaming eyes.[3]

Livestock portraits became a favorite among Englishmen of the period. Many a country estate and English drawing room boasted paintings of obese cattle in the foreground of a bucolic country landscape. Some of Britain's best artists were kept busy drawing commissioned works of prizewinning cattle. Popular magazines of the day always included engravings of cows suitable for framing in the homes of the British working class. The artists were often instructed to accentuate the bodies of these creatures to show off their fat. The artist Thomas Bewick complained that he had once lost a commission because he refused to add "lumps of fat here and there" when the animal before him had "no such protrusions." Some of these prize-winning cattle were so fat that their own legs were unable to support their massive girth and they often had to be wheeled into the shows.[4]

While the landed gentry professed to be interested in improving the general quality of British livestock, far greater attention was paid to the outward appearance of their prize animals and their family histories. Early on, attention turned to lines of descent. Breeders were obsessed with genealogy. Countless hours were spent tracing lineage and ensuring purity of bloodlines. The aristocracy became consumed with the question of pure stock. Animals were identified by name and listed in a registry that included detailed information on their ancestry as far back as records existed. For the gentry, whose own claim to rank and title depended solely on bloodlines, the question of purity in their prizewinning cattle became paramount as well. The most important consideration was "the length of time there had been a succession of best blood, without any inferior blood intervening."[5] The aristocracy's near-fanaticism on the question of purity was echoed in its colonial policies abroad. English philosophers and naturalists, including Charles Darwin and his cousin Sir Francis Galton, championed race theory and the new "science" of eugenics, arguing that the superior Aryan race should not be allowed to mix with the inferior black and aboriginal races of the world, lest it be contaminated by impure bloodlines.

Prizewinning cattle served as a physical metaphor for the wealth and prestige of the British ruling class. Cattle had figured prominently in the wealth of the English people as far back as any could remember. In Roman times even Caesar had noticed that "cattle constituted the true wealth of the Britons."[6] Now that England was, itself, a great imperial power, the lords' cattle were shown off to the world and their own countrymen as a visible token of England's newfound greatness. Historian Ritvo writes that these overfed, overstuffed creatures with stump legs, giant girth, and shortness of breath were the "ostentatious evidence of their owners' power of consumption."[7] In consuming their cattle, they symbolically consummated their role as rulers of the world. Here was a new secular ritual, the eating of flesh marbled with the fat of colonial privilege. Marbled beef became both the symbol of affluence and a measure of taste.

The desire for fatty beef, at first a privilege of the rich, soon became an aspiration of the middle and working classes. Ritvo says that the butchers of London

> bought the most celebrated carcasses and put them on display in their shambles, where the public could gaze on them, one last time before they were purchased by great ladies who liked to serve roast that could be identified by name.[8]

Eating fatty beef served as an initiation rite for aspiring Englishmen. The taste for fat was synonymous with the taste for opulence, for power and privilege, for the values that made these island people the feared and envied rulers of the world. Marbled beef brought the bourgeoisie and later the working class into the colonial fold. By consuming the fatty flesh of the bovine, these other classes signaled their willingness to take part in the colonial regime. This modern-day baptism of beef aligned the classes in common pursuit. Now the English people, at large, would live off the "fat of the land." Between the late eighteenth and early nineteenth centuries the weight of cattle more than doubled in England. By the mid-nineteenth century the rest of western Europe had caught up with the new British breeding standards.

The practical aspects of breeding fatty cattle were left to breeders like Robert Bakewell, who once boasted that he could produce "beasts who would put on fat in the tail."[9] Still, it was the rich, with their eccentric preoccupation with prize cattle, who established the culinary standard for the English middle and working classes, and later people on the European continent and the Americas, as each were initiated into the fruits of colonialism.

By the latter half of the nineteenth century, the British home market was hungering for fatty beef. As noted earlier, the pasture-lands of Scotland and Ireland were overgrazed and unable to keep up with the growing demand for beef among the working and middle classes of the new industrial cities of England. British bankers and businessmen began to look elsewhere for greener pastures. Their attention soon turned to tales of tall grass on the western plains of North America. In the early 1870s, reports began filtering back to the London financial houses about vast stretches of rangeland west of the Mississippi River ideally suited for the grazing of cattle.

The timing of the British financial invasion of the American west couldn't have been more propitious. In the years immediately following the Civil War, the western frontier had been colonized and converted to pastureland to graze beef cattle for the northern and eastern markets of America. The buffalo had been eliminated from the western range and the aboriginal population subdued and sequestered onto reservations, leaving the prairies an open grassland, ready to be exploited.

The story of how the western frontier was transformed into the largest cattle pasture in the world, and then nearly annexed by British financial interests, is among the most sordid and shameful sagas in the history of the American Republic. That story began in the Texas cattle country. It was there on the arid southwestern grasslands that the ground was laid for the conversion of the Great Plains, the British invasion of the American west, and the coming together of a powerful Euro-American cattle complex.

Part Two

HOW THE WEST
WAS WON

11

Rail Links and Cattle Crossings

Most Americans in the early decades after independence had little reason to think in continental terms. The vast tracts of land that lay beyond the Mississippi were of little concern and even less interest. Daniel Webster voiced the sentiments of many of his fellow countrymen when he asked rhetorically:

> What do we want with this vast worthless area? This region of savages and wild beasts, of deserts, shifting sands, and whirlwinds of dust, of cactus and prairie dogs?[1]

Fifty years later, the western prairies had been subdued and colonized. Many of their inhabitants were exterminated. Those spared the gun and the white man's diseases were rounded up and forced onto reservations. The buffalo of the Great Plains had been slaughtered, leaving the rich grasslands of the western range to be used as grazing fields for cattle. By the time the U.S. Census Bureau declared the frontier officially closed in 1890, an area the size of all of western Europe had been transformed into the largest pastureland in the world. In less than half a century, the western wilderness had been converted to a "productive resource," a feat of unparalleled magnitude and scale. Frontier historian Frederick Jackson Turner captured the enormity of what had transpired. Writing in 1890, Turner called the migration onto the plains "the greatest pastoral movement in recorded history."[2]

The American cattle culture was gestated in Texas. The breeding ground was a giant geographical area whose northern apex bordered on San Antonio. The lines of Spanish cattle country descended south-easterly to the Gulf Coast and southerly to Laredo on the Rio Grande.[3] The area proved to be an ideal breeding ground for the bovine. The mild climate and plentiful grass and water combined to make southern Texas the cattle incubator of North America.

In an earlier section we noted that Franciscan priests had been the first to explore the region. By the last quarter of the eighteenth century, the priests had established over fifty missions in Texas and seeded each with herds of cattle. After the Mexican people declared their independence from Spain in 1821, the mission priests of Texas were forced to sign a loyalty oath to the new government. Most refused, abandoning their missions and leaving some of their cattle in the care of local Indians while turning the rest loose in the Texas wild, where the cattle flourished.

In the fight for independence with Mexico in the 1830s, many Spanish ranchers fled south of the Rio Grande, abandoning their herds to the wild as the mission priests had earlier. In 1836, the New Republic of Texas declared the feral cattle to be part of the public domain, thus providing an endowment for ambitious Texans to ex-ploit and build upon.[4] It has been said that "Texans did not create their cattle industry, they simply took it over."[5] Young "cowboys" began rounding up strays along the banks of the Rio Grande. Herds of 300 to 1,000 head were driven inland to Missouri and Ohio and along the Gulf Coast into New Orleans for sale. Even with the increase in roundups, the cattle population continued to multiply. Some 100,000 head roamed Texas in the 1830s. Three decades later, on the eve of the Civil War, the cattle population had increased to over 3.5 million.[6]

During the Civil War, the North captured the Mississippi River, cutting off the movement of Texas cattle east to feed Confederate troops. The longhorns multiplied, and by the end of the war, south-ern migrants, hoping to rebuild their lives on the frontier territory of Texas, found cattle grazing everywhere. Meanwhile, the war had devastated southern herds. The Union armies had further depleted the stock of cattle in the northeast and middle Atlantic states to feed their troops. Suddenly, and rather unexpectedly, the country turned its attention to the Texas longhorn.

Feral Spanish longhorn cattle bore little resemblance to their well-bred shorthorn relatives in the east. For decades the longhorn was hunted more often than it was herded. Texans said of the cattle that they were "wilder than deer," and "fifty times more dangerous to footmen than the fiercest buffalo."[7]

Colonel Richard Irving Dodge recounted the story of the chance encounter between a Texas longhorn and a regiment under the command of General Taylor. A soldier shot at the animal, whereupon the bull charged the entire column, and "put to flight an army which a few days after covered itself with glory by victoriously encountering five times its numbers of human enemies."[8]

It was said that the longhorn had the nose of a bloodhound. Cowboys in search of water would put their lives in the hands of these canny animals, who could sense an oncoming shower fifteen miles away and a hidden stream or water hole forty miles distant. The longhorn was unmatched as a scavenger; unlike other bovines, it could feed upon the leaves of trees. Legend tells of the story of one steer whose skeleton was found hanging upside down high up in an elm tree. According to its owner, it had climbed up the limbs and out onto the branches "like a squirrel to eat the buds, and just accidentally hung himself." These agile animals could raise their forefeet onto cottonwood limbs to reach the leaves, and they often used their horns to pull down the blossoms of the Spanish dagger. Historian Daniel Boorstin writes:

> They could live on prickly pear, and when there was no grass, they browsed like deer on the shoots of trees and bushes. They were supposed to have the limber neck of a goat, a mouth that could chew and a stomach that could digest the thorns of cactus and chaparral.[9]

Their most salient feature, as Boorstin and others observed, was their high degree of "mobility."[10] Fast, restless, always on the go, they embodied the frontier mentality. They moved with the fat of the land, depleting the wild grasses and other flora of the western landscape. These were the "swampers," the semiwild cattle of the coastal plains of Texas who were rounded up, corralled, branded, and driven north to the abattoirs of New Orleans and Kansas.[11]

While more than a few enterprising ranchers trekked north from Texas all the way to Iowa and Illinois to get their cattle to northern markets, the trip up the middle of the country was far too dangerous and long for the cattle, despite their extraordinary mobility. Weight loss, natural calamities, and outlaw attacks all took their toll on the stock, often leaving the herds emaciated and depleted at journey's end. Getting surplus Texas cattle to hungry and eager northern customers became a commercial challenge. The solution came in 1867 when a young entrepreneur, Joseph McCoy, hit on the idea of linking Texas cattle with the eastern railroads that were just extending their rails into the outskirts of the western prairies.

The north-south cattle trails met up with the east-west rail link in the dusty little one-street town of Abilene, Kansas. McCoy described the town as "a very small, dead place, consisting of about one dozen log huts, low, small, rude affairs, four-fifths of which were covered with dirt for roofing."[12] It was in this primitive frontier town that the north-south and east-west byways of America first intersected, connecting the four coordinates of a great continent. Cattle stepped over the divide and onto the railcars, thus changing the course of America's history.

The twenty-nine-year-old Illinois cattle buyer convinced the Kansas Pacific division of the Union Pacific Railroad to construct a rail siding for a cattle pen at the remote Abilene depot and to pay him a commission on every carload of cattle shipped. McCoy then successfully lobbied the governor of Kansas, persuading him to lift the quarantine on Texas cattle entering the state. (Outbreaks of "Texas fever," a serious cattle disease, had led states like Kansas to curtail or ban shipments of cattle from the Lone Star State for fear of contaminating local herds.)[13] After persuading the Illinois legislature to amend state law to allow shipments of his cattle into that state, McCoy set about the task of constructing cattle pens and advertising his scheme among the Texas drovers. On September 5, 1867, McCoy shipped twenty railroad cars of cattle east from Abilene. By 1871, Abilene was processing 700,000 longhorn steers annually, all bound east for the abattoirs of St. Louis and Chicago.[14]

The bold venture had succeeded. The Illinois businessman had brought the southern drovers together with the northern buyers, cementing a new north-south business arrangement, marking the first effective commercial rapprochement since the Civil War. Before the war, "cotton was king." Southern slave plantations produced bales of cotton destined for the northern and European textile markets. The new arrangement challenged the long-standing hegemony of king cotton. Cattle were about to become king, with southern ranchers providing livestock for the northern beef market and the leather tanneries of New England.

Throughout the 1870s, the Chisholm Trail stretching from Texas to Abilene was trafficked by herd upon herd. The longhorns generally covered ten to twelve miles a day on their three-month trek north to the rail link. The herds were driven by young cowboys, a cheap labor pool composed of southern youths, blacks, Mexicans, and Indian itinerant labor. Working conditions on the drives were tough, and pay was subsistence-level. The average cowboy made between $25 and $40 per month and was expected to work a twelve-to-eighteen-hour day for three months at a time.[15] Wranglers, cooks, and trail bosses fared little better.

The new north-south cattle complex expanded in the 1870s. The demand for beef, tallow, and hides seemed nearly insatiable. The North, rebounding from the war, began to rebuild and expand its industrial base. The new urban middle and working classes basked in postwar prosperity and created even greater demands for beef. The number of Texas cattle was inadequate to the growing demand, forcing ranchers to search out new grazing lands for the herds. The western plains lay waiting. Two formidable obstacles had to be cleared, however, before the plains of North America could be used for pasture. Their native inhabitants, the buffalo and the Indians, had to be moved aside to make room for the great pastoral invasion.

12

The Great Bovine Switch

What was there befor

The western range makes up over 40 percent of the land surface of the continental United States.[1] It stretches upward from Texas into Oklahoma, Kansas, Colorado, Arizona, and New Mexico; north into the Dakotas, Montana, and Wyoming; and west to Idaho, California, and Oregon. Much of the western range was relatively treeless, with the exception of cottonwoods and other shrubbery growing along the streams and rolling hills that occasionally break up the landscape. The prairie grasses—blue bunch wheat grass, buffalo grass, and dozens of other varieties of grass, shrubs, and native flowers—stretched like a sea of green across the range. Prairie rodents were everywhere on the plains—ground squirrels, pocket gophers, mice. Hawks and golden eagles kept watch high over the plains. Herds of pronghorn, mule deer, and elk crossed over the fields. Predator species—coyotes, wolves, and bobcats—ruled over the grassy domain. In terms of sheer size, the western plains are rivaled in grandeur only by the great plains of the Eurasian steppes.

The plains are ruled by extremes. The scorching hot winds of summer can nearly sear the flesh. Icy northern winds make the winter months bitter cold. In the spring, torrential rains turn riverbeds into raging rapids. In the dry summer months, the rivers turn into mud flats, then parched gullies. Cyclones and electrical storms are com-

mon occurrences. The air is often so charged with electricity that
the night sky will light up from the tiny "tapers of light" emanating
from the points of the horns on the heads of cattle. The Great Plains,
writes western historian Edward Dale, is "a land where nature seems
to operate on a gigantic scale."[2] A daunting and desolate place, the
plains were looked on as "the Great American Desert" in the early
years of the republic.[3]

A short two decades after the surrender of the Confederacy at
Appomattox, the western range had been tamed and transformed to
suit the requirements of husbandry and commerce. The area was
reconsecrated as "cattle country" and thought of as the world's premier pastureland.

Western wild grasses were unique and enjoyed a distinct advantage over the grasses of the east. They were resilient to drought and
unlike the eastern grasses did not need to be "cured" in barns over
winter. Western grasses dried out on the open ground, providing a
rich and nourishing source of hay for winter grazing. Marveling at
the "wonder grass," historian Daniel J. Boorstin asked rhetorically,
"Who could imagine a fairy-tale grass that required no rain and
somehow made it possible for cattle to feed themselves all winter?"[4]
Unfortunately for the cattle ranchers, the grasslands were already
occupied by buffaloes and Indians. As long as they remained on the
land it could not be successfully converted to pasture and effectively
exploited by the newly emerging ranching complex.

why the west

The promise and challenge of the plains country was recognized
early on. Legend has it that upon learning about the successful win-
tering of steers on the grasslands near Fort Keogh in 1876, the com-
manding general of the garrison, General Nelson Miles, predicted,
"When we get rid of the Indians and buffalo, the cattle . . . will fill
this country."[5] It soon became apparent that getting rid of the Indians
could best be accomplished by eliminating buffalo from the western
plains, cutting off their primary means of survival.

Cattlemen joined ranks with eastern bankers, the railroads, and
the U.S. Army in a systematic campaign to exterminate the bison
of the western range. The task was enormous. Buffalo herds black-
ened the plains. Herds of tens of thousands of head were common.[6]
A visitor could watch an uninterrupted stampede of several hours'
duration without a break in the chain. Giant dust clouds could be
seen miles away as the bovines thundered over the distant horizon.

Bison gone

William Hornaday tried to capture the spectacle in words. He wrote, "It would have been as easy to count or to estimate the number of leaves in a forest as to calculate the number of buffaloes living at any given time during the history of the species previous to 1870."[7]

Just a few years later, the buffalo were eliminated entirely from the western range after thousands of years of habitation. In their place were 600,000 head of cattle grazing peacefully on the same "short grass" that just a few years earlier had provided fodder for the massive herds of plains bison.

In his now classic monograph, Hornaday dates the demise of the American buffalo to the migratory movement of Texas cattle into the northern plains.[8] The railroads and the United States Army had helped clear the way for the Spanish longhorns. By 1869, the Union Pacific Railroad had divided the plains buffalo into a northern and southern herd. Between 1871 and 1874, the southern herd was decimated at the hands of buffalo hunters like Buffalo Bill, most of whom were under contract with the railroads and army to supply buffalo meat for rail employees and soldiers.[9] The northern herd was eliminated several years later, leaving the plains wide open for cattle.

The mass extinction of the American buffalo remains, to this day, one of the most gruesome tales in the ecological history of the country. The slaughter was sudden and decisive, ending 15,000 years of continuous existence on the plains virtually overnight. Some observers, who experienced the spectacle firsthand, wrote moving accounts. Colonel Richard Irving Dodge reported that near his army post in Kansas, buffalo were limitless in number as late as the winter of 1871. By the fall of 1873 Dodge wrote:

> Where there were myriads of buffalo the year before, there was now myriads of carcasses. The air was foul with a sickening stench, and the vast plain, which only a short twelve months before teemed with animal life, was a dead, solitary, putrid desert.[10]

Dodge estimated that over 4 million buffalo had been slain.

On the Texas plains over 1,500 hunters and skinners fanned out over the prairie, shooting every buffalo in sight. One frontiersman, S. P. Merry, said that "there were hunters everywhere . . . you could hear guns popping all over the country." Hides were heaped up along wagon trails and rail sidings across the Texas plains country. One merchant "had four acres . . . blanketed with bales of hide" waiting to be carted by wagon to Fort Worth." At the rail terminal at Fort Worth, 60,000 hides were piled along the siding in the spring of 1876 waiting to be shipped back east.[11]

New tanning methods for treating buffalo hides had been devised in 1871, making the skins commercially valuable. Buffalo hunters usually received between $1 and $3 per hide. The hides were often tanned with the fur on and made into coats, robes, and overshoes. Many of the hides were purchased by the British army, which regarded buffalo leather more highly than calf leather because of its elasticity and flexibility. Buffalo leather was even used to make belts for industrial machinery and could be seen in the finest homes as padding and covering for furniture. It was considered the best leather for carriage tops, sleighs, and hearses.[12]

Buffalo were slaughtered en masse. Hunters often competed with each other to see who could "bag" the most game in the least time. While movie accounts show the buffalo hunter in pursuit of a stampeding herd from atop his mount, most buffalo hunters preferred the "still hunt," killing their prey from cover.[13] In that way, the carcasses would not be strewn over the plains but concentrated, making it easier to skin them.

Every buffalo hunter hoped to achieve the coveted "stand." Occasionally an entire herd of buffalo would stand their ground and allow the riflemen to shoot them down, one by one, without moving position. John Cook, a buffalo hunter of some renown, described the stand in detail:

> I now had what I had so often heard about but had never actually seen before, "a stand." . . . After I killed twenty-five that I knew of, the smoke from my gun commenced to hang low, and was slow in disappearing. . . . Even while I was shooting buffaloes that had not been shot at all, some would lie down apparently unconcerned about the destruction going on around them. I fired slowly and deliberately.[14]

The shooting went on for an hour and a quarter, and when it was over, eighty-eight buffaloes were dead and many others lay wounded, the field a sea of blood.

Other hunters reported similar experiences with the "stand."

Hornaday reported that the buffaloes would often "cluster around the fallen ones, sniff at the warm blood, bawl around in wonderment, and do everything but run away."[15] Colonel Richard Irving Dodge's account is perhaps the most graphic and revealing:

> Attracted by the blood, they collect about the wounded buffalo. Another bullet is now sent in; another buffalo plunges, stops and bleeds. The others still stare and, seeming to think the wounded animals responsible for the unusual noise, concentrate their attention on them. Again and again, the rifle cracks. Buffalo after buffalo bleeds, totters and falls. The survivors stare in imbecile amazement.[16]

Buffalo hunting became a popular sporting event during the period, and the railroads began advertising cheap excursions across the plains, promising easterners that they could shoot buffalo to their heart's content from the comfort and safety of a moving train. One observer described the hunt:

> The rate per mile of passenger trains is slow upon the plains, and hence it often happens that the cars and buffalo would be side by side for a mile or two. . . . During these races the car windows are opened, and numerous breech-loaders fling hundreds of bullets among the densely crowded and flying masses. Many of the poor animals fall, and more go off to die in the ravines. The train speeds on, and the scene is repeated every few miles.[17]

The buffalo were left to rot, their remains scattered along a narrow line stretching for hundreds of miles along the rails. In May 1872, the *Denver Rocky Mountain News* condemned the sport shoots on the plains:

> The carcasses of the animals, in every stage of decomposition, which have been wantonly shot from the passing trains, are seen on either side of the track, all along where it passes through the buffalo ranges. It would be a good idea for the general division superintendents to enforce a rule prohibiting the firing of guns from the train.[18]

For wealthy easterners and European royalty, special buffalo game shoots became the rage in the 1870s. Buffalo Bill Cody, the best-known of the buffalo hunters, recounted a shooting match that had been arranged between himself and another famed buffalo hunter, named Comstock, for the entertainment of a group of wealthy sports enthusiasts from St. Louis. Cody remembered that he had killed thirty-eight to Comstock's twenty-three on the first run. He attributed his victory to his finesse in corralling the creatures, allowing him to increase his count. "I had 'nursed' my buffaloes, as a billiard player does the balls when he makes a run." After "the run" the visitors from St. Louis celebrated by setting out "a lot of champagne, which they had brought with them and which proved a good drink on a Kansas prairie."[19]

Cody's most celebrated guest on the prairie was the Grand Duke Alexis, the son of Czar Alexander II. On January 13, 1872, the Russian noble and his entourage joined Lieutenant General George Custer, General Philip Sheridan, and Cody for a sport hunt on Red Willow Creek near North Platte, Nebraska. Buffalo Bill lent the prince his favorite running horse, Buckskin Joe, and rode alongside him to provide the appropriate instructions. The prince was a quick learner, and after a few false starts he downed his first buffalo. The prince was "elated at his success," said Cody in his memoirs. The *Kansas City Times* remembers that the prince

> leaped from the saddle in a transport of astonishment, turned the horse loose, threw the gun down, cut off the tail as a souvenir and then, sitting down on the carcass, waved the dripping trophy, and, as Custer later stated, "let go a series of howls and gurgles like the death-song of all the fog horns and calliopes ever born." . . . The Russians came galloping up to see what was the matter. They first solemnly embraced their prince by turns, then fell into each other's arms. The trophy was passed from hand to hand till all were plastered with blood and dirt.[20]

Not everyone approved of the buffalo shoots on the prairies. One newspaper of the period chastised the unfolding spectacle on the plains, calling it "wantonly wicked." The paper condemned "killing these noble animals for their hides or to gratify the pleasure of some Russian Duke or English lord."[21]

While history books often explain away the mass slaughter of the bison as an act of wasteful exuberance, the facts point to a clear and systematic policy designed to replace the buffalo with the steer and the Indian with the cowboy. Historian Eric Ross says, "It was an

absolute prerequisite for the advance of cattle raising on the Great Plains: and it was widely considered necessary to end the resistance of the Plains Indians."[22] General Philip Sheridan, the commander of the Armies of the West, summed up the strategic thinking of the period in remarks to the Texas legislature:

> These men [the buffalo hunters] have done . . . more to settle the vexed Indian question than the entire regular army has done in the last thirty years. They are destroying the Indians' commissary; and it is a well-known fact that an army losing its base of supplies is placed at a great disadvantage. Send them powder and lead if you will; but for the sake of lasting peace let them kill, skin, and sell until the buffalo is exterminated. Then your prairies can be covered with speckled cattle and the festive cowboy who follows the hunter as a second forerunner of an advanced civilization.[23]

The buffalo were exterminated on the Great Plains by the end of the 1870s. Their sun-bleached bones could be seen scattered across thousands of miles of grassland, glistening under the prairie sun. In fact, so many millions of skeletons scarred the prairie killing fields that they became a source of commercial value. The "white harvest," as it was called by the commercial scavengers, became a boom business. Buffalo bones brought up to $8 a ton.[24] The bones were transported east, where they were ground up for phosphorus fertilizer. "Fresher bones" were made into bone char and used in the sugar-refining process to eliminate the brownish coloration of sugar.[25] Some of the bones were made into bone china. Horns and hoofs were made into buttons, combs, knife handles, and glue.[26] Buffalo hunters and homesteaders eked out a living on the bone harvest for several years. Tragically, many Indians were forced to become bone scavengers as well. They collected the skeletal remains of the buffalo and carted them off to the nearest railhead, where they received the white man's money.[27]

In one Dakota town, a young banker, M. I. McCreight, described his job buying bones from the "redman":

> In the distance, he recalled, the townsmen could see the wagon trains of the Indians as they followed the winding trails that led over the prairies toward the market. In front of each slowly moving caravan strode the chief . . . followed by a motley group of men,

women, children and dogs. . . . About half a mile outside the town, the visitors halted . . . and made camp. Then the chief and his councilors walked into town and inquired what price was being paid for bones. On being told that the rate was six dollars a ton, they went back to the camp and brought in their loaded carts to be weighed. From the scales they drove their carts to the railroad siding and dumped their contents. After receiving their money, the Indians swarmed into the stores to spend it. Only after the last dime was gone did the visitors break camp.[28]

At the Kansas Pacific railhead at Hays, Kansas, bones were often piled ten feet high along several miles of railroad siding. At the Dodge City depot of the Sante Fe line, bones were piled up for miles—so many bones that the railhead could not provide enough boxcars to haul them east. The buffalo bone trade became such an integral part of the commercial life of the prairie that in Kansas people were fond of saying that buffalo bones were legal tender in Dodge City.

Some westerners made their fortunes on the bone harvest. Month after month, miles of boxcars would start the long slow haul east filled with skeletons. The Santa Fe line alone shipped 1,135,300 pounds of bones in 1872, 2,743,100 pounds in 1873, and 6,914,950 pounds in 1874.[29]

By the early 1880s, the white man's strategy of eliminating the "Indians' commissary" had succeeded beyond anyone's wildest expectations.[30] Even the skeletal remains of the great bison of the plains had been carted off, removing any last telltale sign of their former presence on the prairies. Now only Spanish longhorns and English shorthorns could be seen grazing along the grasslands, attended to by cowboys on mount.

The Indians of the plains were never able to recover from the swift and deadly blow aimed at their source of sustenance. Many Indian tribes, dazed by the massive carnage, thought it a sign from the gods of their wrongdoings. Some, like the Omaha Indians, could not accept the fact that the herds were gone. They continued to believe, for a short while, that they must be hiding in caves or "beyond the horizon." Tribal shamans attempted "to call the herds forth from their remote places with ritual ceremonies." The ceremony was called "anointing the Sacred Pole" and required buffalo meat as a sacrifice. Because there were no buffalo left, the tribal leaders took the last little money they had collected from federal land transfers and purchased thirty head of cattle, which they killed as an offering to the gods. When this failed, they bought more cattle, repeating the ritual over and over again until they ran out of money to buy more cattle for sacrifice. Defeated, spiritually and physically, they finally resigned themselves to cultivating small plots of land, raising enough maize, chickens, pigs, and cattle to sustain their lives.[31]

The Kiowa experienced a similar fate. The tribe had always sacrificed a buffalo as an offering at its yearly sun dance, the most sacred of its animal rituals. In 1881, the sun dance had to be postponed for two months while they searched the plains for buffalo. They finally stumbled upon a lonely survivor wandering on the plains and killed it for the ceremony. The next year, not a single buffalo could be found.[32]

The last one

13

Cowboys and Indians

Indian tribes had lived in a symbiotic and sustainable relationship with the bison on the Great Plains of North America for thousands of years. The Native Americans hunted the buffalo, killing just enough to provide themselves with food, clothing, and shelter. Buffalo were the mainstay of their existence, as cattle were for so many European cultures. Unlike their bovine relatives from Europe, however, the buffalo could not be easily domesticated; they remained a hunted animal. The U.S. Army, the railroad, and the ranchers hoped that by eliminating the bison from the prairies, they could starve their adversaries into submission, thus reducing their own losses and shortening the conflict on the plains. The "enemy" were individual tribal nations, each a guardian over a small swath of the sea of grass that stretched from the Missouri River to the Rocky Mountains and beyond. The Comanches lived in western Texas and Oklahoma. To the north, in Oklahoma, Kansas, and Colorado, lived the Kiowas. To the north and east were the Osage. Farther north, in the Dakotas, Montana, and Wyoming, the Cheyenne ruled. Most of the northern plains was Sioux country. To the west were the Blackfoot. In the Great Basin between the Rocky Mountain ranges, the Utes, Paiutes, Shoshones, and Washoes resided. The southwest was populated by Pueblos, Hopis, Apaches, and Navajos.[1]

In the early years of the western campaign to clear the Indians from the plains, government troops occasionally engaged in barbarous acts of wanton violence. At Sand Creek, in Colorado Territory, troops under the command of Colonel John M. Chivington of the 3rd Colorado Cavalry charged a sleeping camp of Cheyenne villagers in the early morning hours of November 29, 1864. Their chief, Black Kettle, rushed from his tent waving both an American flag and a white flag of surrender. Chivington ignored the plea of surrender and massacred men, women, and children in the village. An interpreter gave an eyewitness account at a subsequent military inquiry into the incident:

> They were scalped, their brains knocked out; the men used their knives, ripped open women, clubbed little children, knocked them in the head with their guns, beat their brains out, mutilated their bodies in every sense of the word.[2]

Between 200 and 500 Indians died that day. When Chivington was asked at the military inquiry why he had opened fire on children, he is reported to have said, "Nits make lice." Later, Colonel Chivington "appeared on a Denver stage where he regaled delighted audiences with his war stories and displayed 100 Indian scalps, including the pubic hair of women."[3]

By 1870, the War Department had shifted its emphasis from killing Indians to starving them into submission by eliminating their "commissary"—the plains buffalo. The starvation policy proved to be the superior military strategy. Weakened and demoralized by the wholesale slaughter of the bison, entire Indian nations surrendered with only scattered instances of resistance. Military casualties were fewer in number than popularly believed. According to official government records, in the twenty-five years of military action on the western plains, the number of Indians killed or wounded totaled 5,519 while the army listed 932 officers and enlisted men killed in action and 1,061 wounded. The army also listed 461 civilians killed and 116 wounded during the entire western campaign.[4]

The policy of starving the plains Indians into submission was so successful that by the beginning of the 1880s, most tribes had been driven onto reservations, where they were closely "watched over" by government agents and the U.S. military. With the buffalo eliminated, the Indians became totally dependent on government rations to survive. Feeding these new wards of the state became a major business of the government, as well as a new commercial opportunity for the fledgling western ranching interests. The buffalo eaters of the plains became the new beef eaters of the western range.

By controlling the source and distribution of beef, the government was able to exert near-total control over tens of thousands of native Americans. At the same time, the new beef-rationing policies provided a new commercial market for cattle.[5] The Indian Department of the federal government purchased large amounts of beef from western ranchers, establishing a precedent for future government support programs. In 1880 alone, the government contracted for 39,160,729 pounds of western beef "to be delivered on the hoof at 34 Indian Agencies in ten western states at prices from $2.23 a hundredweight at the Fort Belknap agency in Montana to $3.74 at Los Pinos Agency, Colorado."[6] Some estimates of the amount of beef purchased by the government for distribution to the reservations range as high as 50 million pounds a year.[7]

Having killed off the buffalo and squeezed the Indians off the plains so they could graze their cattle, ranchers then turned around and sold beef to the government to feed the hungry Indians whose source of food they had eliminated. This is the story of how so many western ranchers made their initial fortunes, something rarely mentioned in the history books. Edward Dale writes:

> There can be no doubt that this market was a factor in promoting the growth of ranching on the plains and that a number of important cattlemen laid the foundations of their large enterprises by securing lucrative government contracts to supply Indians with beef.[8]

The history of the period is a running account of enterprising western ranchers conspiring with corrupt Indian agents to artificially hike up prices on beef contracts destined for the reservations while "finagling" on the quantity and quality of beef actually delivered. The "Beef Ring" in Washington was notorious among the post–Civil War lobbies for feeding at the public trough.

As if this weren't enough, western ranchers, emboldened by their new commercial successes, went a step further, usurping not only the "free grass" of the plains, but even the land set aside for Indian reserves. The ranchers regarded the newly "emancipated" prairies as public domain and viewed themselves as "tenants by sufferance."[9] In those early decades, the government had not yet exercised control over the use and occupancy of public lands, leaving the ranchers millions of acres of "free grass" on which to pasture their herds. Some of the ranching outfits grazed herds of 50,000 to 100,000 head on the plains in the early to middle 1880s. To cut the expense of transporting cattle consigned to the Indian Department for distribution to the reservations, many ranchers simply brought their herds directly onto the reservations and grazed them "on site," before handing them over to the government agents.[10]

Some of the most-traveled cattle trails crossed through Indian reservations, and many a drover took the opportunity to pasture his head for several days or weeks, fattening them up for the remaining trip to the Kansas railheads. One such reservation, the home of the Cheyenne and Arapaho Indians, intersected the two best-known north-south trails, the Chisholm and the Western trails. The reservation covered 4.3 million acres and had been set aside by the government in 1869 to "house" 3,500 Indians.[11] By 1880, ranchers in pursuit of new pastureland began invading a section of the reserve called the Cherokee Outlet. In the following years, ranchers sought permission from the government to graze their herds on Indian land, some even offering to lease the land for a token fee of 10 cents per head of cattle.[12] The Interior Department continued to deny permission, with little effect. Cattle poured onto the reservations, devouring the grasslands. Meanwhile, the Indian tribes living on the reservations were literally starving. Government beef rations were inadequate, and the Indians, trapped on the reservations, became eager prey to still another rancher scam. They agreed to allow the herds to continue grazing on their lands in return for beef. On December 12, 1882, the chiefs of the Cheyennes and Arapahos filed a formal request with the government seeking to lease 2.4 million acres of reservation land to cattle ranchers for a fee of less than 2 cents an acre. Half of the revenue raised was to go to buying young cattle for the Indians to raise.[13]

The Department of the Interior, while never formally recognizing such agreements, established an informal policy condoning the makeshift arrangement. In a letter to all the parties involved, the Secretary said:

While the Department will not recognize the agreement or lease you mention, nor any other of like character, to the extent of approving the same, nor to the extent of assuming to settle controversies that may arise between the different parties holding such agreements, yet the Department will endeavor to see that parties having no agreement are not allowed to interfere with those who have.[14]

The government's unofficial "wink" opened the way for widespread graft and corruption. Ranchers begin to curry favor and make payoffs to willing chiefs throughout the western rangeland, securing grazing rights, often for a fraction of the real market value of the land. The larger ranching companies were generally able to secure the most favorable arrangements. Within a few years, the Indian reservations on the plains had been carved up into "spheres of influence," leaving western ranchers in virtual control of the vast western rangelands. Tensions between Indians and whites over broken agreements and unkept promises mounted, finally forcing President Cleveland to intervene in 1885 and order the removal of all cattle from the Cheyenne and Arapaho reservations.[15]

This first sustained controversy between cattle ranchers, Indians, and the government over the use of western rangeland had another, more long-lasting effect. Ranchers banded together, creating the Cherokee Strip Livestock Association, the first of several powerful cattle associations that would come to dominate the politics of cattle country in the decades ahead. Today, over a century after their first attempt to lease public lands at below market value, ranchers, aided by powerful cattle associations, continue to enjoy favored treatment, leasing over 270 million acres of public land in the American west for cattle grazing at a fee per acre that is well below the market value of the land.[16]

14
Grass Is Gold

Generations of American schoolchildren have listened with rapt attention to romantic tales of the great gold rush of 1849. Few are aware of the other rush west as thousands sought their fortunes on the grasslands of the plains. The slogan "free grass" set the imagination of the country afire in the 1870s. Not since the enclosure of the British and European commons had the western world eyed such an expanse of free grass. Eastern bankers and speculators proclaimed that "grass is gold."[1] As word of the "emancipation" of the plains spread east, investment money began to flow west, first in a trickle, then in a flood. Euphoric reports of windfall profits fueled the fire. Virtually overnight, the attention of the country turned to the grassland of the Great Plains. There were fortunes to be made on the "Great American Desert." Everywhere, it seems, there was talk of beef. Immigrants trekked west to the plains to find their green pot of gold. Bankers sent their representatives to the western range to make deals. A new kind of "cattle fever" swept the land, as Americans set their minds to becoming the greatest beef empire in world history.

Not everyone was pleased with the opening up of the western

range. Eastern cattlemen were particularly bitter over the new turn of events, which was forcing many of them out of business. General James S. Brisbin wrote of their plight in *The Beef Bonanza; or How to Get Rich on the Plains*:

> Our eastern farmers are giving up the cattle breeding. They cannot compete with plains beef, for while their grazing lands cost them $50.00 to $75.00 and $100.00 per acre, and hay has to be cut for winter feeding, the grazing lands in the west have no market value, and the cattle run at large all winter—the natural grasses curing on the ground and keeping the stock fat even in January, February and March.[2]

Nowhere was the interest in the western rangeland more intense than in England. The British, as mentioned earlier, were the great beef eaters of Europe. With their newfound wealth as a colonial and industrial power, they had money to spend. As we noted earlier, Scotland and Ireland had already been turned into a pastureland to graze cattle for the British market, but even these lands could not keep up with the growing demands of the British aristocracy, middle classes, and military, whose appetites for beef seemed to have no bounds. An anthrax epidemic on the European continent spread to Ireland and England in the 1860s, devastating domestic herds and raising the price of scarce beef even further on the British market. The British turned to the Americas, north and south, to supply them with additional beef. Shipments of live cattle and salted beef across the Atlantic grew steadily in the 1860s. Still, trade was limited. The opening up of the western range proved both an enormous commercial opportunity and a technological challenge. Here was a new pastureland of great potential that could more than meet the British demand for beef. The question was how to effectively connect the grazing fields of the American west with the British consumer 5,000 miles to the east. The answer came in the 1870s with the westward expansion of the American railroads, the invention of new refrigeration technologies, and an influx of financial capital from abroad.

British companies played a major role in financing the building of America's transcontinental railroads in the 1870s and 1880s. The

Scottish American Investment Company Limited, of Edinburgh, invested millions of dollars in American rail expansion.[3] The expansion of the railroads onto the Western plains helped facilitate the shipment of greater amounts of beef east toward the English market. Indeed, moving cattle by rail from west to east became a primary commercial objective of the new railroads. Historian Eric Ross points out that "burgeoning livestock shipments stimulated a dramatic expansion in railroad mileage."[4]

At the same time the rails were being laid across the western plains, new technological innovations made it possible, for the first time, to ship fresh beef across the Atlantic. Refrigerated shipping established the all-important technological link needed to fashion a Euro-American cattle complex for the coming century.

A young inventor from New York, John I. Bates, experimented with hanging beef carcasses in refrigerated rooms by using ice-cooled air circulated by large fans. In June 1875, Bates shipped ten carcasses to England. They arrived fresh and sparked a flurry of interest among British investors. Timothy Eastman bought up Bates's patent that same year and launched an ambitious campaign to ship refrigerated carcasses to Britain. By the end of the year, he had shipped over 206,000 pounds of beef. In the following year, he began shipping a million pounds of beef per month. By the end of that year, the Eastman operation was providing the British Isles with 3 million pounds of fresh beef every month. Other companies followed Eastman's lead, and soon ocean steamers packed with fresh, refrigerated American beef were ferrying east to English ports on a daily basis; nearly every steamer between New York or Philadelphia and England carried American beef.[5]

By 1880, cheap American beef was beginning to edge the more expensive Scottish and Irish beef off the British market. English consumers were ecstatic over the new supply of fresh beef. According to some accounts, "near riots occurred in Liverpool and Dublin when the masses eagerly attempted to purchase the cheap meat."[6] Many ranchers in the north country, however, were incensed and began to fight back in what became known as the battle between "heather" and "short grass" country—an allusion to the merits of Irish and Scottish pastureland versus the western plains of North America.[7]

It wasn't long before British and Scottish financiers began to catch the "cattle fever" that had already swept over America.

The drawing rooms buzzed with the stories of this last of bonanzas; staid old gentlemen who scarcely knew the difference betwixt a steer and a heifer discussed it over their port and nuts.[8]

Flushed with tales of the fabulous fortunes being made on the American grasslands, the British government set up a Royal Commission on Agriculture and sent two representatives to the American west to make a firsthand assessment. They returned with glowing accounts of the grasslands of the Americas, which were covered with "self-made hay."[9]

The rush to capitalize and colonize the American west was on. The British set up giant cattle companies across the plains, securing millions of acres of the best grasslands for the British market. While the West was made safe for commerce by American frontiersmen and the U.S. military, the region was bankrolled, in part, by English lords and lawyers, financiers, and businessmen who effectively extended the reach of the British beef empire deep into the short grass of the Western plains.

First came the Anglo-American Cattle Company, Limited, which was registered in May 1879 with £70,000 of capital.[10] Several months later, the Colorado Mortgage and Investment Company of London, Limited, was launched. It purchased 10,000 acres of rangeland north of Denver. A year later, the Prairie Cattle Company, Limited, was capitalized with £200,000 under the chairmanship of the Earl of Airlee. These "armchair cowboys" purchased large tracts of land along the watercourses in Colorado and New Mexico. The Texas Land and Cattle Company, Limited, was chartered in December 1881 with £240,000. It purchased property in south Texas and then bought up herds grazing along the Horseshoe Range. In 1882, the Matador Land and Cattle Company was formed. It quickly purchased 60,000 head of cattle, 300,000 acres of land, and range privilege on over 1.8 million additional acres of western range. That same year the Missouri Land and Livestock Company, operating out of Edinburgh, began operations in Missouri and Arkansas. Still another Scottish-American Company, the Western American Cattle Company, was chartered with £220,000 and began ranching operations on the northern branch of the Cheyenne River in western South Dakota and Wyoming. In 1883, Western Ranchers, Limited, another British firm, took up residence in western Dakota Territory. Other British and Scottish companies were formed in the 1880s, fanning out into every available niche on the western plains. There was the Swann Land and Cattle Company, the California Pastoral and Agricultural Company, the Wyoming Cattle Ranch Company, the Cattle Ranch and Land Company, the Arkansas Valley Land and Cattle Company, and the Maxwell Cattle Company, to name just a few.[11]

While many of the British investors hired Scottish or American managers to run their new ranching operations, more than a few English lords built their own "castle on the prairies," expensive estates adorned with the best of English furnishings, stocked with the finest European wines and delicacies, and boasting a full complement of servants and livery.[12] Many of the ranch homes on the prairies served as summer retreats or vacation houses for the British ruling class, who entertained an entourage of family friends and acquaintances with hunting trips and fishing and wilderness excursions. A British cattle representative, Morton Frewen, built an elegant castle for his New York society wife, Clara Jerome, in Traving, Wyoming. In the 1880s their home became a favorite summer vacation spot for the elite of the British aristocracy, many of whom were investors in the British-owned Powder River Cattle Company.

Cheyenne, Wyoming, became a favorite retreat for British investors in the Prairie Cattle Company. British and American cattle barons formed the exclusive Cheyenne Club, where "members wore ties and tails" and enjoyed the finest European cuisine, served by a French chef. Many British gentlemen continued to have the London paper sent to them regularly to keep up with business and social matters back home.[13] Their presence on the plains seemed quite strange in a country that just a few years earlier was teeming with wild bison and Indian tribes.

Many of the stockmen's associations, which had been organized by American ranchers in the 1870s to protect their economic interests before state legislatures and in Washington, became little more than "mouthpieces for foreign cattle barons."[14] They were powerful voices. In New Mexico, cattle associations controlled 40 million acres of land and owned over 1.5 million cattle. The Texas Livestock Association had over 500 members and owned over a million head. The largest, the Wyoming Stockmen's Association, controlled over 500 square miles, worth upward of $150 million. By the mid-1880s,

British financial interests dominated the associations, turning much of the west into a quasi-colonial outpost of the British Empire.[15] The stockmen's associations came under increasing attack. Said one critic:

> With the help of eastern and British capital, they [the stockmen's associations] have expanded all of a sudden into confederacies dangerous alike to private enterprise and to public liberty. The government of the cattle states and territories is virtually in their hands. They hold the key to thousands of square miles of the public estate, and have shut small settlers out of it. They control the local legislatures, and a judge whose interpretation of the law does not suit them has a very precarious tenure of office.[16]

By 1884, American public opinion began to turn against the British takeover of the west. Angry editorials appeared in daily newspapers and agricultural journals. The *Drover's Journal* of Chicago warned of the far-reaching consequences of the British land grab:

> The line should certainly be drawn at non-resident aliens who take their large profits to foreign countries. It is said that over 20,000,000 acres have already been secured by foreign capitalists and corporations in tracts of 50,000 to 3,000,000 acres each. . . . It is certainly not wise and not right to permit foreign speculators to get possession of it in large tracts, to the exclusion of our citizens who may wish to settle upon and cultivate it.[17]

Anti-British sentiment was running high in the summer of 1884, when both the Democratic and Republican conventions included planks in their campaign platforms calling for curbs on "alien holdings" in the United States. In the Presidential campaign that year between James C. Blaine and Grover Cleveland, Blaine galvanized the anti-British mood of the country with his slogan "America for Americans."[18]

A bill was introduced into the House of Representatives that year that would prohibit the English and other Europeans from buying up any more of the American west. The bill's sponsors argued that the continued buying up of America's grasslands by "foreign noblemen" would lead to "a system of landlordism incompatible with the best interests and free institutions of The United States." The bill condemned this new form of "absentee landlordism" and warned that America was in danger of becoming a colonial territory of the British Empire. The committee sponsoring the legislation concluded with a ringing plea that "American soil should be owned exclusively by American citizens."[19] The introduction of the bill failed to calm the nerves of an increasingly xenophobic public who saw the country being sold out from under them.

15

The Politics of "Corned Beef"

Corn

Public protest and Congressional concern, though vocal, did little to stem the tide of British investment in the western rangelands. By the mid-1880s, much of the American west belonged to British and Scottish bankers and businessmen, and an assortment of English noblemen. The British brought with them far more than their capital. They also brought their unique taste for "fatted" beef. The British consumer insisted on heavy beef, richly marbled with speckles of fat. To meet that need, the cattle barons of the American West and Midwestern farmers came up with a unique scheme. For the first time in agricultural history, they brought together cattle production and grain production into a new symbiotic relationship, one that would fundamentally alter agricultural practices and food distribution patterns for generations to come.

Farmers in the midwest had already begun experimenting, on a small scale, with feeding surplus corn to cattle as early as the 1830s. Because of its unusual topography, the Ohio Valley became an experimental laboratory for the new entrepreneurial scheme. Ohio enjoyed a rich soil base and favorable climate for growing corn. Northern Indiana, on the other hand, was unsuited for corn production but made ideal pastureland for cattle. So much corn was being produced in the Ohio Valley by the 1830s that local farmers

and businessmen hit on the idea of shipping Indiana cattle into the state to be fed a rich diet of corn before being taken to slaughter at the Cincinnati abattoirs. The Miami Valley in southwestern Iowa and central Kentucky became the first major cattle-feeding region.[1] As population density increased, and more and more public land was enclosed and put under the plow, cattle ranchers were forced to move west to the open ranges of Illinois and Iowa.[2] The corn followed the cows west, continuing the new symbiotic relationship between grass and feed. On the eve of the Civil War, cattle were being shipped regularly from the prairies of Iowa to Illinois to be fattened on corn before being sent to St. Louis and Chicago for slaughter.

By the time the Great Plains were "liberated" for cattle grazing, the historical conditions were ripe for a wholesale change in agricultural practices—the bringing together, on a mass scale, of animal husbandry and grain production. The railroads had linked the western range with the midwestern states, bringing pastureland and corn country together. Here were two great agricultural regions of the world, existing side by side—a premier grazing land and a rich grain-producing region. By the 1870s, the midwest was awash in corn. In 1871, the corn crop was so abundant that farmers increased their demand for feeder cattle from the Great Plains.[3] Says anthropologist Eric Ross:

> The raising of cattle on the plains was . . . quickly assimilated into the established interregional symbiosis with corn-producing states to the east with their constant need of cheap, grass-fed cattle to fatten on their surplus grain.[4]

"Free grass" and "surplus corn" came together in the 1870s largely to suit the palate of the British consumer, who insisted on fatty beef. There is no doubt, say western historians like Edward Dale, that the heavy demand for beef in Britain spurred "closer relations between the ranchmen of the Great Plains and the cattle feeders of the cornbelt."[5] In 1876 the Commissioner of Agriculture formalized the new relationship in government policy:

> Let the vast areas of pasture in the border states and territories be employed with breeding and feeding the cattle until they are two years old, and then let them be sent forward to the older sections

to be fed a year on corn and rounded up to the proportions of foreign demand.[6]

The new symbiosis won over the British, who quickly began to turn their allegiance from Scottish and Irish beef raised on heather to grass and corn-fed American beef. The royal family, the Lord Mayor of London, the Governor of the Bank of England, and other persons of rank all praised the quality of American meat.[7] By the 1880s, America was responsible for a majority of the beef imported to England.[8] It was at this moment that British financiers stepped in with massive amounts of capital, buying up much of the western range and cattle industry, as well as making heavy investments in the corn-belt states, all in an effort to gain control over the fledgling grain-fed cattle complex. This novel new ranching enterprise would soon alter the agricultural and economic relationships of nations and eventually wreak havoc on the environment of the planet.

Within five years of the British "invasion" of the western range, beef exports to England had increased in value to nearly $31 million. In the period between 1884 and 1886, 43,136 tons of fresh beef were shipped to the British Isles. It should be noted that not everyone shared equally in the new beef glut. The middle and upper classes in England consumed the lion's share of the American corn-fed beef.[9] The military consumed much of the rest—each soldier was guaranteed 12 ounces of meat per day. Working-class Britons were still largely excluded from the beef culture, being able to afford only small amounts and inferior cuts. Within working-class families, the little beef that was consumed was distributed unevenly, the adult males receiving most of the available supply, while women and children received little or no meat.[10]

The English demand for fatty beef, the western ranchers' need to fetch top dollar for their prairie steers, the midwestern corn farmers' desire for feeder cattle on which to unload surplus corn, and the British financiers' interest in capitalizing on their new colonial venture all worked together to create a new Euro–American cattle complex. Slowly, Americans adopted the British taste for fatty beef, partially in response to the supply-driven considerations of plains ranchers and midwestern farmers who continued their lucrative arrangement, mixing free grass with surplus corn.

An economic depression swept the country in 1884. Then, in the winter of 1886 and 1887, the plains were hit with a devastating series of winter storms, killing tens of thousands of cattle. Some ranchers lost up to 70 percent of their herds.[11] The great storms of 1886 crippled the cattle industry and bankrupted many of the cattle barons. The larger British and American companies survived and reorganized.

By 1900, the western grasslands were already overstocked and overgrazed. Ranchers could no longer afford to feed their steers on grasslands for five to six years.[12] At the same time, the corn-belt states continued to produce surplus corn, making it more practical to feed cattle for only a year or two on the grasslands and then transfer them to midwestern feedlots for fattening on corn before being sent to market.

What had started with the peculiar British taste for fat-laced cuts of beef steadily grew into a new commercial relationship unlike any other in agricultural history. After 1900, fluctuating grain prices began to affect the price of beef as more and more cattle were fattened on corn. At the same time, the yearly fluctuation in cattle production and consumer demand for beef began to seriously affect the price of grain. In fact, the grain market was becoming so dependent on beef that "without the ruminant market, grain prices would decline sharply."[13]

To help ensure American consumer acceptance of fat-speckled beef, the United States government devised a grading system to measure the value of beef. The system, which was established in 1927 by the United States Department of Agriculture (USDA), graded beef on its fat content and started with the assumption that fatty beef was of higher value and preferred by consumers over leaner cuts of beef. The British taste for fat had finally been adopted by the United States government as a standard for judging the value and price of beef sold to American consumers.

The quality grades, which are stamped on all cuts by USDA inspectors, are prime, choice, select, standard, commercial, utility, cutter, and canner. The grades are determined by "the amount and distribution of finish [fat] on the animal."[14]

Prime is the highest quality and is generally served in the best restaurants and sold by specialty butcher shops. Choice is second in quality and is the preferred grade purchased by most consumers because it is high in fat content but cheaper than prime. Select beef has less fat and is less preferred, rarely showing up on supermarket meat counters. The other grades of beef are primarily used in processed meats like hot dogs and lunch meats or by institutional food services. The lower grades of beef are also used in pet foods.

The grading system is less than scientific and is open to abuse and error. A federal beef inspector walks down the line of hung carcasses in the slaughterhouse chill room peering into an open slit between the twelfth and thirteenth rib to examine the rib-eye muscle. He examines the marbling—the flecks of fat interspersed throughout the meat—and the texture and color. He also checks the cartilage to assess the age of the animal. The entire examination takes less than fifteen seconds, after which he slaps the carcass with a metal stamp designating the grade. It is not uncommon in some of the more highly automated packing houses for an inspector to grade 330 carcasses an hour. It's no wonder that the General Accounting Office (GAO) found that one out of every five carcasses is misgraded by federal inspectors.[15]

By favoring fat over lean beef in its grading system and pricing policy, the USDA has helped sustain the grain-fed cattle complex of North America for the better part of a century. G. M. Ward succinctly summarizes the partnership that has emerged between the government, cattle ranchers and corn farmers:

> Because of the more favorable price, the choice grade is the predominant goal of feeders, and thus it is apparent that the existing grading system has imposed a structure on the industry which in turn has institutionalized consumer tastes and demand for grain-fed cattle.[16]

The grain-fed cattle complex grew slowly until the eve of World War II. Just before the war, only 2.2 million cattle, or about 5 percent of the nation's beef cattle, were being fed on grain, much of the prime and choice meat going overseas to the British and continental markets or being consumed by America's middle and upper classes.[17] After the war, new agricultural techniques greatly increased agricultural production in the United States. The introduction of special monocultured grain crops into the fields, the increasing use of petrochemical fertilizers and pesticides, and the mechanization and automation of the agricultural production process greatly increased yields. Between 1945 and 1970, agricultural yields increased by 240 percent, the greatest rise in agricultural output in U.S. history.[18] The vast surpluses of corn, according to a report on the postwar cattle industry sponsored by the Rockefeller Foundation, "made possible a livestock production system based on grain feeding and is still providing relatively inexpensive meat to the American consumer."[19]

Between 1950 and 1990, the number of cattle in the United States increased from 80 million to 100 million, most of them primed on grass and then fattened on corn.[20] To stimulate the consumer market for fatty beef, Safeway and other grocery chains began touting the superiority of prime and choice cuts. The increased consumer demand, in turn, further stimulated the development of huge commercial feedlots across the midwest, the plains states, and California, where cattle were fed a rich diet of corn and other grains to produce the marbled flesh that could qualify for the prime and choice USDA stamps of approval.

By 1989, about half of the nation's output of grain-fed cattle in the United States had been "finished" in 198 giant automated "beef factories" scattered throughout the western states.[21] Some of these commercial feedlots handled more than 50,000 cattle. Special federal tax incentives in the 1970s encouraged even more investments in feedlot operations. Affluent Americans, including well-known personalities like John Wayne, invested in limited partnerships "which bought livestock, placed them in feedlots, and then sold them for club members."[22]

It should be pointed out that cattle are not physiologically well suited to eat large amounts of high-energy grain. A heavy grain diet disturbs the normal functioning of microorganisms in the rumen, resulting in a range of digestive diseases, the most common being "rumenitis-liver abscess complex." Approximately 8 percent of all the cattle slaughtered in the United States have abscessed livers.[23]

Today, a century after the first efforts to combine the free grass of the plains with the surplus corn of the midwestern grain belt, 106 million acres of U.S. agricultural land is used to grow 220 million metric tons of grain for cattle and other livestock.[24] In the United States, livestock, again mostly cattle, consume almost twice as much grain as is eaten by the entire population.[25] Globally about 600 million tons of grain are fed to livestock, much of it to cattle.[26] If worldwide agricultural production were shifted from livestock feed to grains for direct human consumption, more than a billion people on the planet could be fed.[27]

The grain-fed beef complex has forced a fundamental change in the dynamics of human social relations at the most basic of all social levels. The question is now one of survival itself, of who eats and who doesn't, of how the millions of acres of available land on the planet are used, and for whom.

huge cattle #s

Thesis

cows eat all grass

16
Barbed Wire and Land Scams

The euphoria over free grass was short-lived. Perhaps American ranchers and their foreign financiers suspected, though dimly, that the great bonanza of the plains could not long be sustained. As early as 1862, the federal government had passed the Homestead Act, in part to ease the growing population pressure in the east by encouraging the western expansion of settlers. Soon after the government and the cattlemen pushed the buffalo and Indians off the plains to make room for steers, hordes of farmers began arriving on the edge of the grasslands, asserting their own claims on the public domain.

Still, in the interim, the boom years of the 1870s and early 1880s, the cattle barons enjoyed near-hegemony over public lands. Having dislodged the Indians from their ancestral commons, the ranching empires of the west declared a right of sovereignty over vast tracts of public land. The notion of "range rights" was widely accepted. If a rancher expropriated a local stream, his right to exclusive claim over all the land drained by that stream was accepted by other ranchers. This was an informal code of the plains without legal entitlement. In these early years, some ranching empires claimed "range-rights" to public lands as large as the states of Massachusetts and Delaware.[1]

Range Rights

As long as the cattle barons could afford to maintain small armies of hired guns to protect their spheres of influence, little could be done to thwart their control over the grasslands.

Then in the 1880s, a revolutionary new invention made its way west to the plains, changing forever the dynamics of power on America's rangeland: Barbed wire facilitated the enclosure of public lands in the United States. Josphen Glidden had devised this new kind of fencing a decade earlier. He had apparently come up with the idea after his wife implored him to put a fence around her garden to protect it from neighborhood dogs. Glidden "borrowed his wife's coffee grinder to use as a reel for the smooth wire and with the aid of an old grindstone to bend it, placed short pieces of wire with sharp points around the smooth wire." He was granted a patent on his invention on November 24, 1874, and opened up a small manufacturing plant in DeKalb, Illinois.[2]

At first, western cattlemen resisted the new invention, fearing it would be used against them by farmers anxious to protect their holdings against unlawful encroachment. Cowboys complained that barbed wire injured their horses and cattle and restricted their free movement across the plains. They called the new fencing the "devil's hatband."[3] It wasn't long, however, before some of the larger cattlemen began to use barbed wire themselves, as a way of protecting their spheres of influence. Charles Goodnight, a Texas cattle baron, fenced in over 3 million acres of "public range" with illegal fences and agreed to remove them only after President Theodore Roosevelt intervened years later. Other cattlemen followed suit, fencing off millions of acres of public land to which they had no legal title. The demand for wire grew so fast in the west that by 1880 over 80.5 million pounds of fencing had been sold.[4] The plains were crisscrossed with Glidden's amazing fences.

Ranchers remained divided on the benefits of barbed wire. While some favored its use to protect herds against crossbreeding with inferior stock or to hold feral diseased cattle at bay, others viewed the invention as a fetter to their free access to water and land. A Texas trail driver expressed his thoughts on the subject in 1884:

In 1874, there was no fencing along the trails to the North, and we had lots of range to graze on. Now there is so much land taken up and fenced in that the trail for most of the way is little better than a crooked lane, and we have hard times to find enough range to feed on. . . . fences, sir, are the curse of the country.[5]

While ranchers divided into two opposing camps, the "free-grass men" versus the "fenced-range men," battles also raged between cattlemen and farmers.[6] The cattle barons favored the old Spanish laws that required farmers to fence in their property. Most western states passed open-range laws giving cattle the freedom to roam and putting the responsibility on settlers to fence in their crops. Farmers, understandably, favored English common law, which required the owners of livestock to enclose their animals inside fencing while leaving farmers' fields unfenced.

Fence-cutting wars broke out on the western prairie in the early 1880s. In Texas alone, more than half the counties reported fence cutting and the burning of pastureland by late 1883.[7] During that autumn and winter, night riders destroyed over $20 million worth of barbed wire.[8] On several occasions, gunfights ensued, leaving many cowboys dead. On October 4, 1883, the *Dodge City Times* in Kansas reported:

> Blood was shed in the southern part of Clay County [Texas] on the 4th over the cutting of Sherwood's fence. A man named Butler said to be a leader in the cutting business, was killed and several others wounded—supposed to have been done by parties guarding the fence or by line riders.[9]

More than a few local and state governments attempted to prevent the fencing in of public land, as did officials of federal land offices. For years, they were outflanked and outarmed by the cattle barons, who relied on a combination of political muscle and hired range warriors to maintain their sovereignty over the public domain. Thousands of acres of government land were enclosed by ranchmen in Texas and Montana. Cattle companies enclosed entire counties in southwestern and western Kansas. The Carlisle Cattle Company, a British company, enclosed a large section of Wyoming's public land. Other cattle companies enclosed public land in Nevada and New Mexico.[10]

Finally, responding to public pressure, especially from the growing number of farmers pushing west into the plains country, the U.S. Congress passed a law in 1885 designed to prosecute anyone who fenced in public land for private use. Even after the passage of the legislation, many observers were fearful the cattle companies would simply ignore the statute altogether, flaunting the directives of the federal government. Editors of the New York business journal *Bradstreet's* quipped: "It will be interesting to note the outcome of the attempt to determine whether the Government and settlers, or whether the cattle companies are in charge."[11]

In August of the same year, President Cleveland issued a proclamation against "unlawful fences" on the western range and made it clear that if they were not removed he would be forced to send in the army to destroy the fencing.

Many of the cattle companies that had spearheaded the enclosure of U.S. public lands were British. They included the Prairie Cattle Company and the Arkansas Valley Land and Cattle Company, both of which were accused of "fencing one million acres of Colorado land illegally." The British were taken aback by the sudden turn of events in America and began wondering about the wisdom of their initial investments in the western rangelands. The *Economist* railed against Fleet Street for its naiveté and chicanery:

> On the advice of unscrupulous Americans who decoyed them into this kind of investment, they believed in their innocence that the "cattle interest" of the west was strong enough to defy the laws of the country. They took possession of millions of acres of land to which they had no more right than to the City Hall in Broadway. They laid out thousands of pounds of sterling in fencing . . . which will now have to be cleared away. They attempted to get control of the whole grazing area by . . . making fraudulent entries on them. . . . Our land speculators in the far west cannot be surprised at bringing down a storm of unpopularity on their heads when they fly in the teeth of laws intended to protect settlers, or worse still, endeavor to undermine them. They have not dealt honestly with the American land system or the American people, and hence the prejudice they have raised against themselves all over the States.[12]

Even with the new government restrictions, British and American cattle companies were often able to circumvent the laws by engaging in a number of unethical and illegal schemes. Many of the cattle companies took advantage of the Homestead Act, which was enacted to provide 160 acres of public land to every small farmer. The cattle concerns secured title to the 160 acres of land immediately surrounding their ranch house or watering hole, while continuing to graze their herd on thousands of acres of publicly held land around them. Others took advantage of the Timber Culture Act, which was enacted in 1873 and granted each claimant an additional 160 acres of public land on the condition that one-quarter of the land be planted with trees as an environmental safeguard. Many ranchers took the land; few planted any trees.

Of all the legislation passed by the government to distribute public land, none was more flagrantly abused and misused than the Desert Land Act of 1887, which awarded land to anyone willing to improve irrigation on the site. According to historian Wallace Stegner, the legislation "could hardly have been better devised to help speculators and land-grabbers. . . . Fraud was almost never provable, but it was estimated that 95 percent of final proof titles were fraudulent, nevertheless." The Union Cattle Company of Cheyenne simply "plowed a thirty-five-mile-long furrow, called it an irrigation ditch" and secured title to over 33,000 acres of public land.[13]

Other cattle companies bought up land from the railroads, then preempted public land next to it. The British-based Swann Land and Cattle Company bought 500,000 acres of land from the Union Pacific Railroad Company, which was heavily financed by British bankers, and then proceeded to fence in an additional 500,000 acres of public land.

Government investigations subsequently declared that between 4.4 million and 7.3 million acres of public land were fraudulently expropriated by cattle companies in the 1870s and 1880s. In 1887, Congress passed legislation banning foreign companies or domestic firms that were more than 20 percent foreign-owned from obtaining more land on the western plains. Still, even this gesture proved virtually ineffective in reversing the process of foreign domination of the western range. The Scottish-American Mortgage Company simply bypassed the statute by recording its landholding in the names of American citizens. Other companies had their cowhands claim title to lands under the Homestead Act and other various government land distribution acts and then, for a small fee, bought out the deeds.

The expropriation of the western plains was unlike any settlement process before or since in American history. Historian Benjamin Hibbard summed up the spirit of the times:

Haha

> All told, it was the most unmistakable, wholesale, shameless instance of land grabbing that has yet been practiced in America. Companies with headquarters in eastern cities and even in England fenced in as much land as they wanted and some had the effrontery to claim in court that a man had a right to as much range as he could fence.[14]

In 1916, the federal government passed the Grazing Homestead Act, which granted 640 acres of public land to each rancher, specifically for grazing livestock. By 1923, "31.4 million acres of public domain in virtually all the western states and territories, excluding Texas, had been filed on by livestock raisers under the Grazing Homestead Act."[15]

The enclosure of public lands did little to curb the power of the corporate cattle barons. In fact, where government legislation didn't specifically favor the cattlemen, ranchers simply turned the laws to their advantage, by either legal or extralegal means. The government continued to turn a deaf ear to complaints of farmers and others whose rights were systematically trampled by the ranching interests.

The cattlemen's associations' final triumph came in 1934 when President Franklin D. Roosevelt signed the Taylor Grazing Act into law.[16] Ostensibly, the law was supposed to allow for the improvement of public land by leasing it to ranchers who would take collective responsibility for its management and improvement. In reality, the act succeeded in transferring tens of millions of acres of public lands to private leases in return for a token permit or lease fee.

The powerful western cattle associations had been lobbying for a public lease policy for over sixty years. When the idea was first publicly floated at a cattle convention in St. Louis in the 1870s, one prescient publication, the *Statist*, warned that "under this leasing system, the Cattle King of the West would be transformed into a magnate of tenfold power and the importance of an English Duke."[17]

That prediction has long since become a reality. Today, 30,000 ranchers in eleven western states graze cattle on approximately 300 million acres of public land—an area equivalent to the fourteen east-

ern seaboard states, stretching from Maine to Florida, or 16 percent
of the land surface of the lower forty-eight states. From the very
inception, the fee for permit holders was so low it amounted to a
virtual government handout. When the Act commenced in 1936,
cattlemen paid 5 cents per month per head of cattle.[18]

Those receiving a permit retained exclusive rights to use the parcel
of public land allocated to them. More important, the permit could
be held by the leaseholder's family in perpetuity—that is, handed
down to each succeeding generation. The government awarded the
permits to ranchers who owned "base property" near public land,
guaranteeing that the same cattle companies that had long enjoyed
free grass would continue to do so, albeit at a nominal fee.

Today, permit holders are paying only $1.81 a month per cow
for the right to graze on America's public lands. The Reagan administration estimated the market value for pasturing cattle on the same
grasslands to be between $6.40 and $9.50 per month.[19] In 1989,
western ranchers paid only $35 million to graze their cattle on vir-
tually the entire publicly owned western range of the continental
United States at a fraction of the cost of leasing the equivalent private
land.[20] The Taylor Grazing Act represented one of the biggest give-
aways of land in modern history. Few constituencies before or since
have been so completely subsidized by the American taxpayer, a fact
rarely raised in the public debates over welfare programs administered by the federal government.

Cattle ranchers benefit not only from the token leasing fees but
also from the market value of the licenses. Although a rancher cannot
sell his permit, he can sell his base property, and because the permit
generally remains affixed to the property, the value of his holdings
is magnified manyfold by the exclusive grazing rights that accompany it. Ranchers have made hundreds of millions of dollars over
the years selling real estate attached to public land permits. A 1984
study conducted by the House Committee on Appropriations detailed the extent of the abuse. The committee pointed to one rancher
who sold his spread for $1 million "over what he would have received
because a permit to graze on public range was attached to his private
property."[21]

Cattlemen receive an additional benefit as lessees of public lands.
Their grazing fees are collected by the Bureau of Land Management,
which uses 50 percent of the monies to finance "range improve-

ments" in the grazing district where the funds are collected.[22] A little more than a third of the collected fees go back to the U.S. Treasury, and the rest is given over to county governments.[23] The United States Forest Service administers a similar program. The improvements that are made are more often designed to advance the commercial interests of the rancher than to upgrade the plain ecosystems, which is the stated intent of the program. For example, in Whitehorse Butte, Oregon, one rancher pays an annual fee of $18,000 for the use of 126,000 acres of public land. The BLM has plans to further subsidize the rancher by building him a water pipeline, drilling him a well, and constructing sixteen miles of fence. The cost of the project was estimated at $174,000, with annual maintenance of the pipeline costing an additional $14,000.[24] Because the permit fees are so minuscule, the revenue raised from the lessee pays for only a portion of the "improvements" made on public grazing land. The rest of the bill is paid for by the American taxpayer. In 1989, for example, the BLM and the Forest Service spent $35 million more on administering the program than the program took in.[25]

BLM "improvements" include paying for stock ponds, the seeding of exotic grasses, building fences, herbicide spraying, posting of signs, and other conveniences. In 1985, the BLM and the Forest Service completed a seven-year study on the public grazing program on the western range and concluded that the present system amounts to a multimillion-dollar giveaway.[26]

The real story of how the west was won bears little resemblance to the storybook accounts handed down to generations of young Americans. Behind the facade of frontier heroism and cowboy bravado, of civilizing forces and homespun values, lies a quite different tale: a saga of ecocide and genocide, of forced enclosures of land and people, and the expropriation of an entire subcontinent for the exclusive benefit of a privileged few.

The enclosure of the American plains was not unlike the earlier enclosure movements in Tudor and Elizabethan England and on the European continent in its impact on native populations and the environment. In Tudor England, in the early sixteenth century, the landed gentry joined forces with the newly emerging merchant class to force peasants off their ancestral commons to make room for sheep, whose wool was beginning to fetch a high price in the new textile markets. The English Commons had been farmed collectively for centuries under various tenancy arrangements. The majority of peasants enjoyed the right to belong to the land, including the right of access to common fields and pastures. Beginning in the 1530s, landlords forced the enclosure of commonly held lands, turning the commons into private grazing lands for the pasturing of sheep. Denied access to the land, rural peasants became a new disinherited class, unable to use their ancestral grounds to sustain themselves and their progeny. Many migrated to the new industrial cities, where they became the first generation of unskilled laborers. Others fought back, in a futile attempt to regain their lost status. Sir Thomas More captured the tenor of the times in his book *Utopia*. "Sheep devour people," he proclaimed as the landlords and merchants continued to move sheep onto land that a few years earlier had been tilled by peasants to feed their families.

In America, millions of Indians were driven off their ancestral commons on the great American plains by ranchers and the federal government, to make room for the pasturing of cattle to serve the burgeoning new beef markets of America and Europe and the leather-tanning and tallow industries. The buffalo was exterminated and Indians were forced onto reservations, where, half starved and weakened by the white man's diseases, they were provided with meager government rations, barely enough to survive.

In the American west, "cows devour people." They also devour the environment. As in England, where the overstocking and overgrazing of sheep quickly depleted the soil, causing long-term damage to the flora and fauna of the British countryside, the onslaught of cattle onto the western plains has devastated the grassland, destroying millions of acres of land and undermining native ecosystems—an issue we will explore in greater detail in Part Five.

The transformation of the American plains from a pristine range to a commercial pastureland in less than a generation is, without a doubt, one of the greatest business transactions in world history. Few Americans are aware that the west was won for cattle and that western ranchers joined with British banking interests to colonize a vast stretch of the American plains, creating a powerful Euro-American cattle complex. Even fewer Americans are aware that today cattlemen and cattle companies across the great western range enjoy access to millions of acres of public land and that they are virtually subsidized by the American taxpayer in their endeavors. The notion of the fiercely independent western cattlemen, the frontier knights who blazed the trail for the westward expansion of civilization, is little more than myth, nurtured by the cattle barons themselves and perpetuated by a slew of dime-store novels and western movies.

"cows devour people"

" " " " enviro

Biggest buss. trans ever

Part Three

THE
INDUSTRIALIZATION
OF BEEF

17
The Beef Trust

Distributors

Cattle — Corp. power

In the years following the Civil War, the American cattle complex became inescapably linked to corporate power, exercised at every level of society—from the control and use of land and resources to the processing and distribution of food to various classes and groups of people. While we have already discussed the forces that colonized the land for the cattle culture, we also need to examine an equally formidable force: the people and businesses that institutionalized power over the distribution of beef and cattle products in America.

The consolidation of control over the grazing lands and cornfields of America in the 1870s and 1880s was accompanied by the emergence of a second locus of power, centered in the meat-processing cities of Chicago, St. Louis, Cincinnati, and Kansas City. A new generation of mostly American businessmen and entrepreneurs moved quickly to concentrate their power over the abattoirs, rail routes, and distribution outlets, making themselves the sole arbiters and exclusive power brokers between the cattle-raising concerns of the west and midwest and the final consumers of beef products in the east and abroad. In 1850, the United States was processing $12 million worth of red meats. Just seventy years later, the red meat industry was worth $4.2 billion and was among the country's largest contributors to the gross national product. It was also the nation's second-largest employer.[1]

Beef was king in America, and a handful of companies virtually controlled the meat-packing industry. The success of the companies lay in their ability to take advantage of new innovations in rail refrigeration and to undermine competition and monopolize markets. The refrigerated railcar, like the refrigerated transatlantic steamer, revolutionized the beef industry. George H. Hammond, a Detroit meat-packer, began shipping frozen dressed beef east to wholesale meat merchants in Boston in 1869. In 1871, he opened up a packing plant in Indiana just across the state line from Chicago and only miles away from the giant Union Stockyard. By 1875, Hammond was making regular shipments of refrigerated beef to New England, where local butchers were more than willing to pay a premium of 2 cents more per pound for fresh beef.

One of the Boston beef merchants who sold Hammond's cuts of beef locally, Gustavus Swift, was so impressed with the profit margins that he opened up his own packing house in Chicago in 1877 and began shipping refrigerated beef east. In 1878, he hired a Boston engineer, Andrew Chase, to design a more efficient refrigerated train car. The Swift-Chase car, as it became known, was far more reliable, allowing him to turn a limited trade into a national market. By slaughtering the steers in Chicago and shipping only dressed beef, Swift saved millions on transportation costs. Sixty percent of the weight of each live steer shipped east was of no economic value and merely excess baggage, which increased costs. Swift "could ship three dressed carcasses for what it cost to ship one live steer," and by transporting trimmed frozen carcasses, Swift "undercut eastern slaughterhouses by as much as 75 cents a hundredweight."[2]

Swift's overnight success spurred imitators. Philip and Simeon Armour launched their own refrigerated beef business in 1882. By 1886, their company accounted for nearly a quarter of Chicago's beef trade. Nelson Morris joined the competition in 1884, and became the third-largest fresh beef producer in Chicago. Hammond by that time was the fourth-largest producer. In 1901, Armour purchased the Hammond Company, increasing its hold on the industry. The Cudahy Packing Company and Schwarschild and Sulzberger (later known as Wilson & Company) entered the market in the late 1880s, rounding out the big five companies, later known as the Beef Trust.

On the eve of World War I, the five companies controlled over two-thirds of the fresh beef output of the United States and half of its total red meat production.[3] Like the British and American cattle barons who relied on a combination of deceit and coercion to plunder the plains, the meat-packers of Chicago conspired in violation of federal law to fix prices and control markets. Even after the passage of the Sherman Antitrust Act, the Chicago meat-packers continued their activities, flaunting the directives and warnings of the federal government. A government investigation conducted in 1893 disclosed that executives of the big five meat-packing companies

> met regularly [in Chicago] in a suite of rooms. . . . rent for these rooms and other expenses connected with these meetings were apportioned among the packers in proportion to their shipments of dressed beef. At these meetings, the territory was divided and the volume of business to be done by each packer was apportioned upon the basis of statistics compiled . . . penalties being levied when one of them exceeded his allotment in any territory.[4]

After the United States Supreme Court issued an injunction against the pool in 1903, three of the big five companies—Armour, Morris, and Swift—created a new entity called the National Packing Company in a move to circumvent the letter of the law. The new company began purchasing its competitors and related businesses in an attempt to gain hold of the entire food-processing industry in the United States. By 1911, the National Packing Company had become so powerful that it was dubbed "the Greatest Trust in the World" by the popular press.[5] Muckraker Charles Edward Russell warned the public that the National Packing Company was amassing

> greater power than ten Standard Oil companies. Reaching out, absorbing industry after industry, augmenting and building, by great brute strength, and by insidious, intricate, hardly discoverable windings and turnings, day and night this monstrous thing grows and strengthens until its grip is at the nation's throat.[6]

Although the National Packing Company successfully rebuffed several criminal indictments by the government, it was dissolved in 1913, but not before still another meat pool was formed, this one international in scope. Armour, Swift, Morris, and Sulzberger joined together with British and South American companies "to control shipment of meat to the United States and Europe." By that time the big five meat-packers were operating plants in Brazil, Argentina and Uruguay and exporting meat to Europe and North America.[7]

By the end of World War I, the beef trust controlled much of the American economy. According to federal investigations, the big beef packers held interests in livestock companies, railroad terminals, railroads, stockyards, machine supply companies, warehouses, land development companies, public utilities, publishing houses, sporting goods companies, banks, and hundreds of other businesses, with assets totaling billions of dollars.[8]

Under threat of still another government indictment for antitrust violations, the big five agreed to a consent decree in 1920, requiring them to dispose of many of their holdings both in the meat industry and in related fields.[9] The consent decree proved to be a temporary hindrance but fell short of posing an effective long-term obstacle to the big meat-packers. By 1935, Armour and Swift had regained control over 61 percent of the meat sales in the country. Two decades later, in 1957, a Congressional report concluded that "economic concentration in meat packing was as great as before the consent decree."[10]

From the very beginning of America's industrial experience, the beef-packing companies played a dominant role in establishing the contours of American commerce. In the early decades following the Civil War and in the first half of the current century, they were an omnipresent force, continually dictating the terms of engagement for American capitalist development. In their operating style, marketing practices, and relations with the federal government, the beef-packing giants set the pace and tone for American business practices in the twentieth century. Their reach extended into every area of modern business life. Nowhere was their influence more felt, however, than in the production process itself.

The beef packers were the first industry to successfully employ mass production techniques, division of labor, and the assembly line in their manufacturing process, becoming a model for the automotive industry and the rest of American industry in the twentieth century. Their rational method of organization, with its emphasis on speed, efficiency, and utility applied to the manufacturing of meat and the

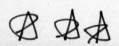

manipulation of men, helped create the conditions for the emergence of a new cattle complex bearing all of the essential characteristics of modern industrial production. Twentieth-century industrial life began with the introduction of the "disassembly line" in the packinghouses of Chicago's Union Stock Yards.

Set tone.

for

20ot Cat

Beef Packers

18

The Disassembly Line

America emerging as Top DOS (handwritten)

The post–Civil War era marked the beginning of America's emergence as an industrial power. Rail links and telegraph wires crisscrossed the continent, bringing together raw resources, an immigrant work force, and waiting urban markets into a powerful commercial phalanx. Foundries and factories clustered around riverways and lakes in the northeastern and midwestern states, their chimneys bellowing with spent energy, a sure sign of the prosperous future that lay ahead. Everywhere there was discussion of power-driven tools and new methods of production. Legions of men and women were recruited to work in the new industrial factories, where they were instructed in the arts of machine labor and factory production. Daily rounds gave way to the punch clock and work schedules, and the craftsmanship of generations became lost amid the hustle and bustle of machines and men stamping out identical products, all uniform, predictable, cheap, and anonymous.

A relatively new temporal value arose from obscurity to become the dominant time orientation and organizing principle of the new industrial era. Efficiency became a means, then a goal of the new order. Men were consumed, even obsessed, with finding new ways to maximize output in the minimum time, while exerting the min-

Efficiency (handwritten)

imum labor, energy, and capital in the process. Speed replaced quality as the modus operandi of the new mass production culture.

It was inside the giant Union Stock Yards of Chicago that much of the new "industrial" way of thinking was born. While most economic historians have been drawn to the steel and automobile industry for clues to American's early industrial genius, it was in the slaughterhouse that many of the most salient innovations in industrial design were first used. The huge packing plant on Chicago's south side dwarfed most of the industrial factories of the day. It was enormous, comprising over a square mile. Companies like Armour and Swift employed 5,000 or more men in their facilities inside the yard.[1] By 1886, over a hundred miles of track surrounded the yards, with trains unloading carload after carload of western longhorns onto the planks and into the sprawling pens.[2] Everywhere the eye could see, there were cattle milling, moving, being separated and corralled into designated areas, to await their last walk up the chutes, high atop the slaughterhouse. "So many cattle no one had ever dreamed existed in the world," wrote Upton Sinclair in his book *The Jungle*.[3]

The packinghouses were the first American industry to create the assembly line. Unable to keep pace with the flood of cattle coming in daily from rail links scattered across the Great Plains, and anxious to meet the beef needs of both easterners and a growing foreign market, the packinghouse giants hit on the idea of streamlining the process of slaughter by the use of a novel device, the conveyor belt. An early publication, financed by one of the meat-packing companies, described the process:

> The slaughtered animals, suspended head downward from a moving chain, or conveyer, pass from workman to workman, each of whom performs some particular step in the process.[4]

The speed with which an animal could be killed, dismembered, cleaned, and dressed with the new assembly-line production was extraordinary. For example, in the older process, a steer would be stunned and stuck and left to bleed on the ground. It would then require three men to drag the beast along the floor to a crosstie, where it was propped up to allow the head to swing free. The process often took more than fifteen minutes. By the first decade of the twentieth century, a single "shackler" could hoist seventy carcasses

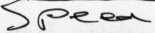

Speed

each minute "simply clipping the shackles around the hind foot, while steam power does the rest."[5] Henry Ford later reminisced that "the idea [for his automobile assembly line] came in a general way from the overhead trolley that the Chicago packers used in dressing beef."[6]

The partial replacement of machines for men in the slaughter process forced a new reality upon the body politic—the increasing neutralization and detachment of the act of killing. For the first time, machines were used to speed along the process of mass slaughter, leaving men as mere accomplices, forced to conform to the pace and requirements set by the assembly line itself.

Speaking of the new process of detached, mechanized killing, historian of technology Siegfried Giedion remarked:

What is truly startling in the mass transition from life to death is the complete neutrality of the act. . . . It happens so quickly, and is so smooth a part of the production process, that emotion is barely stirred. . . . One does not experience, one does not feel; one merely observes.[7]

The disassembly line introduced the pivotal concepts of modern industrial production: division of labor, a continuous production flow, mass production, and above all, efficiency. The bovine had been reduced still another notch on the great chain of being. Desacralized as well as dismembered, this icon of otherworldly generativeness was transformed by the new high priests of efficiency— Gustavus Swift, Philip Armour, and the like—into a standardized production unit. Hoisted onto chains and hooked onto rails, these noble creatures, venerated by much of western culture for the first few thousand years of recorded history, were hurried along from station to station, where they were hacked at, cut up, severed, divided, reduced, and reconstituted, ending up as disembodied cuts of meat at the end of the line.

It's no wonder historians of a later period were more comfortable extolling the virtues of the assembly line and mass production in the automotive industry. The mental deadening of assembly-line workers, though unsettling, was at least a step removed from the bloodletting on the "kill floor." In the newly mechanized abattoirs of Chicago, the stench of death, the clanking of chains overhead, and the whirr of disemboweled creatures passing by in an endless procession overwhelmed the senses and dampened the enthusiasm of even the most ardent supporters of the new production values.

Production workers fared poorly on the new disassembly line. Jobs Working conditions in the slaughter houses were Dickensian. Men were forced to work in dimly lit rooms with poor ventilation and even poorer sanitation. Laborers often stood in pools of stagnant water, full of effluent and blood. Management did not provide cafeterias, or even medical stations, in the early years. Workers hurriedly ate their meals, often near their workstations, while surrounded by the stench of dying animals and the sight of limbs and carcasses being severed, sawed, and sectioned.

Cuts were commonplace, especially on the killing floor, where workers brandished an array of knives and saws. With little or no medical attention available, laborers were forced to dress their own wounds as best they could without slowing up operations on the line. Infection and disease were widespread—the highest of any industry in the country. Tuberculosis and pneumonia spread through the chill rooms. In Chicago, thirteen men died of the diseases at the Swift plant alone between 1907 and 1910.[8]

The disassembly line undermined the job security and independence of the skilled butchers. With butchering now divided into mindless tasks that required little or no apprenticeship or skill, packinghouses turned to the large pool of immigrant and black laborers to man the workstations on the line. By the first decade of the twentieth century, the skilled butcher had all but been eliminated in the Chicago yards. He was replaced by "killing gangs" often numbering as many as 157 men divided into 78 different "trades," each worker performing a minute task over and over again. Commentators marveled at the efficiency of the new production method, which transformed the process of division of labor into a near science. "It would be difficult to imagine another industry where division of labor has been so ingeniously and microscopically worked out," remarked the labor economist John R. Commons. "The animal has been surveyed and laid off like a map."[9]

Management hoped that by dividing up tasks into smaller and smaller operations they could effectively eliminate any remaining worker control over the conduct and pace of work while at the same time speeding up production on the floor. They were successful on both fronts. A management publication explained the new approach to butchery:

> There is no room for individuality or artistry in beef butchering. The worker does not decide where or how to make his cut; he does not look at the animal and make an appropriate decision. All cuts are by the book; the instructions are very exact.[10]

In 1908, Armour introduced an automated conveyor system on the cattle-killing floor, forcing the laborers to work at the pace set by the machinery. A trade journal at the time heralded the breakthrough:

> Instead of the men going to the work, the work came to them. And they must keep steadily and accurately at work, for it keeps coming, and each man must complete his task in an appropriate time or confess himself incompetent for the job.[11]

Production increased dramatically in the decades following the introduction of the disassembly line. In 1884, five splitters handled 800 head of cattle in a ten-hour day. By 1894, four splitters were handling 1,200 head a day. Upton Sinclair was awed by the "furious intensity" of the splitters. They appeared almost possessed as they hacked away, splitting the backbone of steer after steer. So fast was the pace of dismemberment that they severed the carcasses "literally upon the run."[12]

Stripped of their humanity, forced to work in an environment that was as hazardous as it was hellish, packinghouse laborers fought back, demanding better working conditions and better pay. Some of the bloodiest labor battles of the waning years of the nineteenth century and the opening decades of the twentieth century were fought between the fledgling beef-packing unions and the Beef Trust. In 1894, the tiny Chicago Stockyard Butchers' Union struck the big five packers. Thousands of workers walked off the job, only to be replaced by scabs. The reaction was swift and violent. Scab workers were beaten by the strikers as they tried to enter the factory gates. The police were called in to quell the uprising, and President Grover Cleveland dispatched federal troops, crippling the efforts of the striking union.[13]

In 1896, the American Federation of Labor, then under the iron hand of Samuel Gompers, encouraged the formation of the Amalgamated Meat Cutters and Butcher Workmen of North America, the first nationwide union of packinghouse workers. By 1903, Amalgamated had successfully negotiated industry-wide agreements that included 15 percent pay raises and increased work gangs to accommodate the production line speedups.[14]

Emboldened by their new clout, union organizers overstepped, demanding significant wage increases at a time when the economy was in recession and unemployment had doubled. The packers balked, and the union struck. Fifty thousand workers walked off the job. Riots broke out in the major packing towns—Chicago, Omaha, and Kansas City. The companies kept the plants operating with waves of new immigrant laborers and poor blacks. Within months, union strike funds were depleted. Dispirited, members quit the strike and the union in droves. Finally, Jane Addams, the Chicago social reformer, intervened with J. Ogden Armour, pleading for an end to the conflict. The company agreed to rehire former workers at a reduced wage. Defeated, many accepted the offer, leaving the union "high and dry." Within a few years of the disastrous defeat at the hands of the Beef Trust, the union membership had dropped from 56,000 to a low of 6,000 members. In the ensuing years, Amalgamated regrouped, regaining members and clout till its rolls swelled to 100,000 in a labor force of 161,000.[15]

The union mounted a second nationwide strike in 1921. Fifty-five thousand workers in thirteen packing locations around the country walked off in December of that year. Unfortunately, as was the case in the 1904 debacle, the union had chosen to strike during an economic downturn. With unemployment running high, management found it relatively easy to marshal a scab work force and keep its operations running. A court order was handed down, outlawing "peaceful picketing" of the plants.[16] Two thousand police were called in to enforce the decree, setting the conditions for a bloody confrontation. Captain Russell of the Chicago Stockyard Police explained his troops' marching orders.

The patrolmen have been instructed not to shoot unless necessary. They have been advised to use their clubs and fists freely. However, they have also been told that if the occasion should arise for shooting, they must shoot quickly and accurately. That policy has had excellent results already.[17]

On December 7, strikers and their families gathered along Ashland Avenue across from the plants, throwing rocks and shouting epithets at the mounted police. The police opened fire, killing at least one striker and wounding nine others. Amalgamated lost the strike, capitulating to the packinghouse giants on February 1, 1922, just two months after the walkout. They regrouped once again and by the late 1930s were finally successful at organizing industry workers and negotiating lasting agreements with the major beef companies.[18]

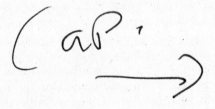

19
Modern Meat

Shift in control

Changes in the beef industry after World War II provided an opportunity for new companies to challenge the long-standing dominance of the big five meat-packers. While the cast of companies changed, coercion and corruption continued to characterize the policies and practices of the new industry leaders.

The meteoric rise of "factory" feedlots in the 1950s and 1960s, the new automated slaughtering processes, and the popularity of precut packaged beef shifted the locus of power from the older, more staid meat-packing operations to more aggressive firms. Many of the newer companies established highly automated meat-processing plants in rural areas close to the commercial feedlots to cut transportation costs and take advantage of a cheaper, nonunion, rural labor pool. The giants of the industry, mired down by old equipment, spiraling shipping costs, and expensive labor agreements, found themselves increasingly unable to compete with the upstart companies.

In 1970, the old Union Stock Yards on the south side of Chicago were shut down, a telling sign of the success of the new more decentralized meat-processing strategy.[1] Trucks and interstates had largely replaced railcars and rails, and much of the cattle-slaughtering business was now scattered across the midwest and plains states. Of

change

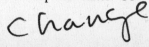

the original big five operations, only Swift remained in a leadership position as brash and aggressive new firms like Iowa Beef and Excel moved to fill the post–World War II vacuum in the beef industry.

Iowa Beef Packers, now the nation's largest beef processor, set the pace in the 1960s. Taking a lesson from Gustavus Swift and the early meat-packers, who had saved costs by shipping refrigerated carcasses rather than live steers, IBP went a step further, shipping precut boxed beef instead of carcasses. The savings were enormous, allowing IBP and its imitators to gain a dominant hold over the industry in less than a decade. IBP executive Dale Tinstman explained the company's strategy: *Boxed Beef*

> There is a lot of wasted space in a modern truck or railcar filled with chilled sides of beef. A side of beef has an awkward shape— it can't be neatly packed, and a side has a lot of bone and trim that will never go into the meat case. It was logical to move to boxed beef.[2]

Boxed beef also appealed to the new supermarket chains that were opening up in suburban malls along newly paved highways. Retailers were anxious to cut labor costs, and consumers appreciated the convenience of prepackaged beef. The number of retail butchers dwindled in size by the 1980s, their ranks primarily made up of specialty butchers servicing the gourmet trade and a smaller number servicing older, inner-city ethnic communities. The new beef processors were also able to save additional dollars by retaining the trimmed fat and other waste materials in the slaughtering process and using them in the preparation of by-products.

IBP saved on labor costs at its processing facilities by maintaining an aggressive anti-union stance. It located its facilities in nonunion states—Iowa, Nebraska, Kansas, and Texas—and fought any hint of union encroachment with an arsenal of legal and illegal tactics. Its success was copied by other new entrants into the beef trade in the 1960s.

Journalist David Moberg describes the various means used by IBP to cripple organized labor:

> Rather than ship carcasses to urban wholesalers or supermarket chains, it cut up the animals and sold "boxed beef" that eliminated

skilled, well-paid butchers. It ruthlessly fought the packinghouse unions, breaking strikes, signing sweetheart contracts with unions like the Teamsters or National Maritime Union and, where unionized, accepting only contracts below the rates at established packers. . . . It was efficient and ruthless.[3]

The unions fought back. In 1979, the two major packing unions, United Packing House Workers of America and the Amalgamated Meat Cutters and Butcher Workmen, joined forces with the Retail Clerks International Union to form the United Food and Commercial Workers Union (UFCW). From its new base of operation, the union took on IBP and the other new anti-union packers. The two forces locked horns in 1982 at IBP's Dakota City Plant. The union struck to achieve contract "parity" with other meat-packing companies. The confrontation between IBP and the workers turned ugly when the Nebraska National Guard was called in to "quell picket-line violence."[4]

Other strikes followed, including a long protracted battle between UFCW Local P-9 and the George A. Hormel packing plant in Austin, Minnesota. The Hormel strike was bitter and violent and required the intervention of the Minnesota National Guard to maintain order. This new generation of worker walkouts, with its strikebreakers, pitched battles at the factory gates, and the stationing of military peacekeeping forces, is reminiscent of the struggles at the turn of the century when a largely immigrant labor force squared off against the big five Beef Trust to demand representation and improved working conditions.

Little has changed in the meat-packing industry since Upton Sinclair's telling account of working conditions in the slaughterhouses at the turn of the century. Working conditions are still hazardous and unsanitary. Workers are still mercilessly exploited by management. The companies continue to foster inhumane practices on the kill floor and in the chill rooms. The conditions are often primitive, even ghoulish. Says Eleanor Kennelly of the UFCW, "A meat-packing plant is like nothing you've ever seen or could imagine. It's like a vision of hell."[5] It's no wonder that employee turnover is as much as 43 percent a month at some plants.[6]

Companies often encourage turnover, pitting migrant workers from Mexico against Asian boat people for menial, demeaning, and

turnover

dangerous jobs. High turnover helps insulate the companies against union organizing.

> More importantly, for union organizing, the system of turnover prevents employees from becoming knowledgeable, from becoming more sophisticated, because they're simply not there long enough.[7]

Turnover is fueled by the high rate of personal injury, the second-highest of any occupation in America. (Only the logging industry has a higher rate of injuries.) In 1988, 45,000 workers in the beef-packing industry were injured on the job out of a work force of 135,000 men and women—a rate of injury three times the national average of other American industries. The Occupational Safety and Health Administration (OSHA) has estimated that in some packing plants the injury rate exceeds 85 percent.[8]

The rate of injuries has climbed dramatically in the past five years as a result of the streamlining of production and the increased speed of the disassembly lines. The pace is dizzying. Workers now make thousands of "cuts" a day on the kill floor on lines that process up to 300 cattle per hour. Some cutters are forced to make five cuts every fifteen seconds.[9] Companies like IBP minimize the problem of injury, preferring to think of it simply as another cost that needs to be factored into the production process. An IBP spokesman explained, "Once we push the button in the morning, we don't want the chain to stop. If it stops, it costs money. We want to pump the tonnage through."[10]

In 1987, the Labor Department imposed a $2.59 million fine on IBP for falsifying records on safety violations and worker injuries. The company "willfully failed to report" 1,038 instances of job-related injuries and illnesses in one of its many facilities. In 1988, OSHA announced it was fining John Morrell & Company $4.6 million for "egregious" and "willful" health violations at its plant in Sioux Falls, South Dakota.[11]

While the working conditions on the kill floors and the chill rooms of the nation's packinghouses are hellish, the living conditions of many meat-packing workers are equally nightmarish. Packing plants are often located on the outskirts of small rural towns. Migrant packing workers, like migrant agricultural workers, lead a largely nomadic existence, continually moving from one meat-packing town to another. Workers often live in overcrowded and squalid trailer parks, without adequate plumbing and sanitation. Infant mortality and illiteracy are among the highest of any occupational group in the nation. Workers and their families are often discriminated against by local communities, who view them as outsiders and interlopers.

> These workers have no ties with their community. Their relations with the community are hostile. They are ostracized. They put a strain on the community resources. The hospitals are reluctant to treat indigents. The schools dislike teaching English to non-English-speaking children. . . . The day-to-day existence of this new breed of workers is subhuman. The system of turnover flourishes by making the living and working conditions intolerable, and by causing the deterioration of small towns.[12]

Immigrants

IBP and its competitors seized upon the rural poor and the new immigrant groups flooding into the country from Mexico, Central and South America, and Southeast Asia, building corporate empires on the backs of a cheap pool of largely unorganized workers. By 1988, IBP was slaughtering 29 percent of the cattle in the U.S. and controlled 35 to 40 percent of the boxed beef trade.[13]

IBP's success was not solely attributable to its timely innovations and exploitive labor practices. During its rise to dominance the firm garnered a reputation for dirty dealings, including behind-the-scenes payoffs and strong-arm tactics. In September 1974 the company and its founder and chairman, C. J. Holman, were convicted of conspiring with a New York City Mafia figure to steal their way into the lucrative New York meat market, the world's largest beef center, by paying bribes and kickbacks to commercial beef operators and union officials.

The Mafia virtually controlled the New York City beef trade in the 1970s. Their representative, Moe Steinman, entered into an illegal agreement with IBP at a clandestine meeting held in a hotel suite in 1970. In return for regular payments to Steinman and another of his colleagues—totaling millions of dollars over an eight-year period—IBP would be "guaranteed" the inside track to New York wholesalers and retailers. The *Wall Street Journal*, which broke the story, reported:

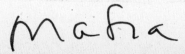

Consequent to the meeting in the Stanhope Hotel, Iowa beef would reorganize its entire marketing apparatus to allow Steinman's organization complete control over the company's largest market and influence over its operations coast to coast. In 1975 Iowa Beef would bring Moe Steinman's son-in-law and protégé to its headquarters near Sioux City to run the company's largest division and throw his voice into vital corporate decisions.[14]

The *Journal* concluded that "because of their hold on Iowa Beef, the racketeers' control of other segments of the meat industry would expand and harden. And as a result of all of this, the price of meat for the American consumer . . . would rise."[15]

In 1981, IBP was bought out by Occidental Petroleum for $800 million.[16] Occidental's board chairman explained his company's interest in the beef industry by predicting that "food shortages will be, to the 1990s what energy shortages have been to the 1970s and 1980s."[17]

IBP's chief imitator and rival in the 1970s was the MBPXL Corporation, headquartered in Wichita, Kansas. In 1978, Cargill Industries, the largest privately held grain company in the world, purchased the company, changed its name to Excel, provided it with much-needed capital, and relocated its processing facilities to Dodge City, Kansas.[18] Cargill's decision to add beef-processing operations to its corporate portfolio reflected the trend toward vertical integration in the 1970s. It also signaled the ultimate consolidation of the beef industry, bringing cattle, grain, beef processing, and marketing together in a single cattle complex.

Still another food company giant, Con-Agra, burst onto the cattle scene in the 1980s, buying up Swift and other smaller firms in the beef industry. Con-Agra owns or has interlocking financial interests in grain processing, feed and fertilizers, farm chemicals, global commodity trading, frozen foods, and retail operations. In 1989 Con-Agra's Red Meat Company's annual sales topped $7.5 billion.[19]

Today the new big three in the beef industry exercise significant control over virtually every stage of the beef process. They own many of the seed companies whose strains are used to grow the grain to feed the cattle. They also produce many of the farm fertilizers and chemicals that are applied to the soil and the feed crops. They even own an increasing share of the cattle herds and feedlots. The big three raise one-fourth of all the cattle they slaughter, or nearly 17 percent of all the cattle slaughtered in the United States. It is estimated that by 1995, 30 percent of the nation's cattle being slaughtered will be controlled by these same three companies in joint ventures with the nation's commercial feedlots.[20] Finally, IBP, Excel, and Con-Agra dominate the slaughtering process itself, being jointly responsible for slaughtering 70 percent of all feedlot cattle in the United States.[21] The new Beef Trust exercises far greater control of the beef industry than its predecessors could have imagined possible.

New Beef Trust

Con Agra

"New Big 3"

20

The Automated Jungle

Product [handwritten]

Most Americans know little of the desperate plight of slaughterhouse workers in the United States. They know even less about how the beef products they consume are produced and packaged. It was in 1904 that novelist Upton Sinclair wrote his devastating exposé of the beef-packing industry. *The Jungle* shocked the nation with its graphic descriptions of the unsanitary conditions in the slaughterhouses of Chicago. Readers were horrified by what they read:

> Whenever meat was so spoiled that it could not be used for anything else, they [the packers] either canned it or else chopped it into sausage. . . . There was never the least attention paid to what was cut up for sausage; there would come all the way from Europe old sausage that had been rejected, and that was moldy and white—it would be dosed with borox and glycerine, and dumped into the hoppers, and made over again for home consumption. There would be meat that had tumbled out on the floor, in the dirt and sawdust, where the workers had trampled and spit uncounted billions of consumption germs. There would be meat stored in great piles in rooms; and the water from leaky rooms would drip over it, and thousands of rats would race about on it. It was too dark in these storage places to see well, but a man could run his hand over these

Fuchindisgusting [handwritten]

piles of meat and sweep off handfuls of dried dung of rats. These rats were nuisances, and the packers would put poison bread out for them; they would die, and then rats, bread and meat would go into the hopper together.[1]

The vivid picture that emerged sparked an immediate public reaction. Outraged, the United States Congress acted swiftly, passing the Pure Food and Drug Act of 1906, barring adulterated or mislabeled food (and drugs) from interstate commerce. The Congress also passed a Meat Inspection Act that year, mandating ante- and postmortem federal inspection of all classes of livestock and red meats in interstate and foreign commerce. The Act empowered the USDA to "require sanitary equipment, conditions, and methods in the slaughtering and packing establishments to prevent the use of harmful chemicals and preservatives and of misleading labels, and to regulate the transportation of meat in interstate and foreign commerce."[2]

Little has been written about the sanitary conditions in the slaughterhouses since the turn of the century, and most Americans believe that the meat they consume poses no serious health threats. The public's ease was shaken momentarily in the 1960s when Congressmen Neal Smith of Iowa began calling attention to health conditions in meat-processing plants unregulated by the federal government. Many of the giant beef packers—Swift, Armour, and Wilson—were bypassing federal inspection statutes by processing up to 25 percent of the red meat in "intrastate plants" and then shipping the products only within the state, thus avoiding interstate commerce and federal inspection.[3]

Some twenty-two states had no requirements for ante- or postmortem examination of livestock. Eight states had no inspection standards. The conditions in many of the intrastate facilities were deplorable. According to an internal USDA report that was leaked to the press and the public, USDA inspectors in Delaware had uncovered both "rodents and insects, in fact many vermin had free access to stored meats and meat product ingredients." In North Carolina, an observer reported, "snuff-spit [and] sausage meat fallen on the same floor . . . was then picked up and shoved into the stuffer." In Norfolk, Virginia, federal authorities found "abscessed beef and livers, abscessed pork livers, parasitic livers mixed with edible products." In Congressional hearings, legislators were told of the

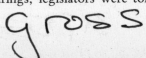

widespread practice of buying what the packers called "4D live-stock"—dead, dying, diseased, and disabled—to cut expenses. In 1967, President Lyndon Johnson signed into law the Wholesale Meat Act, requiring states to develop meat inspection standards comparable to those regulating interstate commerce.[4]

Though neither the Congress nor the public suspected it at the time, the irony of the new 1967 legislation was the widely held assumption that federal inspection laws and practices were indeed adequate and a proper model upon which to base intrastate standards. The fact is, despite the federal laws, unsanitary conditions in the nation's beef-packing plants were widespread. In a 1985 report, the National Academy of Sciences announced that current federal inspection procedures were inadequate to protect the public from meat-related diseases. The NAS report recommended that "newer technologies . . . and modified slaughtering and dressing techniques be developed and implemented to reduce infectious and other hazardous agents."[5]

Surprisingly, the NAS recommendations were never acted upon. Instead, the USDA and the meat-packing industry joined forces, creating a wholly new inspection procedure designed to weaken even further the few safeguards that had been built into the oversight process.

The USDA and several of the giant meat-packers are currently experimenting with a new inspection process called the Streamlined Inspection System (SIS), which virtually eliminates the role of the federal meat inspector in the examination of beef carcasses destined for interstate and foreign commerce. The goal of the high-speed inspection process, which is currently being used in some of the major beef-packing facilities in the United States, is to increase online production by 40 percent.[6] To reach that objective, the USDA has sacrificed many of the inspection procedures that have been used for decades to ensure minimum health and safety standards.

Under the new experimental SIS system, federal meat inspectors no longer inspect every carcass on the production line. Instead, packinghouse workers conduct only random checks—sometimes checking as few as three carcasses out of 1,000. The new process, which relies on the company to do spot inspections on a random basis, has been universally condemned by federal meat inspectors. One inspector likened the new process to "a doctor looking at three people in a town of 1,000 and, because these three were healthy, they would say the whole town was healthy."[7]

The SIS pilot program is designed to mimic the quality-control procedures employed in other industries. Cattle, however, are not products that can be tested randomly for production defects. Each steer is unique. Federal meat inspector Stephen Cockerham described the obvious difference in an affidavit submitted to the USDA, criticizing the new system:

> The meat industry deals with live animals each one individual, each one capable of contracting disease. We are not talking about machine parts stamped out of a press and checked for uniformity.[8]

Under the new SIS process, federal meat inspectors are stripped of most of their authority. Their inspection is relegated to a backup for the quality control staff of the company. In their new, reduced capacity, federal inspectors examine less than 1 percent of the carcasses, whereas they used to examine every animal that came down the line. Federal inspectors no longer make regular checks of the carcasses for signs of disease. The kidneys are no longer checked separately, nor are the lymph nodes, tongues, lungs, and heads, unless a company employee first flags a problem. Federal inspectors participating in the pilot program no longer check products or equipment for microbic contamination. They are not allowed to condemn a carcass that has been spotted for early cases of diseases such as actinomycosis. Federal officials are no longer stationed at the rail inspection area, the location best suited to spot symptoms of cancer and multiple abscesses. At the kidney-carcass inspection station, USDA inspectors can no longer tag a carcass for arthritis or insects. They no longer inspect walls, trailers, or rendering rooms for unsanitary conditions. They are not even allowed to touch all the necessary parts of the carcass to check for signs of disease. Instead, the carcass is viewed from behind a mirror "through fifteen feet of steam and fog" as it whizzes by.[9] With the carcass covered with blood and debris, a visual check from behind a fogged mirror is often a useless exercise.

No longer able to touch and feel a carcass, inspectors cannot diagnose disease and spot many contaminants. One USDA inspector said that "because we no longer palpate or feel the tongues, cactus thorns and associated abscesses are getting through. We miss the flukes, abscesses, lungs and measles, because we can't palpate the diaphragm . . . or hearts and cheeks."[10]

Standards have been relaxed all along the line to allow dirtier, diseased carcasses to squeeze by the review process. Under the new system, there is no maximum number of defects per carcass. A defect counts as a smear only if it measures 3 to 7.9 cm. Blood clots now count as a defect only if they measure more than 2 cm. Mucosa on a single carcass must exceed 2 cm to be scored. Stains caused by oil, grease, and rust are also acceptable if the measure is under a range of 3 to 7.9 cm. Scar tissue caused by healed ulcers, liver spots, and sawdust are not even scored but allowed to pass on through the inspection process. Hemorrhages must be greater than 2 cm to be scored.[11]

USDA officials justify the new lax procedures and reduced standards, arguing that the beef need not be free of all contaminants but merely be "aesthetically acceptable." According to the agency, "carcasses whose degree of cleanliness are . . . within the action level are not injurious to health."[12] Carol Tucker Foreman, former Assistant Secretary of Agriculture in the Carter administration, voiced the concerns of many when she dryly remarked:

> The thousands of people who have suffered food poisoning after eating beef will, no doubt, appreciate that their beef was aesthetically acceptable, even though it made them ill. "Lovely to look at dangerous to eat" is not a standard that is likely to help beef sales.[13]

Whistle blowers within the federal meat inspection service estimate that under the new SIS program, the rate of unwholesome beef getting the USDA stamp of approval has jumped markedly. The system is designed to fail, say many federal meat inspectors, because it is based on the faulty premise that the companies can be trusted to police their own product. While company employees check the carcasses, federal meat inspectors spend much of their time checking paperwork.[14] Federal meat inspector Michael Beacom put his finger directly on the problem:

> The intent of the SIS is to turn the responsibility of wholesome meat products over to the company and its employees. The employees take their orders and get their paychecks from the company.

The company's purpose is to make more profit. Why would the USDA want to turn over the responsibility of meat inspection to . . . the owners of the meat-packing industry, whose number-one concern would be profit?[15]

Employees know that if they trim a carcass to remove impurities it will cost the company money and eat into its profit. Workers concerned with keeping their jobs are, more often than not, likely to let the contaminated beef slip through so as not to arouse the ire of management. Jim Dekker, a federal meat inspector, vented the frustration and concern of many of his colleagues in a formal affidavit submitted to the USDA on the new SIS program.

The whole idea of meat-packing companies policing themselves is ridiculous. I've heard the comment that it is like having the fox guarding the chicken house, and that is exactly the truth.[16]

Foreigners

Company employees are often so inexperienced that they are unable to identify contaminated beef even if they try to perform their job. Many are from Mexico, Latin America, and Southeast Asia, and are barely able to speak English. Turnover, as already mentioned, is so high in the processing plants that quality-control employees come and go before they are versed in even the most rudimentary procedures. Said one USDA inspector, "People are hired off the street and certified as soon as they can hold a knife." Many of the companies prefer illegal aliens as quality-control staff because they speak only Laotian or Spanish. That way the "trimmers don't understand what the USDA inspector is saying."[17] In one plant, quality-control employees were so badly informed about procedures that they finally asked a USDA inspector what it meant to put a government tag on a kidney. "They did not know the tag means the food is condemned and must be removed."[18]

So poorly trained are the quality-control staff that in one pilot program they failed to spot fifteen out of fifteen tonsils infected with measles because they didn't know where the tonsils were located on the animal, or even what they looked like. In another SIS program, quality-control personnel failed to identify "a piece of hide two inches wide and fourteen inches long from cattle that had been lying in manure which was caked on the skin." One corporate employee,

Cook meat well!

observing the SIS process, warned that the quality-control inspectors "were so poorly trained that they could not recognize infection until the pus came oozing out of abscesses."[19]

USDA officials have reacted to the criticism by warning the public to make sure they cook their meat well. Bemused over his own agency's cavalier attitude, Dekker responded sardonically, "I suppose if abscess, dirt, manure, fecal material, or any other contamination is cooked long enough it will not hurt you."[20]

Companies have been caught falsifying records and reports, suppressing data, and deliberately allowing diseased meat to get by the line and onto the market. The Government Accountability Project, a public interest organization that has closely monitored one corporate quality-control program, interviewed quality-control officials "who described having multiple sets of books on product violations—one for the USDA, one for the permanent corporate records, and one that was 'eyes only,' for company management. The records for USDA were the least honest."[21]

Often the companies will reroute cattle and make cosmetic changes to hide incidences of disease. USDA inspectors report that companies split up shipments of diseased cattle to "reduce the odds of sick animals showing up in the sample by slipping them into shipments of healthy cows."[22] Other inspectors tell of cattle coming onto the kill floor with high fevers. Normally the cattle are not supposed to be slaughtered when ill. Under the new regime the cattle are simply hosed down until they cool off to an acceptable temperature, then killed. The incidences of fever never show up on the corporate records. Said one federal inspector:

> I worked at [a major cattle slaughter firm] in private industry before coming to USDA and we had standing orders not to write it down if we found problems. There seems to be a general practice in the industry not to make a record of bad news.[23]

Rinses are also being used to mask contaminated carcasses. Carcasses are supposed to be washed down to rinse the dust off during the disassembly process. However, according to federal meat inspector Dora Fries:

The pre-washer adds water to the carcass and covers up dirt. Have you ever taken a piece of warm tallow [beef fat], put some fecal matter on it, washed it with pressure like the pre-washer has, then you look at it, it looks clean. Take a sharp knife and slice very thinly and see all of the fecal matter buried in the fat yet. I have done this test. Why else did they put in a pre-wash but to cover up fecal matter and add water so the carcasses will weigh more. The pre-washer does not wash off dirt, it just buries it in the fat.[24]

Recently twenty-four USDA inspectors sent a joint letter to the National Academy of Sciences raising concerns on the wholesomeness of the U.S. beef supply. Their letter concluded, "In good conscience, we can no longer say that we know USDA approved beef is wholesome. . . . USDA advertises the SIS as fewer inspectors looking at less meat on more carcasses at faster line speeds, all without lowering public health standards. We don't buy it."[25]

In 1990, federal meat inspectors from around the country flooded the USDA with affidavits describing abuses throughout the new SIS program. Under the new regime, noted one inspector, "inspectors are expected to check thirty livers per minute. The reality is that after two seconds—when the liver gets past them they don't know whether it is wholesome or not." Said another, "The first commandment [of SIS] is Never Stop the Line. . . . It has reached the point that inspectors can't even stop the line to clean measles off surfaces where other cattle are worked on, which means we can expect cross-contamination of that disease." Under the new SIS program, federal inspectors no longer have the authority to even stop the line if they spot a problem. "All they can do is complain. . . . It's like a police officer trying to stop a robbery without a gun."[26] Unless the company itself agrees that a problem exists or a violation of law occurred, the federal inspector is helpless to take remedial action.

The standards have been so compromised, says another USDA inspector, that "meat whose disease symptoms previously would have forced it to be condemned, or, at most, approved for dog food, now gets the USDA seal of approval for consumers."[27] Inspectors cite the case of "water bellies," cows that are clogged up and cannot urinate. "There is the equivalent of buckets of urine in their briskets,

shank, and bellies. It just floods out when the cow is slaughtered."[28] Under the new system, cow bellies are no longer condemned, but are routinely approved for human consumption.

Cattle with "peritonitus," a bloody mucuslike fluid in the carcass cavity, are routinely approved, whereas under the previous system they would have been condemned.[29] Even cattle with pneumonia and arthritis are routinely approved. According to one USDA inspector, "Veterinarians are now approving cattle that wheeze loudly as they're breathing before slaughter and whose lungs are filled with fluid, that have scar tissue and abscesses running all up and down the sides of the lungs, and stuck to their ribs, and have . . . popped blood vessels in kidneys that are no longer functional."[30]

Some cattle have been approved "that are stuffed with regurgitated food that was oozing out." Fecal smears up to a foot long, along with hair, grubs, adhesions, flukes, and ingesta, are all getting by the line. One USDA inspector remembered instances where he "could see the contamination due to feces and hair from four feet away, mostly on the brisket, armpits, and foreshanks."[31]

Not surprisingly, the increased level of fecal contamination in beef has paralleled the rise in reported cases of salmonella across the country. The incidence of salmonellosis has doubled in the last sixteen years.[32]

More than half the outbreaks, according to the Center for Disease Control, are traceable to meat and poultry. Food poisoning, such as salmonellosis, causes over 2,000 deaths per year and 500,000 hospitalizations, costing hundreds of millions of dollars in additional health care services and other costs.[33] One of the pilot plants that had gone seven years without having a single shipment of beef returned by customers for salmonella reported three returned shipments in the first four months of the SIS experimental program.[34] Other foodborne diseases are also increasing as a result of unsanitary slaughterhouse conditions, including staphylococcus infection and listeriosis.[35]

The descriptions given by the USDA meat inspectors of conditions in some of the nation's biggest slaughterhouses are appalling. They tell of cows being slaughtered that were dead on arrival at the plant—their bodies so icy cold that their hearts couldn't adequately pump out the blood.[36] Carcasses are sent down the disassembly line with their insides full of extraneous objects—rust flakes, broken teeth, nails, claws, rings, tags, and rosin.[37]

In some of the plants the pace on the disassembly line is so fast that cactus thorns remain on the cow's tongues because workers don't have time to remove them.[38] Belts become so clogged with grease that they stop running. Instead of cleaning away the filth, employees simply sprinkle salt on the grease until the system can be made operational.[39] The pressure to keep the disassembly line moving is so great that in one plant, management refused to stop the line even "when they were dripping hydraulic oil onto products" and then refused to tag the carcasses as contaminated.[40]

Walls in the rendering rooms are caked with scum and mildew, with grease dripping down from the equipment onto the workers. The plants are infested with cockroaches, some up to two inches long. Some of the meat being processed is so old it is "green when trimmed."[41] This is often meat that was already sent back from the supermarkets because it was unwholesome. The meat is simply recycled.

Contaminated heads, called "puke heads" because they are filled with rumen content, are now being salvaged and reworked by company employees and no longer have to be submitted to USDA inspectors for reinspection. The result is that in some plants, more than 24 percent of the "puke heads that are reaching the head boning table for boxing are contaminated with hair, dirt, hide, and ingesta."[42] "It's a little unsettling," says USDA inspector Michael Anderson, "knowing that somewhere tonight some family is preparing to chow down on hamburgers, chili, etc. that contains ground-up trimmings from a head or heads like this."[43]

Under the old system, federal inspectors "used to keep the floor shining." Now, with their authority reduced, the kill floors are often "full of guts, urine, and feces, and general muck, sometimes to the point of being so slippery it's dangerous to walk."[44] The gore and filth attract large numbers of rats. In some of the plants, "hunting and killing rats turned into something between sport and a bad joke for the inspectors. Company employees told us that rats were all over the coolers at night running on top of meat and gnawing at it."[45]

Some meat processors and wholesalers are beginning to speak

discuss

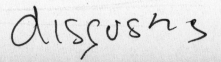

out publicly, concerned over the rise in substandard meat being shipped from the packing plants. John Krusinski's Finest Meat Products, a plant that processes beef into Polish sausages, became so distraught over the quality of beef being sent from some of America's major meat-packers, including Monfort, Iowa Beef, and Excel, that he aired his grievances in 1989 on Cleveland television. He told of meat shipped to his plant that "was obviously sour and full of bacteria. It stank and had pus from abscesses. Routinely the meat stinks so bad that government inspectors tell us to air it out."[46]

Krusinski submitted one shipment of beef to laboratory tests and found excessive coliform bacteria in the beef. The beef also had excessive yeast counts. The meat had so deteriorated, said Krusinski, that when he attempted to "grind and cook the meat in this condition, it just falls apart, and pus comes out like foam."[47] Many slaughterhouses cover up putrefaction by putting phosphate in the meat. Krusinski said that when he complains to the packinghouses, "they basically tell me to take it or leave it. They threaten that if I continue to complain they will not ship any products."[48] The meat processor explained why he decided to speak out despite the risk:

> My own family, including my grandchildren, eat the meat products prepared by my firm. Both as a matter of professional integrity, and loyalty to my family and community, I cannot remain silent while USDA allows an inexcusable deterioration in the quality of beef produced at major slaughterhouses.[49]

In the interest of speeding up production, cutting costs, and improving profit margins, the American beef industry and the USDA have seriously undermined the safety and health standards of the nation's slaughterhouses. Today, millions of Americans and consumers in countries around the world are purchasing cuts of beef unaware of the potential health threat posed by the meat they are consuming.

While traditional foodborne diseases are on the rise, new cattle diseases are also being discovered. The new diseases are not even monitored by quality-control inspectors, or USDA meat inspectors, because no direct causal link has yet been found to human disease. Although USDA officials continue to argue that these new diseases are host-specific and pose no immediate threat to human beings, epidemiological studies suggest at least the possibility of a causal connection and the need for more detailed studies.

Bovine spongeform encephalopathy (BSE), also known as "mad cow disease," broke out in British herds in 1986, and by 1990 had affected some 16,000 cattle from 7,000 herds. The disease eats away at the cow's brain, causing it to become spongelike in appearance. The disease drives the animals mad, requiring them to be destroyed. Scientists suspect that BSE, which is incurable, is caused by feeding cattle offal from sheep infected with scrapie.

Although the disease has not yet been proved to affect human health, its discovery caused an uproar in Britain, leading to a ban on beef in more than 1,000 British schools, for fear the disease might spread to humans. Within weeks of the first reported outbreak of BSE, nearly one in every four British consumers stopped eating beef, crippling the domestic beef market.[50]

Even more troubling is the discovery of two cattle diseases in the United States that are now widespread and suspected of having possible causal links to human diseases. Bovine leukemia virus (BLV) is an insect-borne retrovirus that causes malignancy in cattle and is found in 20 percent of the cows and over 60 percent of the herds in the United States. BLV antibodies have been found in human leukemia patients. BLV has also been found to infect human cells in vitro. Moreover, increasing epidemiological evidence suggests a possible link between BLV and some forms of leukemia. Studies have shown higher incidences of human leukemia in counties with a high percentage of cattle infected with BLV. Similar studies in Sweden and the Soviet Union have linked BLV outbreaks and increases in human leukemia. Scientists have also discovered a close link between BLV and HTLV-1, the first human retrovirus ever shown to cause cancer. HTLV-1 causes a rare and fatal form of leukemia known as T-cell leukemia. BLV and HTLV-1 share a common gene. The gene, whose function is to replicate the virus, is identical in both BLV and HTLV-1.[51]

In recent years a second cattle virus has been discovered in American herds. The virus, which was first isolated in domestic cattle in the 1970s, is called bovine immunodeficiency virus because its genetic structure is so closely related to the HIV or AIDS virus. Scientists have successfully infected human cells with BIV, and at least one study suggested that BIV "may play a role in either malignant or slow viruses in man." The USDA Animal and Plant Health Inspection Service, working with the National Institutes of Health, has been quietly engaged in investigating the potential links between BIV and human disease since 1987. In a formal response to a petition submitted by the Foundation on Economic Trends, Dr. James Wyngaarden, then director of the NIH, and Bert Hawkins, administrator of the Animal and Plant Health Inspection Service, reported that "cattle sera from herds in different localities in the U.S. are being collected to screen for BIV infection." The agency directors also announced that they were in the process of developing "sensitive assays to screen human sera of individuals at some risk of exposure to the virus, either through occupation or some other means."[52]

In 1991 the USDA released the results of its four-year investigation on BIV to the Foundation on Economic Trends. The findings are disturbing. According to the USDA, the cow AIDS virus is widespread among dairy cows and beef cattle and is suspected of suppressing the animals' immune systems, making them susceptible to a wide range of diseases, including mastitis and lymphosarcoma. The USDA says that it does not yet know "whether exposure to BIV proteins causes human sera to . . . become HIV positive." The USDA is continuing its investigations.[53]

Meanwhile the cow AIDS virus is continuing to spread among American cattle with no cure in sight. The economic impact of BIV on the beef and dairy industries is likely to be devastating in the years to come as more and more cattle become infected with cow AIDS and succumb to a range of opportunistic and parasitic diseases stemming from a weakened immune system.

Despite increasing anecdotal evidence linking bovine leukemia virus and bovine immunodeficiency virus to potential human health risks, the USDA has steadfastly refused to check slaughtered meat, milk, and dairy products to see if they contain antibodies to these retroviruses. Every day, Americans consume beef and dairy products from cows, some of which were infected with bovine leukemia virus and cow AIDS, without any assurance that the products are safe.

Changes in the nation's meat inspection system are similar to the changes that have taken place in other areas of the meat industry, where the drive for increased efficiency and profit has resulted in the inhumane treatment of both animals and workers, as well as increased health risks to the consumers of beef products. Now the same highly industrialized approach to men and meat is being exported to other countries in a systematic effort to create a global cattle complex. This ambitious undertaking, spearheaded by global corporations, international lending institutions, and national governments, represents the culmination of the long westward expansion of cattle cults across the Indo-European and American landscapes. The consolidation of the world's beef industry into a single global complex is already having a profound effect on the earth's ecosystems and economic systems.

COW AIDS

21

The World Steer

The final chapter in the 500-year saga to colonize the Americas with cattle came after World War II. Nation-states and multinational corporations began the process of joining North, Central, and South America into a single cattle complex, a vast grazing operation stretching 6,000 miles from the Great Plains of North America to the rich grasslands of the Argentine pampas.

British investment houses invaded the grasslands of South America at the same time they were establishing cattle companies on the American plains. As was the case in North America, the pacification of the plains Indians and transatlantic refrigeration provided the impetus for a massive infusion of British capital into the grasslands. By 1880, British and Scottish firms already owned over 20 percent of the cattle on the pampas.[1] Over the next two decades, British financiers moved quickly to create an elaborate cattle complex in South America, just as they had done earlier in Ireland and Scotland and were doing concurrently in North America. Historian S. Hanson describes the process:

> In the River Platte region, livestock, improved by the continuous heavy import of British blooded animals, moved on British-owned railroads to British-equipped and financed plants, from which the

146

finished product was shipped on British steamships to England, for a long time the only import market.[2]

By the turn of the century, 278 refrigeration ships were regularly crossing the Atlantic transporting South American beef to England and Europe.[3] Some British merchants made fortunes off the Argentine trade. The Vestey family of Liverpool dominated much of the Argentine trade in the late nineteenth century and went on to establish Dewhurst Limited, the largest chain of retail butcher shops in England.

While Argentina provided much of the beef for the British aristocracy and middle class, Uruguayan cattle were used to make the famed "Liebig extract" of meat, a cheap beef spread sold primarily to the English working class. For many Englishmen, the extract served as their main source of animal protein. In the 1880s, over 150,000 head of Uruguayan cattle were slaughtered and rendered into Liebig spread at the English-owned factory at Fray Bentos on the Uruguay River.[4]

The increasing demand for beef in post–World War II Europe and the United States spurred renewed interest in the land of Latin America. In the 1960s, with the help of loans from the World Bank and the Inter-American Development Bank, governments throughout Central and South America began to convert millions of acres of tropical rain forest and cropland to pastureland to raise cattle for the international beef market. Between 1971 and 1977 alone, over $3.5 billion in loans and technical assistance was pumped into Latin America to promote cattle production.[5] Much of Central America was turned into a giant pasture to provide cheap beef for North America. In South America the Amazon rain forests were cleared and burned to make room for cattle grazing, largely to supply the beef needs of England and Europe. The speed of conversion has been staggering and rivals the earlier invasion of the North American plains and Argentine pampas.

The "cattlization" of Central and South America is part of a systematic effort by multinational corporations to create a single world market for the production and distribution of beef. Industry analysts are already beginning to bandy about a new term, "the world steer," the bovine analogue of the world car.[6] Transnational corporations, eager to create what Peter Drucker and others have called

B 5 Buss

the global shopping center, are moving to gain control over every aspect of the beef business in hopes that a worldwide vertical integration of operations will allow them to optimize resources and maximize market potential.

Multinational corporations are beginning to assemble cattle the way they assemble cars, bringing together inputs—seeds, grain, pharmaceuticals, cattle embryos, cattle, automated slaughtering processes, wholesale marketing, and retail distribution—from various countries into a single coordinated operation. The world steer is already a near-reality, and North, Central, and South America are fast becoming the world's primary grazing lands and abattoirs.

A critical step in the creation of a "world steer" cattle complex is the standardization of the final products. Political scientist Steven Sanderson lists the most important factors: "Immunity from major contagious diseases, certain marbling characteristics of the meat, standardized cuts of beef, and so forth."[7] The beef industry is entering a new era, "in which the meat on consumers' tables will have been developed in Europe and North America, bred in Latin America, fed with export grains from the key producing countries, slaughtered under international standards, and consumed in the communities most removed from their point of origin."[8]

The institutionalization of the world steer is deeply affecting the economies of developing nations. Countries like Mexico are hardest hit by this newest form of neocolonial exploitation, as more and more land is converted to pasture to graze cattle destined for the U.S. market. Mexico ships large numbers of live cattle to the United States, where they are fattened on grain in Texas feedlots and slaughtered for domestic consumption.[9]

At the same time, countries like Brazil are using more and more land to produce feed for livestock. Much of the feed is being exported to feed livestock in Europe, Russia, Japan, and the United States. Central and South American cattle are for the most part grass-fed. In Brazil, 23 percent of the cultivated land is currently being used to produce soybeans, of which nearly half are for export. The implications are enormous and far-reaching. An acre of land can generally produce over 1,200 pounds of white corn per year. When the land is seeded with soy, far less corn is available for human consumption, resulting in higher grain prices. The price increases fall disproportionately on the poor. For example, black beans, long a staple of the

Lands

Brazilian peasant diet, are becoming more expensive, as farmers have switched to growing soybeans for the more lucrative international feed market.[10]

Mexico is devoting an increasing amount of its agricultural production to sorghum to feed cattle and other livestock. Twenty-five years ago, livestock consumed less than 6 percent of Mexico's grain. Today at least one-third of the grain produced in the country is being fed to livestock. This in a country where millions of people are chronically undernourished.[11]

In all the countries of Central and South America that are becoming captives of the world steer process, the poor are the ultimate victims of the quest to optimize resources and maximize market penetration. The attempt to create a single world market for cattle and beef is likely to have powerful repercussions on the political fortunes and futures of these developing nations, further compromising the already marginalized status of the rural poor. Says Sanderson, "Therein lies the most significant political aspect of the internationalization of cattle production: the existential threat to the peasantry in countries with a large, poor rural population dependent upon agriculture for survival."[12]

The fate of the peasant community in the immediate future appears grim. While beef exports have been declining in recent years in many Latin American nations, they continue to provide these countries with one of their few entry cards into the global market. At the same time, many of the countries of Central and South America are using more and more agricultural land to grow soy, sorghum, and other feed grains, much of it for export. Forced to choose between feeding people and feeding livestock, the landed aristocracy and urban power elites have chosen the latter course, impoverishing millions of *campesinos* in the process. Even then, local agricultural production in some countries is already being strained beyond capacity, requiring more dependence on foreign feed, much of which is provided by the same multinational corporations that own or control the domestic herds, slaughterhouse facilities, and marketing and distribution channels in the Latin American countries. Several years ago, the USDA estimated that "Latin American countries will suffer deficits in feed and provide a burgeoning market for United States feed grains . . . largely due to increases in cattle production."[13] That prediction came true in some countries in the 1970s and 1980s. Companies like Quaker Oats and Purina moved aggressively to fill the vacuum left by the shortfalls in local feed production.

With rain forests being converted to pasture and cropland being converted to feed grain, the rural peasants find themselves displaced and disinherited, without any means to secure their survival. Modern cattle raising is a very capital-intensive and labor-saving industry. While peasant agriculture can often sustain a hundred people per square mile, the average rain forest cattle ranch "employs one person per 2,000 head of cattle and this . . . amounts at best to one person per twelve square miles."[14] Landless and desperate, millions of peasants have migrated to overcrowded urban areas, seeking what little employment is available. Most have had to settle for meager government handouts and live hand to mouth on the streets or on the city outskirts in makeshift shanty towns. Many have begun the long trek north along the Pan American Highway, hoping to find a better life in northern Mexico. Millions have crossed over the Rio Grande into the United States in the past two decades, changing the cultural dynamics of the entire southwestern part of the country.

Today, a majority of the children in the Los Angeles public school system are Hispanic. Much of the Latinization of the United States culture is directly attributable to changing land-use patterns in the rest of the Americas, where cattle grazing and feed grain production have replaced subsistence agriculture, turning a continent into pastures, agricultural fields, and abattoirs for the international beef trade.

The Poor

Part Four

FEEDING CATTLE AND
STARVING PEOPLE

22

Cattle Everywhere

1,000,000,000 Cows

Cows everywhere. There are over one billion cows alive today.[1] They are grazing on six continents. A quarter of the earth's landmass is used as pasture for cattle and other livestock.[2] The productivity of the world's grassland is highly variable. On very rich grassland, a cow can be supported for a year on two and one half acres. In marginal grazing land, fifty or more acres of grassland may be required to feed a single cow for a year.[3]

In Australia, the number of cows exceeds the number of people by 40 percent. In South America, there are nine cows for every ten people. In Argentina, Brazil, Paraguay and Uruguay, the cattle population equals or exceeds the human population.[4] The world's cattle population has increased by 5 percent in the past decade.[5]

There are now about 100 million cows in the United States, nearly one cow for every two and a half Americans. With less than 5 percent of the human population of the planet, the United States boasts 8 percent of the cattle population.[6]

Americans tend to think of the United States as a highly industrial, urbanized culture. The fact is that while we are packed together in tight urban corridors, primarily along the seaboards and the north-south axis of the Mississippi, nearly 29 percent of the landmass of the United States is currently used as grazing land, primarily to feed cattle.[7] A third of the land is publicly held and leased out to cattlemen on the western range.[8]

Today, some 200 million human beings in scores of countries around the world are involved in livestock production.[9] North, Central, and South America together produce 43 percent of all of the beef in the world.[10] The United States is the major beef-producing nation, accounting for 22 percent of global output.[11] The USSR produces about 18 percent of the world's beef, followed by Argentina and Brazil, each of which produces approximately 5 percent of all beef products.[12] All of the western European countries combined produce an additional 17 percent of the world's beef.[13]

In the United States, beef is big business. Although the ranching population is less than 0.2 percent of the civilian labor force, beef cattle are a $36 billion industry that accounts for nearly 24 percent of the cash receipts of the United States farm sector and 7 percent of supermarket sales.[14] Cattle production is now the nation's fourth-largest manufacturing industry. The principal cattle-feeding states are all west of the Mississippi—Kansas, Colorado, Nebraska, Iowa, Texas, Missouri, Oklahoma, and California.[15]

In the United States, "beef is king." Some 100,000 cows are slaughtered every twenty-four hours in the United States.[16] In a given week, 91 percent of all United States households purchase beef.[17] People in the southern United States spend slightly more on beef than those in any other region of the country. People in the west spend the least amount. Households in the top 20 percent income bracket spend relatively more for beef than others.[18] Americans currently consume 23 percent of all the beef produced in the world.[19] Today, the average American consumes 65 pounds of beef per year.[20]

Americans are trained, from an early age, to gorge on beef. The statistics are staggering. Consider the hamburger. Children under 7 years old eat an average of 1.7 hamburgers per week. Between the ages of 7 and 13, children eat 6.2 hamburgers per week. Between the ages of 13 and 30, ground beef consumption tapers off slightly to 5.2 hamburgers per week, the protein addiction being filled by more "adult" cuts of beef like steak and roast.[21] Over 6.7 billion hamburgers are sold to Americans each year at fast-food restaurants alone.[22] The average American consumes the meat of seven 1,100-pound steers in his or her lifetime.[23]

While Americans are among the premier beef eaters of the world, the Australians are not far behind. Western Europeans consume half as much beef as Americans, while the Japanese consume only 10 percent as much beef.[24] These figures are likely to change dramatically in the next decade as more and more Japanese consumers join the world's exclusive beef club. Between 1965 and 1990, the Japanese demand for beef rose 3.5 times.[25] In 1989, more McDonald's hamburgers were sold in Tokyo than in New York City.[26] Although beef prices are four times higher in Japan than in the United States, Japanese trade officials expect to see a doubling in beef consumption over the next ten to fifteen years.[27]

Japan is not the only Asian country to join the ranks of the beef-eating nations of the world. In recent years, both South Korea and Taiwan have dramatically increased domestic beef consumption as well.[28] Other developing countries of Asia are expected to follow suit in the coming decade.

In virtually every nation of the world, in the past half century, rising income levels have gone hand in hand with increased meat consumption, particularly beef consumption. The nations of the Organization for Economic Cooperation and Development offer a good case in point. In twenty OECD countries, the proportion of calories coming from animal products rose from 35 to 40 percent during the 1970s, as income levels rose.[29] In some countries, most notably Italy, Spain, Portugal, and Japan, the increase in consumption of animal products was dramatic and virtually paralleled the rapid rise in the country's gross national product.[30]

The relationship between rising income and increased meat and beef consumption is just as pronounced within each nation. In a detailed study conducted in over fifty countries, higher income groups consistently derive more of their fat, proteins, and calories from animal sources than do lower income groups.[31] In Jamaica, one of the poorer nations in the world, beef is the number one source of protein for the wealthiest 25 percent of the population, while wheat flour ranks a lowly seventh. For the poorest 25 percent of the population, however, the figures are nearly reversed. Wheat flour is the number one source of protein, while beef ranks thirteenth. In Madagascar, the wealthiest families consume twelve times as much animal protein as those at the base of the social pyramid.[32]

Beef eating, in most countries, is a form of privilege, a visible sign of wealth and status. Among nations, entrance into the beef club represents power and, from a geopolitical perspective, is every bit as significant in determining a nation's status in the world as the number of its tanks and ships or the rise in its industrial output.

Power relationships between nations and within nations during the whole of the modern age have often been fought out around the issue of beef. Indeed, as we have already noted, the ability to control the production and distribution of beef has been a critical factor in the very expansion of Western civilization. Everywhere the cattle complex has migrated, it has been responsible, at least in part, for the establishment of new patterns of political dominance. The question of consuming beef, then, extends far beyond the simple issue of "taste" to include the most complex issues of social justice and equity facing our species.

The consumption by a privileged few of grain-fed beef while millions go without the minimum daily caloric requirements is one of the most critical issues confronting contemporary civilization. Understanding the role played by the international beef club in the global food game and the politics of diet is essential to addressing the question of human survival in the coming century.

Beef = Power

23

Malthus and Meat

It has been nearly two hundred years since Thomas Malthus penned his short essay on population. His dire predictions on the relationship between the increase in human population and available land for cultivation helped brand economics the "dismal science." Malthus argued that "the power of population is indefinitely greater than the power of the earth to produce subsistence for man." The British economist said that if left unchecked, population increases in a geometrical ratio, while cultivated land only increases in an arithmetical ratio.[1] Thus, population pressure will always strain the carrying capacity of the earth, leading to soil erosion, depletion of natural resources, famine, and pestilence. The process, Malthus believed, was both inevitable and self-correcting. Whenever population exceeded the ability of the land to sustain it, starvation, war, and disease would ensure an appropriate adjustment in human numbers, until the balance between mouths to feed and available land again came into line.

Malthus's essay had a powerful effect on the thinking of his day, putting a damper on the enthusiastic predictions of Enlightenment thinkers. His note of pessimism provided a strong antidote to the cornucopic visions of progress being extolled by so many of his peers. Unaffected by the new spirit of progress, Malthus remained steadfast

157

in his belief in the inherent limits posed by unlimited population pressure against fixed available land. He wrote:

> The natural inequality of the two powers of population and of production in the earth and that great law of our nature which must constantly keep their effects equal form the great difficulty that to me appears insurmountable in the way to the perfectibility of society. . . . I see no way by which man can escape from the weight of this law which pervades all animated nature.[2]

Of course, humankind did escape the Malthusian grip, at least for a while. The opening up of vast new lands for cultivation and grazing in the New World and new breakthroughs in agricultural technologies, first in the form of improved breeding methods, later in machine technology, and finally in chemical inputs, staved off the day of reckoning. As already noted, the introduction of new plant monocultures, petrochemical fertilizers, and pesticides after World War II resulted in the greatest increase in agricultural output in world history. World grain output increased by more than two and a half times between 1950 and 1984.[3] Economists and agronomists were near-unanimous in their conviction that human ingenuity and new technology would always triumph over the fears and concerns of the skeptics. Their faith was shaken in the 1980s as world population increases began to exert new pressures on a soil base that had already been overworked. World grain output per person fell nearly 7 percent between 1984 and 1989.[4] In Africa, the Near East, and Latin America, food production per person is lower today than at the beginning of the decade.[5] A number of environmental factors contributed to the agricultural crisis in the 1980s. They include "eroding soils, shrinking forests, deteriorating rangelands, expanding deserts, acid rain, stratospheric ozone depletion, the buildup of greenhouse gases, air pollution, and the loss of biological diversity."[6] The high cost of energy and the scarcity of fresh water have also precipitated the decline. Today, the signs of inherent limits that Malthus warned of are beginning to reappear. The technological optimists find themselves on the defensive for the first time as a growing number of young intellectuals and economists join the ranks of the neo-Malthusian school.

With world population expected to increase by 959 million people in the 1990s, fears have been rekindled about the ability to feed the human population in the years ahead.[7] In 1988, worldwide grain reserves fell to their lowest point in recent memory—an estimated fifty-four days' supply.[8] Population experts predict increasing famine in the sub-Sahara of Africa, Bangladesh, and India, and less available grain to feed growing populations throughout Central and South America, China, and parts of Southeast Asia.[9] The long-term future appears even more problematic. The human population is expected to double in less than sixty years, from 5 to 10 billion people.[10] In 1988, scientists from the United States National Academy of Sciences and the American Academy of Arts and Sciences released a rare joint statement warning of the dire consequences that lie ahead as the population surge confronts an escalating series of environmental threats:

> Arresting global population growth should be second in importance only to avoiding a nuclear war on humanity's agenda. Overpopulation and rapid population growth are intimately connected with most aspects of the current human predicament, including rapid depletion of nonrenewable resources, deterioration of the environment (including rapid climate changes), and increasing international tensions.[11]

Despite growing alarm over the problem of too many people fighting for too few resources, little if any consideration is given to one of the most important factors contributing to the crisis. In all of the literature surrounding the issue of overpopulation, scant attention is paid to the fundamental shift in world agriculture in this century from food grains to feed grains, a shift of monumental proportions whose impact has been felt at every level of human existence. A new neo-Malthusian threat looms before us, more frightening and sinister than anything that has come before. The great cattle cultures of Europe and North America have erected an artificial worldwide protein ladder in the past century and a half, with grain-fed beef ensconced on the top rung. Today, the affluent populations of Europe, North America, and Japan are perched atop that food chain, devouring the bounty of the planet.

It seems disingenuous for the intellectual elite of the first world to dwell on the subject of too many babies being born in the second-

and third-world nations while virtually ignoring the overpopulation of cattle and the realities of a food chain that robs the poor of sustenance to feed the rich a steady diet of grain-fed meat. The transition of world agriculture from food grain to feed grains represents a new form of human evil, whose consequences may be far greater and longer-lasting than any past examples of violence inflicted by men against their fellow human beings.

To understand the enormity of the problem it is necessary to examine the biology of the world's food chain and the way it has been manipulated and distorted to serve the interests of a select few.

Chemist G. Tyler Miller sets up a simple food chain to illustrate how the laws of energy operate on living creatures in the evolutionary scheme of nature. The chain consists of grass, grasshoppers, frogs, trout, and humans. At each stage of the food chain, when the grasshopper eats the grass, and the frog eats the grasshopper, and the trout eats the frog, and so on, there is a loss of energy. In the process of devouring the prey, says Miller, "about 80–90 percent of the energy is simply lost as heat to the environment." Only between 10 and 20 percent of the energy that was devoured remains within the tissue of the predator for transfer to the next stage of the food chain. Consider, for a moment, the number of each species that are required to keep the next higher species alive. "Three hundred trout are required to support one man for a year. The trout, in turn, must consume 90,000 frogs, that must consume 27 million grasshoppers that live off of 100 tons of grass."[12]

Today, over 70 percent of the grain produced in the United States is fed to livestock.[13] Unfortunately, of the domestic animals, cattle are among the most inefficient converters of feed. They are energy guzzlers and considered by some to be the "Cadillac" of farm animals. It takes 9 pounds of feed to make 1 pound of gain in a feedlot steer, with 6 pounds of this "consisting of grains and by-product feeds and 3 pounds of roughage."[14] This means that only 11 percent of the feed goes to produce the beef itself with the rest either burned off as energy in the conversion process, used to maintain normal body functions, or excreted or absorbed into parts of the body that are not eaten—like hair or bones.[15] In the total feedlot system, says David Pimentel, "the protein fed to the beef and breeding stock consists of about 42 percent forage with the remainder being grain. Cattle have a feed protein conversion efficiency of only 6 percent.

70% grain to cows

That means that the animal produces less than 50 kg of protein from consuming over 790 kg of plant protein."[16]

By the time a feedlot steer is ready for slaughter, it has consumed 2,700 pounds of grain and weighs approximately 1,050 pounds.[17] Currently, in the United States, 157 million metric tons of cereal, legumes, and vegetable protein suitable for human use is fed to livestock to produce 28 million metric tons of animal protein which humans consume annually.[18]

Cattle and other livestock are devouring much of the grain produced on the planet. It need be emphasized that this is a new agricultural phenomenon, unlike anything ever experienced before. Ironically, the transition from forage to feed has taken place with little debate, despite the fact that it has had a pronounced impact on the politics of land use and food distribution in the past half century. In the United States alone, the figures are shocking. Food economist Frances Moore Lappé notes that 145 million tons of grain and soybeans were fed to livestock in 1979—cattle, poultry, and hogs. Of that feed only 21 million tons were available to human beings after the energy conversion, in the form of meat, poultry, and eggs. "The rest, about 124 million tons of grain and soybeans, became inaccessible to human consumption."[19] Lappé calculated that if the 124 million tons of wasted grain and soy were converted to cash it would be worth approximately $20 billion and if converted to human use could provide "the equivalent of one cup of grain for every single human being on earth every day for a year."[20]

The worldwide demand for feed grain continues to grow, as multinational corporations seek to capitalize on the meat demands of affluent countries. Two-thirds of the increases in grain production in the United States and Europe between 1950 and 1985, the great boom years in agriculture, went to provide feed grain, much of it for cattle.[21]

In the developing countries, the question of land reform has periodically rallied peasant populations and spawned populist political uprisings. Still, surprisingly, while the question of ownership and control of land has been an issue of great public import, the question of how the land is used has been of less interest in the political dialogue. Yet, it has been the decision to use the land to create an artificial food chain, the most inequitable in history, that has resulted in such misery for hundreds of millions of human beings around the

(and v)

world. Lappé compares the productivity of land used to grow food versus feed:

> An acre of cereal can produce five times more protein than an acre devoted to meat production; legumes (beans, peas, lentils) can produce ten times more; and leafy vegetables, fifteen times more. . . . spinach can produce up to twenty-six times more protein per acre than can beef.[22]

The multinational corporations that produce the seeds, the farm chemicals, and the cattle and that control the slaughterhouses and the marketing and distribution channels for beef are eager to tout the advantage of grain-fed livestock. Advertising and sales campaigns geared to developing nations are quick to equate grain-fed beef with a country's prestige. Climbing the "protein ladder" becomes the mark of success and ensures entrance into an elite club of producers who are atop the world's food chain. *Farm Journal* reflects the bias of the agribusiness community:

> Enlarging and diversifying their meat supply appears to be a first step for every developing country. They all start by putting in modern broiler and egg production facilities—the fastest and cheapest way to produce nonplant protein. Then as rapidly as their economies permit, they climb "the protein ladder" to pork, milk, and dairy products, to grass-fed beef, and finally, if they can, to grain-finished beef.[23]

Encouraging other nations to climb the protein ladder advances the interests of American farmers and agribusiness companies. Most Americans might be surprised to learn that two-thirds of all the grain exported from the United States to other countries goes to feed livestock rather than to feed hungry people.[24]

Many developing nations climbed the protein ladder at the height of the agricultural boom, when "green revolution" technology was producing grain surpluses. In 1971 the Food and Agricultural Organization (FAO) of the United Nations issued a report encouraging developing nations with surplus grain to use it to develop a market in feed grain.[25] In those countries where rice was the dominant crop, the FAO suggested switching to coarse grains that could be more easily consumed by livestock. The U.S. government provided further encouragement in its foreign aid program, tying food aid to development of feed grain markets. Companies like Ralston Purina and Cargill were given low-interest government loans to establish grain-fed poultry operations in developing countries, beginning them on the journey up the protein ladder.[26] Many nations followed the advice of the FAO and have attempted to remain high on the protein ladder long after the surpluses of the green revolution have disappeared.

The shift from food to feed continues apace in many nations, with no sign of reversal, despite the growing hunger of an increasingly desperate humanity.[27] The human consequences of the transition from food to feed were dramatically illustrated in 1984 in Ethiopia when thousands of people were dying each day from famine. The public was unaware that at the very same time Ethiopia was using some of its agricultural land to produce linseed cake, cottonseed cake, and rapeseed meal for export to the United Kingdom and other European nations to be used as feed for livestock. Currently, millions of acres of third-world land are being used exclusively to produce feed for European livestock.[28]

The question of privilege and power, of expropriation and exploitation in the modern world, has worked itself down into the very calorie count of every human being on the planet. The disparities are troubling. Three-fourths or more of the diet of the average Asian is composed of grain. Asian adults consume between 300 and 400 pounds of grain a year. A middle-class American, by contrast, consumes over a ton of grain (2,000 pounds) each year, 80 percent of it by way of eating cattle (and other livestock) that are grain-fed.[29] On a daily basis, the average Asian consumes about 56 grams of protein, only 8 grams of which is animal protein. The average American, in comparison, consumes 96 grams of protein a day, 66 grams of it derived from animals.[30]

The question of food vs. feed is likely to play a larger role in the politics of north-south relations in the coming decades. We need only remember that two out of every three human beings on the planet consume a primarily vegetarian diet.[31] With one-third of the world's grain output already going to cattle and other livestock, and the human population expected to increase by almost 20 percent in the next decade, the makings of a worldwide food crisis are already in the offing.[32]

Americans are among the premier beef eaters of the world. We have managed to hoist ourselves to the top of a carefully constructed man-made protein ladder from which we consume the bounty of the planet via an animal intermediary, the steer. Yet the question of entitlement is rarely raised among the American people. Consuming large quantities of grain-fed beef is viewed as a right and a way of life. The underside of the beef culture, in which displaced people search desperately for their next meal, is never brought into the light of day to be scrutinized and agonized over. The beef-consuming people are too far removed from the unseemly side of the cattle complex to know or care how their dietary preferences affect the lives of others and the political affairs of nations.

24

The Sociology of Fat

As populations gain entrance into the grain-fed beef club, they begin to incorporate the fat that has been concentrated at each rung of the protein ladder into their own bodies. The beef-eating cultures of the northern hemisphere are fat, often obese.

Overweight and obesity have long been associated with power and well-being. Among certain tribes of West Africa, pubescent girls of the elite families are taken to special fattening huts where they are force-fed for up to two years, at the end of which they are declared fit for marriage.[1] In imperial Rome, obesity became so widespread that the government passed dietary laws limiting the amount of money that could be spent on food and the number of guests that could be entertained at dinner. In the Middle Ages, gluttony was common among the nobility, who considered it a visible sign of their well-being. The church, on the other hand, frowned upon gluttonous behavior, making it a venial sin. In Dante's *Inferno*, one of the twelve circles of hell is set aside for the gluttons. In the Renaissance, the new opulence was often expressed bodily. Artists of the period painted obese women draped in finery and surrounded by lavish furnishings. Rubens models had to weigh 200 pounds or more before they were deemed suitable to sit for the artist.[2]

The Puritans of the American colonies set an ascetic tone for the

Us = fat

nation's first settlers, opposing indulgences of any kind.[3] Their otherworldly ways were not sufficient, however, to deter later generations of American immigrants from coveting the vast riches of a bountiful continent. The post–Civil War era was a period of unparalleled expansion and growth. Men made their fortunes and celebrated their newfound wealth by gorging themselves with every conceivable indulgence. It is, perhaps, no mere coincidence that the "age of corpulence," as it was referred to by commentators of the time, paralleled the rise of the beef culture.[4] Beef eating was the most visible sign of "the good life." Steak houses were built almost as fast as churches as the "teeming masses" spread west into the "new Europe."

By the twentieth century, America had surpassed England as the greatest beef-eating culture of the world. Not surprisingly, as Americans have come to consume greater amounts of marbled beef speckled with the fat of rich cereal grains, they have become increasingly overweight.

According to the Centers for Disease Control, over 34 million people in the United States are fat, with the people of the midwest and south slightly fatter than those from the west and northeast.[5] Other studies estimate that between 24 and 27 percent of the United States population is overweight.[6] While many things contribute to overweight, including an excess of sugar in the diet and an increasingly sedentary life-style made possible by high technology, the consumption of animal fat is among the most important contributing factors.

Americans have become increasingly heavier in each succeeding decade of the twentieth century. Selective Service data show that men inducted into the army in the 1950s were heavier than men of the same height inducted into the service in the 1940s. The soldiers of World War II were heavier than those who served in World War I.[7] Women are also gaining weight. According to federal government data assembled by the University of Michigan, American women experienced an increase in body mass during the two decades stretching from 1960 to 1980. Among white women in the 25-to-34 age bracket, the number considered obese rose from 13.3 to 17.17 percent. Among black women of the same age the number increased from 28.8 to 31 percent.[8] In the 1980s men and women were between

2 and 8 pounds heavier than men and women of the same age and
height a decade earlier.

The population of every developed nation of the Western world
is overweight. Still, differences exist between countries. In a survey
comparing the populations of the United States, Canada, and England, researchers found that weight differences correlated with differences in relative wealth between the nations. The population of
the United States was the fattest, followed by those of Canada and
England, leading the researchers to observe that

> the ranking of the three countries on overall prevalence of excessive
> weight corresponds to their relative levels of affluence. The impor-
> tant public health question is whether the increased prosperity which
> every country seeks will lead to still greater levels of excessive weight
> among their populations.[9]

Never before in history have so many human beings been so overweight. The grain-fed-beef-eating nations of the northern hemisphere are mired in so much fat that a new phenomenon called dieting
emerged in this century and became an integral part of the sociology
of Western culture.

Although fasting has been practiced in every culture in history,
it has often been associated with purification and relegated to the
sacred realm. People fasted as a form of sacrifice, to pay penance and
appease their gods. Today, people have substituted self for gods and
dieting for fasting, denying themselves food to pay homage to their
own self-image. Americans spend $5 billion a year trying to lose
weight.[10] The great majority of dieters list physical appearance and
beauty as the motivating factor behind their diets. In national opinion
polls conducted over several decades, 44 percent of American women
and 21 percent of American men said they would like to weigh less.[11]
Currently one out of every two women is on a diet "most of the
time."[12] Among the young, dieting has become a near-obsession.
Over 63 percent of all high school girls in the United States are
currently on diets, and 16.2 percent of all boys. Girls spend an average
of eleven weeks every year dieting.[13] In 1987 *Ms.* magazine reported
that "half of all fourth-grade girls diet." Doctors report that children
as young as 5 are preoccupied with taking off "extra pounds" to

improve their appearance. Dr. William Feldman, a medical professor at the University of Ottawa, says that he has been "seeing 5- and 6-year-olds who were preoccupied with their weight. . . . one young girl broke into tears when her mother asked her to go for a swim. The girl said she looked fat in the swimsuit, when in fact her weight was normal for her height."[14]

The near-pathological fixation with being slim has given rise to new eating disorders like anorexia nervosa and bulimia among middle- and upper-middle-class adolescent girls. While a great deal of public attention has been focused on these "eating disorders," the fact remains that voluntary starvation and periodic purging have become the norm for a majority of women and a smaller percentage of men in America. In a *Glamour* survey of 33,000 women, 50 percent of the respondents acknowledged that they "sometimes" or "often" used diet pills; 27 percent used liquid formula diets; 18 percent used diuretics (water-reduction pills); 45 percent used fasting or "starving." Purging the body (often after bouts of binge eating) is also surprisingly common; 18 percent use laxatives for rapid weight elimination; 15 percent engage in "self-induced vomiting."[15]

Anthropologists, sociologists, and psychologists have pondered the reasons for the shift in standards of appearance from corpulence to slimness in the past century. The transition from an agricultural to an industrial way of life, increased urbanization, and new fast modes of transportation and communications all contributed to the demise of small-town life in America, with its sedentary ways of being.

The twentieth century has been the century of movement, of function over structure, of energy over matter. The image of corpulence was ill suited to the new frenetic pace of life. The slower seasonal cycles of an agrarian order were replaced with the fast linear time frame of the assembly line. Mobility replaced community as a standard of security, and everywhere the talk was of efficiency. In architecture and technology, streamlining became the vogue. The Art Deco Chrysler building in New York City and the sleek new roadster presented quite different images than did the Victorian mansion and the steam engine of an earlier age. The shift from industrial technologies to information technologies hurried the transition from brute strength to mental acumen and from body to mind. Fat became less associated with opulence and more with stodginess and slovenly behavior. To be fat was to be lethargic, slow, dull-witted. In a world where time clocks and schedules, scientific principles of management and efficiency had become the prevailing norms, to be fat was to be old-fashioned. Where fat and wealth used to be the standard of success, a new generation was more likely to agree with the Duchess of Windsor, who said, "You can never be too rich or too thin."[16]

In his book *All Consuming Images*, Stewart Ewen aptly characterized the social idea of slimness as a by-product of modernity. Women's fashions began to reflect the new modern sensibilities in the 1920s with the introduction of the "flapper."[17] Designers began to adorn women's bodies with clothing that was sleek and streamlined and that gave the appearance of mobility, speed, efficiency, and motion, the same qualities and standards that were becoming commonplace in the culture. As modern advertising began to emphasize the virtue of slimness, equating thin with beautiful and sexy, the voluptuous standards of the Victorian era quickly became anachronistic. The change in height, body weight, and vital measurements of the famed White Rock Girl provides an accurate measure of the changing image from fat to thin during the course of the past century. "In 1894, a five-foot-four-inch 140-pound model with a 37-inch bust and 38-inch hips represented the ideal form to our great-grandmothers. She was slimmed down first in 1947 to 125 pounds, then again in 1975 when she was reduced to a mere 118 pounds despite having grown to five feet eight inches."[18]

Although slim is the standard to which most Americans and an increasing number of affluent Europeans aspire, the reality is that the well-to-do peoples of the world are the fattest in history and getting fatter. The peoples of the northern clime are the heirs of a 6,000-year legacy of beef eating that has culminated in a pathology of consumption in the past century. Unable to reconcile their historical lust for animal fat with their new streamlined self-image, they remain betwixt and between an orgy of consumption and purging unique in human experience.

25

Marbled Specks
of Death

meat > BAD
fat

In 1917 the Allied Powers threw a naval blockade around the German-occupied territories of northern Europe. The Danish people were particularly hard hit by the blockade. With its normal food supply routes cut, the Danish government was forced to enact a rationing program based on increasing the intake of potatoes and barley and virtually eliminating meat. Overnight, some 3 million Danes were turned into vegetarians, with some interesting results. During the year of rationing, the death rate from disease fell by 34 percent.[1]

The Danish experiment proved very little. It did, however, suggest a possible link between meat consumption and human disease. Today, after seventy years of research, the scientific community and medical establishment have begun to suggest that a diet rich in animal fat and cholesterol increases the risk of the "diseases of affluence"—heart disease, cancer, and strokes. The consumption of large amounts of saturated fatty acids and cholesterol from meat raises serum cholesterol levels in human beings. The cholesterol is carried through the bloodstream as soluble protein molecule aggregates known as low-density lipoproteins or LDLs. The LDLs deposit cholesterol in the cells lining the walls of the arteries and the heart, where they accumulate as plaque, restricting the blood flow. LDLs also stimulate the formation of platelets in the blood, which often clump together to form clots in the arteries.[2] Choice-grade beef has 15 to 19 percent more fat content than select-grade beef and is responsible for a significant amount of the saturated fat and cholesterol in the American and western European diets.[3]

Living atop the protein ladder has turned out to be very precarious. The affluent populations of the northern hemisphere are dying by the millions from grain-fed beef and other grain-fed red meat. Each year the death toll continues to mount for people whose diseases are related to the consumption of animal fat and increased levels of cholesterol. According to the report of the Surgeon General of the United States, of the 2.1 million deaths in the United States in 1987, 1.5 million were related to dietary factors, including consumption of saturated fat and cholesterol.[4] Dr. C. Everett Koop warned the public that diets high in saturated fats and cholesterol played a key role in three of the nation's top ten causes of death: heart attack, cancer, and strokes.[5] As Americans and Europeans continue to gain weight, consuming an inordinate amount of grain-fed beef and other animal fat products, they increase their chances of dying prematurely from one or more of these diseases. The report concluded:

> High intake of total dietary fat is associated with . . . some types of cancer and possibly gall bladder disease. Epidemiological, clinical, and animal studies provide strong and consistent evidence for the relationship between saturated fat intake, higher blood cholesterol, and increased risk for coronary heart disease . . . breast and colon cancer.[6]

The scientific evidence linking overweight to an increase in life-threatening diseases is now compelling. In a twenty-five-year study of 5,000 residents of Framingham, Massachusetts, researchers found obesity to be a critical factor in predicting cardiovascular disease. The scientists conducting the study concluded that "if everyone were at optimal weight, there would be 25 percent less coronary heart disease and 35 percent less congestive heart failure and brain infarction." In a broader study of 750,000 Americans conducted by the American Cancer Society, researchers found similar correlations between overweight, obesity, and death from heart disease.[7]

Other studies have shown a positive correlation between obesity and diabetes. Overweight people are more likely to develop diabetes than lean people, and obese people are more likely to die from the disease than those of normal weight. Scientists suspect that increased susceptibility is due to the fact that fatty tissue is "less sensitive to insulin." Obese individuals are also more likely to develop gallstones. Since cholesterol is the major component in 90 percent of all gallstones, it should probably not come as a surprise that most women who develop gallstones under the age of 50 are 25 pounds overweight.[8]

Now a spate of new studies are connecting red meat consumption to colon cancer, the number two cause of cancer in the United States. Over 100,000 cases of colon cancer are diagnosed each year, and over 50,000 died of the disease in 1990 alone. In a six-year study of 88,751 women from the ages of 30 to 59 years old, the largest study ever conducted on colon cancer and diet, researchers found that women who ate red meat every day are "two and a half times more likely to have had colon cancer than the women who ate meat sparingly or not at all."[9] Dr. Walter Willett, of the Brigham and Women's Hospital of Boston, the director of the study, said of the findings: "If you step back and look at the data, the optimum amount of red meat you eat should be zero."[10] In the beef-eating cultures of the Western world, the incidence of colon cancer is up to ten times the rate of non-beef-eating cultures of Asia and the developing world.[11]

Scientists are also beginning to link red meat consumption with breast cancer. One in ten women in the United States will eventually develop breast cancer. Among women over the age of 44 the incidence of the disease has increased by 2 percent a year since 1960.[12] Researchers at the National Cancer Institute analyzed data from one hundred animal tests and concluded that "both fat and calories" increase the risk of breast cancer. Recent studies of Finnish and Canadian women came to the same conclusion. Most of the women in the studies who developed breast cancer consumed a "consistently higher average percentage of fat-derived calories."[13] Some scientists believe that the increased fat consumption triggers the cancer by stimulating the release of prolactin, a hormone responsible for regulating fat metabolism and lactation.[14] Researchers in the Toronto-based study of the relationship between fat intake and the incidence of breast cancer suggest that reducing saturated fat consumption to 9 percent of total daily calories—fat now makes up over 37 percent of the daily caloric intake in North America—would probably reduce the risk of breast cancer in postmenopausal women by 10 percent.[15] While beef and other animal products are not the only source of fat in the diet, they are a major factor, especially in affluent countries like the United States.

Perhaps the most compelling evidence ever assembled of the relationship between animal fat intake, cholesterol, and human disease came in 1990 when a U.S.–Chinese team published the findings of a massive study of Chinese dietary behavior and health.[16] The study, which the *New York Times* dubbed "the Grand Prix" of epidemiology, followed the eating habits of 8,000 Chinese people in sixty-nine counties spanning twenty-five provinces.[17]

The Chinese people consume 20 percent more calories than Americans, but Americans are 25 percent fatter. That's because 37 percent of the calories in the U.S. diet come from fat, whereas less than 15 percent of the calories in the rural Chinese diet come from fat. Moreover, 70 percent of the protein in the Western diet comes from animal products and 30 percent from plants, while in China only 11 percent comes from animal products and 89 percent from plants.[18]

The Chinese study, like the many others that have been conducted in the West in recent decades, showed a high correlation between meat consumption and the incidence of heart disease and cancer. The researchers found that in counties where meat consumption increased, the rate of cardiovascular disease increased dramatically, in some cases an increase of fiftyfold over the rate of heart disease in regions where animal fat still made up less than 15 percent of the average diet.[19] Incidences of colon cancer also increased with increased consumption of animal fat. According to Dr. Colin Campbell of Cornell University, one of the directors of the unprecedented study, "Once people start introducing animal products into their diet, that's when the mischief starts."[20]

After analyzing the massive volume of data, Campbell offered some sage advice based on his team's findings:

we shouldn't eat meat

Usually, the first thing a country does in the course of economic development is to introduce a lot of livestock. Our data are showing that this is not a very smart move and the Chinese are listening. They are realizing that animal-based agriculture is not the way to go. . . . We are basically a vegetarian species and should be eating a wide variety of plant food and minimizing our intake of animal foods.[21]

The price in human lives of joining the exclusive beef club is high. Recently, the British medical journal *Lancet* reported a dramatic rise in deaths in Japan from the "affluent diseases." The twenty-five-year trend paralleled the rise in beef consumption in that Pacific nation.[22] In the United States, the health costs of maintaining a rich grain-fed-beef diet have reached staggering proportions. Nearly a million people die of cardiovascular diseases each year, diseases that cost their victims over $100 billion annually.[23] Colon and breast cancer cost approximately $20 billion.[24]

The American Heart Association, the American Cancer Society, the National Academy of Sciences, and the American Academy of Pediatrics are just a few of the professional, medical and scientific associations that have urged a reduction in the consumption of animal fat and cholesterol and the shift to a more vegetarian diet high in protein. The National Academy of Sciences panel on diet and disease recommends that Americans reduce their protein intake by at least 12 percent and switch over from animal to plant sources of protein.

> Substitution of soybean protein for animal protein in the diet reduces the level of serum cholesterol in humans . . . and there is evidence that groups eating vegetarian diets have lower average cholesterol levels than the general population.[25]

The American Academy of Pediatrics goes further, suggesting that everyone over 2 years of age should limit consumption of saturated fat to less than 10 percent of caloric intake. Panel chairman Richard Garleton of Brown University says that

> such a population approach should reduce the average blood cholesterol level of Americans at least 10 percent and should result in an approximate 20 percent reduction in coronary heart disease.[26]

Despite repeated warnings over the past two decades, Americans continue to consume a high-protein diet, rich in grain-fed beef and other livestock products. The average American consumes twice the amount of daily protein recommended by the Food and Agricultural Organization (FAO), far more than the body can even absorb.[27]

Because most of the excess protein comes from animal sources, the health risk to the American people remains high. Still, many Americans feel that reducing their consumption of animal-derived protein will somehow compromise their health, making them weaker, less virile. They are unmindful of the fact that just sixty-five years ago, over 40 percent of the protein in the American diet came from grain, bread, and cereal. Now only 17 percent comes from plant sources, while animal protein, which used to supply half of our protein intake, now supplies over two-thirds of all the protein we consume.[28]

Americans and Europeans are literally eating themselves to death, gorging on marbled beef and other grain-fed animal products, taking into their bodies massive amounts of saturated fats and cholesterol. The fatty substances are building up in the bloodstream, clogging arteries, lining cell walls, blocking passages, triggering metabolic and hormonal changes, stimulating cell growth, and rupturing organs. The "good life" promised by the beef culture has metamorphosed into a cruel joke as Americans, overweight and plagued by the diseases of affluence, suffer from their own excesses.

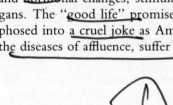

26

Cows Devour People

The Poor

While the rich are dying from the diseases of affluence, the poor of the planet languish for want of the bare essentials of life. The injustice imposed on the world by the twentieth-century protein chain is unprecedented; a billion people gorging and purging, mired in excess fat, while a billion more waste away, unable to provide their bodies with the minimum nutrient requirements necessary to maintain a healthy existence. The rest of humanity, some 3.5 billion people, teeter precariously between salvation and despair, hoping to climb the protein ladder, with the sure result that for every person that makes it to the top rung, still another will be forced to the bottom, where malnutrition and starvation await.

The World Bank estimates that between 700 million and 1 billion people live in absolute poverty around the world.[1] Contrary to popular belief, the poor are getting poorer each year. Forty-three developing nations finished the 1980s poorer than they were at the beginning of the decade.[2] Increased poverty has meant increased malnutrition. On the African continent nearly one in every four human beings is malnourished. In Latin America, nearly one out of every eight people goes to bed hungry each night. In Asia and the

Pacific, 22 percent of the people experience the gnawing pain of perpetual hunger. In the Near East, one in ten people are underfed.[3] Chronic hunger now affects upwards of 1.3 billion people, according to the World Health Organization[4]—a statistic all the more striking in a world where one-third of all the grain produced is being fed to cattle and other livestock. Never before in human history has such a large percentage of our species—nearly 20 percent—been malnourished.

The Age of Progress has been so only for that small portion of humanity living on the northern tier of the planet. For the rest, modernity has brought only hunger and disease and an increasing sense of hopelessness and despair. It is difficult to imagine the enormity of the suffering: five hundred million hungry people in South and East Asia; 160 million in Africa.[5]

Approximately 20 million people die each year around the world from hunger and related diseases. The toll is heaviest on the world's children. "Undernutrition affects nearly 40 percent of all children in developing nations and contributes directly to an estimated 60 percent of all childhood deaths," writes Katrina Galway of the Institute for Resource Development in a report for the United States Agency for International Development (USAID). Over 15 million children die every year from diseases brought on by or complicated by malnutrition.[6]

While millions of American teenagers anguish over excess pounds, spending time, money, and emotional energy on slimming down, children in other lands are wasting away, their physical growth irreversibly stunted, their bodies racked with parasitic and opportunistic diseases, their brain growth diminished by lack of nutrients in their meager diets.

Wasting is a symptom of "acute undernutrition" resulting from a combination of insufficient food intake and a high incidence of infectious diseases, especially diarrhea. Stunting arises from chronic undernutrition and long-term exposure to infectious diseases.[7]

Wasting generally begins immediately after an infant is taken off breast milk. The mother's milk contains vital nutrients that help the baby ward off infectious diseases. The food that replaces mother's milk often does not contain sufficient nutrient value to protect and nourish the growing child. The result is that the baby is more prone

to a range of environmental assaults right at the time he or she is becoming more active.

Most malnourished babies in the third world develop severe diarrhea, the number-one killer of infants in the world today. Diarrhea is usually accompanied by periodic vomiting—both conditions arising out of unsanitary environments, which become breeding grounds for infectious diseases. The diarrhea and vomiting depletes the baby of the few nutrients it has consumed, exacerbating the malnutrition. The baby is limited to a thin, energy-deficient diet, containing little protein and few calories. By the time the child reaches her first birthday, she has contracted one or more chronic parasitic diseases of the intestines. The parasitic invaders rob the child of whatever little protein and calories she has stored up in her body, locking the child into an almost irreversible process of wasting away that will affect the growth of cells, body weight, physical stature, and subsequent brain development.

Chronically malnourished children generally develop smaller body frames and often smaller brains than normal children. If the malnutrition occurs within the first year of their lives, the physical and mental retardation becomes irreversible.[8] Because these children are born of malnourished mothers, chances are they will suffer from congenital malformations at birth, complicated by diminished brain cell development after birth because of inadequate nourishment. "The DNA content of the brains of infants who die of malnutrition, after being born of malnourished mothers, can be as low as 40 percent of that seen in normal newborn infants."[9]

Millions of children in the world today are being denied their genetic inheritance, robbed of their rightful physical stature and mental capabilities—all victims of the cruelest fate of all, malnutrition. It is difficult for most Americans to imagine the specter of millions of human beings with abnormally small heads and bodies, trapped inside a partially developed frame from infancy, unable to reverse their fortunes, to affect their own physical and mental development. These are children who grow up with diminished mental capacity, plagued by physical maladies, so chronically weakened that they remain lethargic and apathetic for a lifetime. For them life is indeed "a short, nasty and brutish affair." Many suffer from a deficiency of vitamin A. The loss of this important vitamin in the diet leads to xerophthalmia, a dryness of the eye, which can lead to lesions and

blindness. Over 250,000 children develop active lesions in both corneas and lose some visual capacity, remaining visually handicapped for life. An additional 6 to 7 million children suffer from hypovitaminosis A, which undermines the child's resistance to infections, especially those of the intestinal and respiratory systems. Millions more suffer from severe anemia, a loss of hemoglobin in the blood. More than 1.5 billion people—30 percent of the human population —now suffer from anemia, making them more susceptible to chronic fatigue and opportunistic diseases.[10]

In malnourished children, all the myriad functions of the body are severely curtailed, making them vulnerable to even minor environmental irritants. Intracellular sodium rises, while intracellular potassium falls. The body experiences a reduction in the rate of protein synthesis and breakdown. It cannot retain sufficient amounts of magnesium, zinc, copper, manganese, selenium or iron. The child is acutely vulnerable to even slight changes in ambient temperatures, causing vulnerability to fever and hypothermia. The immune system barely functions. Open sores never heal, even though the child may not feel any pain. The sores are never swollen or red. There is no pus. The kidney, liver, heart, and other organs weaken and begin to fail.

This is the fate shared by millions of children, primarily in the southern hemisphere of the planet. Their physical, emotional, and mental lives are so dissimilar from those of children in the affluent northern hemisphere that they might as well be from a different genus. We rarely think of their plight; even less do we empathize with their struggle. They are the hordes of suffering humanity whose faces we glimpse only occasionally on a news report. Their existence has been marginalized, reduced to neatly packaged United Nations statistics and reports and filed somewhere conveniently out of sight of our daily routines and concerns. If we think of these people at all, it is generally in shadow terms. They remind us of the dark side of human existence, the netherworld of misery and misfortune that we hope will never be our fate.

The anomaly of rich people dieting and poor people starving, of the human species increasingly separated into two branches, one atop the protein ladder, the other at the bottom, seems more than a bit macabre, even to modern sensibilities, which are often accustomed to naked self-interest and unabashed utilitarianism. In an electronic world, where time has been compressed to near-simultaneity and space shrunk to "virtual reality," where borders are being eliminated to make room for the global market and the global shopping center, humanity has failed to eliminate the most important border of all, the one that separates the haves from the have-nots, those who eat from those who starve. Even in our sophisticated postmodern world of satellite communications and information technology, of space-age weaponry and genetic engineering technology, humanity continues to be divided against itself in the most primitive fashion, with some denying others their right to participate in and be sustained by the earth's bountiful endowment.

The modern cattle complex and the artificial protein chain remain a visible reminder of an earlier consciousness, one weaned on the violence of the hunt, of invasion and usurpation, colonization and greed. The profligate beef-eating habits of the northern people reach far back into the distant past, to the thundering hoofs of mounted horses and herds of cattle making their way west from the Eurasian steppes to ancient Europe, the New World, and places beyond. Now that same thunder is stampeding into the twenty-first century, ramrodded by multinational corporations determined to keep the colonial spirit alive and the world divided. The world steer is fast becoming a reality, ensuring an even greater disparity between the chosen few and the disinherited masses of humanity in the coming century.

The human toll of supporting a worldwide cattle complex and an artificial protein chain has been devastating, and alone would justify a reappraisal of the merits of maintaining a beef culture in the coming century. Yet, these costs are only part of a more profound threat created, in part, by the world steer complex—an environmental threat that is affecting the very survivability of the earth's ecosystems and the biosphere that sustains all of the various forms of life on the planet.

The world's cattle complex is wreaking havoc with the earth's ecology, destroying whole bioregions of the planet in a mad rush to increase the supply of meat. The full impact of modern beef production and consumption can only be weighed and properly understood in light of the effect that modern meat is having on the ecology of the earth. It is here that the legacy of thousands of years of Western cattle expansion has come to the fore, as entire regions of the globe fall victim to hordes of hoofed locusts in search of grass and grain. We need to turn our attention next to the many ways the modern cattle complex has compromised the earth's ecosystems, threatening millions of years of biological evolution in the process of preparing modern meat for market.

World
Steer

Part Five

CATTLE AND
THE GLOBAL
ENVIRONMENTAL
CRISIS

27

Ecological Colonialism

The modern era has been characterized by a relentless assault on the earth's ecosystems. Dams, canals, railroad beds, and more recently highways have cut deeply into the surface of the earth, severing vital ecological arteries and rerouting nature's flora and fauna. Petrochemicals have poisoned the interior of nature, seeping into animals and plants, soaking the organs and tissues with the tar of the carboniferous era. The spent energy of the industrial revolution has choked the skies with layers of gases—carbon monoxide, carbon dioxide, sulfuric acid, chlorofluorocarbons, nitrous oxide, methane, and the like—polluting the air, blocking the heat from escaping the planet, and exposing the biota of the earth to increased doses of deadly ultraviolet radiation.

The scientific community, the governments of the world, and the mass media have devoted a great deal of time and effort to studying and publicizing the impact of these induced human threats to the biosphere, warning of the dire consequences to the planet and civilization of ignoring the mounting entropic bill.

Still, in all of the ongoing public debates around the global environmental crisis, a curious silence surrounds the issue of cattle, one of the most destructive environmental threats of the modern era. Domesticated cattle are responsible for much of the soil erosion in the temperate regions of the world. Cattle grazing is a primary cause of the spreading desertification process that is now enveloping whole continents. Cattle ranching is responsible for the destruction of much of the earth's remaining tropical rain forests. Cattle raising is partially responsible for the rapid depletion of fresh water on the planet, with some reservoirs and aquifers now at their lowest levels since the end of the last Ice Age. Cattle are a chief source of organic pollution; cow dung is poisoning the freshwater lakes, rivers, and streams of the world. Growing herds of cattle are exerting unprecedented pressure on the carrying capacity of natural ecosystems, edging entire species of wildlife to the brink of extinction. Cattle are a growing source of global warming, and their increasing numbers now threaten the very chemical dynamics of the biosphere.

This once-sacred animal of bygone years has taken on a pestilent guise, swarming over the great landmasses of Europe, the Americas, Africa, and Australia like hoofed locusts, devouring the endowment of millions of years of evolutionary history. Sequestered in artificially enclosed urban and suburban environments, most Americans and Europeans are simply unaware of the devastation wrought by the world's cattle. Now numbering over a billion, these ancient ungulates roam the countryside, trampling the soil, stripping the vegetation bare, laying waste to large tracts of the earth's biomass.

We have already traced the colonial partnership of people and cattle that helped subdue the Amerindian populations and harness the untapped energies of the Americas. The seeding of the Americas and other lands with cattle had another effect, every bit as far-reaching as the commercial one. While cattle were used to colonize the New World, transforming it into a pastureland to serve the beef and hide markets in Europe, another more profound kind of colonization took place, one destined to affect future generations long after the passage of the colonial moment in world history. The transplantation of cattle into the New World fundamentally transformed the ecology and topography of North, Central, and South America. Accompanying the bovine was an entire ecological complex made up of Old World grasses, weeds, cereal grains, and legumes. The European grasses, weeds, and grains flourished in the Americas, usurping habitat after habitat, successfully altering much of the indigenous ecology. Just as men and cattle colonized native populations and territories, European plants effectively colonized the biology of the new continents, turning the Americas into an ecological stepchild of Old Europe.

As early as the sixteenth century, Friar Bartolemé de Las Casas wrote of large herds of European cattle devouring native vegetation in the West Indies and the spread of thistles, ferns, nettles, nightshades, sedge, and plantain of Castilian origin.[1] By 1555, European clover had spread across Mexico, providing a familiar carpet of Old World grass for Spanish cattle to graze on. The European plants spread across the New World landscape, usurping native grasses and providing a convenient ecological marker for the steady advance of European colonists and cattle. The familiar sight of wild oats, chess, bromes, Italian ryegrass, and common foxtail growing along the hillsides and valleys of northern Mexico and the California coast surprised later Spanish and English settlers.

Many of the plants arrived with the first cattle, as seeds lying dormant in their stomachs or nettled in their hides. Spanish priests spread seeds on their journeys, planting small communities alongside streams and on the sides of hills. They seeded the Americas with Old World vegetation as far north as San Francisco and as far south as the Argentine pampas. Black mustard, for example, was introduced into California by the Franciscan friars as early as the sixteenth century. American explorer John Frémont was surprised to see redstemmed filaree, a European weed, growing in the Sacramento Valley in 1844. He reported that it was "just now beginning to bloom, and covering the ground like a sword of grass." According to ecological historian Alfred Crosby, by 1860 over ninety species of European weeds had taken root in California alone.[2]

In his book *Ecological Imperialism*, Crosby gives an account of the symbiotic relationship between Old World cattle and grasses that led to the near-total Europeanization of New World ecosystems. Although there exist over 10,000 different species of grass, less than forty "account for 99 percent of the sown grass pastures of the world," notes Crosby.[3] Most of these grasses are native to Europe, North Africa, and the Middle East and have been used as forage for domestic herds of cattle since the first millennia of the Neolithic revolution. These grasses developed in close consort with cattle, each adapting to the other over the long period of Western history.

When European colonists transported cattle to the New World, their grasses accompanied them. These grasses proved far more resilient than native grasses, because they were more tolerant of open

sunlight, bare soil, and close cropping and were used to being trampled by cattle. Often feral cattle swept into a new ecosystem, devouring everything in their path. In the process, they inadvertently
cleared the way for their Old World plant companions, which took
advantage of the stripped niches by taking root in the barren ground.
Crosby explains the process:

> They [the plants] possessed a number of means of propagation and
> spread. For instance, often their seeds were equipped with hooks
> to catch on the hides of passing livestock or were tough enough to
> survive the trip through their stomachs to be deposited somewhere
> further down the path. When the livestock returned for a meal the
> next season, it was there. When the stockmen went out in search
> of his stock, they were there, too, and healthy.[4]

Cattle, then, played a critical role in changing the ecology of the
Americas. Even before the human invasion, cattle helped seed the
new lands with Old World vegetation, paving the way for the "civilization" that followed. The bovine and its plant complex were,
indeed, the original pioneers, the trailblazers of the New World.

In North America, the westward push across the Appalachian
Mountains into the midwest was accompanied by the steady march
of white clover and bluegrass, both of European origin. When the
first English colonists arrived in Kentucky, they were greeted by the
sight of European grass, which had arrived years earlier, having
hitched a ride on the coats of traders, horses, and mules.[5] The settlers
called the European vegetation Kentucky bluegrass.[6] Later, the wagon trains heading west also served as vehicles for the spread of
European grasses, including common hemp, corn cockle, barberry,
and Saint-John's-wort.[7] A pioneer traveling through Illinois in 1818
recalled:

> Where the little caravans have encamped as they crossed the prairies,
> and have given their cattle hay made of these perennial grasses, there
> remains ever after a spot of green turf for the introduction and
> encouragement of future improvers.[8]

From these oases European weeds spread out across the midwest,
Europeanizing much of the Mississippi region. For a time, the Old
World grasses were held up at the foot of the Great Plains. Like the

cowboys and the cattle, they had to wait for the government and military to rid the plains of the buffalo and the Indian before they could make their advance. Crosby points out that the buffalo grass and grama grass that were native to the plains were more resistant to invasion, having successfully adapted to another bovine species over the millennia.[9] The extermination of the buffalo provided the ecological vacuum for the continued westward march of European cattle and grasses.

Today, of the 500 or so most important weeds found in North America, 258 are immigrants from the Old World—177 from Europe, the rest from the Mediterranean and North Africa.[10]

A similar seeding took place throughout South America. European cattle spread out over the grasslands, devouring the local flora, while simultaneously depositing European seeds in their droppings. Peru was overrun by a European clover called trébol in the sixteenth century. The clover provided ideal forage but spread so quickly that the Inca Indians found themselves "in competition with trébol for crop land."[11]

On his famous trip to South America on the *Beagle*, Darwin visited the grasslands of Argentina, where he noticed an abrupt change from "coarse herbage" to "a carpet of fine green verdure." Darwin wrote: "The inhabitants assured me that . . . the whole was to be attributed to the manuring and grazing of the cattle."[12]

In 1877, Carlos Berg reported some 153 European plants flourishing in Patagonia. The wild artichoke became so ubiquitous and dense in Argentina, Uruguay, and Chile that it often made hundreds of square miles impenetrable by horse or foot. Darwin wrote, "I doubt whether any case is on record of invasion on so grand a scale of one plant over the Aborigines."[13] The giant thistle, a Mediterranean biennial, grew up to seven feet tall and flourished everywhere, eliminating much of the natural flora. When it dried, it was often prone to fire. W. H. Hudson, a British naturalist, remembers massive fires raging out of control when he was a young child living in Argentina. By 1920, less than one-quarter of the wild plants growing on the Argentine pampas were native.[14]

Old World plants accompanied the cattle complex into colonial territories around the world. The British navy set anchor in Australian waters in 1788, unloading two bulls and six cows.[15] By 1830, the herds exceeded 371,000. A generation later, Australia was populated with millions of cattle, many of them feral, running wild on the frontier.[16] In 1836, the explorer Thomas T. Mitchell was surprised to see cattle trails so wide and hard-packed around frontier water holes that they "resembled roads." The feral cattle were as surprised to see people. Mitchell recalls their first encounter: "We were soon surrounded by a staring herd of at least 800 head of wild animals." Meeting up with the descendants of their own European herds out on the frontier was a quite unexpected yet comforting experience. Mitchell recalls that "the welcome sight of the cattle themselves delighted our longing eyes, not to mention our stomachs."[17]

The British brought hundreds of Old World plants with them, seeding every available ecological niche. White clover flourished in the moist climate of Melbourne, "often destroying other vegetation." Other grasses, including knotgrass and red sorrel, were such aggressive colonizers that they pushed native flora out of many pastures. Wild oats, a common weed in Europe, took up residence along the Australian Alps. In Tasmania, European snakeweed accompanied the colonists and their cattle.[18] In New Zealand, Old World weeds leaped ahead of the colonists, preparing the settlers with a ready-made European landscape. William Colonso, a naturalist, recalled his shock at stumbling across a specimen of burdock in a remote region of the island. He "gazed on it with astonishment, much like Robinson Crusoe on seeing the print of a European foot in the sand."[19]

By the middle of the nineteenth century, 139 plants of Old World origin were growing wild in Australia. One hundred years later, Australia was populated by 381 immigrant plants. As in the Americas, many native grasses were unable to survive the heavy grazing and trampling of the European bovine. The Australian kangaroo grass, which once grew so tall that it reached to the "very flaps of the saddle," was virtually wiped out by the plant invaders of Europe, and now survives only in small clumps around railroad embankments, cemeteries, and other man-made refuges.[20] By the 1930s, according to the botanist A. J. Ervart, European plant species were establishing themselves in Victoria "at the rate of two per month." Today, according to Crosby, "most of the weeds of the southern third of Australia, where most of the continent's population lives, are of European origin."[21]

The European cattle complex has transformed much of the ecology of the planet. The steady westward march, which began thousands of years ago on the Eurasian steppes, has changed forever the natural evolutionary history of whole continents. Mounted horsemen, cattle, and Old World plants have invaded the great landmasses of the Western world, colonizing native people, subduing and exterminating native flora and fauna, and seriously undermining the genetic diversity on several continents. The invaders have Europeanized whole ecosystems and enclosed vast areas of the global commons in pursuit of commercial gain.

Now the pressure of increased cattle against both natural and artificially imposed ecosystems, as well as the growing reliance on feed grains to support a burgeoning livestock population, is spawning still another environmental change, this time on an even grander scale. Whereas earlier invasions devastated native plants and animals and introduced nonnative species into New World habitats, today's assaults are destroying the very biosphere itself, threatening the future stability and viability of entire bioregions of the world. Cattle are among the major environmental threats facing the planet today. Their role in undermining the earth's biosphere needs to be examined and assessed if humanity is to have any hope of restoring the health and well-being of the planet's ecosystems in the twenty-first century.

28

Tropical Pastures

Since 1960 more than 25 percent of the forests of Central America have been cleared to create pastureland for grazing cattle.[1] By the late 1970s two-thirds of all the agricultural land in Central America was taken up by cattle and other livestock, most of it destined for export to North America.[2] While American consumers saved, on the average, close to a nickel on every hamburger imported from Central America, the cost to the native environment was overwhelming and irreversible. Each imported hamburger required the clearing of 6 square yards of jungle for pasture. "The innocent-looking beef cow," says Joseph Tosi, "is at the center of a destructive ecological cycle that is strangling Central America."[3] In 1979 the United States was importing 110 thousand tons of beef from the Central American countries. By 1990, Central American beef exports to the United States had declined to 48,000 tons per year. Still, cattle grazing continues to play a major role in deforestation throughout Central America.

The creation of a vast cattle complex in Central America has enriched the lives of a select few, pauperized much of the rural peasantry, and spawned widespread social unrest and political upheaval. Over half the rural families in Central America—35 million people —are now landless or own too little land to support themselves, while the landed aristocracy and transnational corporations continue to gobble up every available acre, using much of it for pastureland.[4]

In Costa Rica, the landed gentry cleared and enclosed 80 percent of the tropical forests in just twenty years, turning half of the country's arable land into cattle pastures. Today 2,000 powerful ranching families own over half the productive land of Costa Rica.[5] They are grazing nearly 2 million cattle on the land. Although beef exports to the United States declined in the 1980s, overall beef production continued to remain high. In Guatemala, less than 3 percent of the population owns 70 percent of the agricultural land, much of it used for cattle ranching.[6] Nearly one-third of Guatemala's beef production was exported to the United States in 1990. In Honduras the amount of land devoted to cattle pastures increased from just over 40 percent in 1952 to over 60 percent in 1974. Total beef production in that tiny nation tripled between 1960 and 1980 to 62,000 metric tons annually.[7] In 1990, over 30 percent of the beef produced in Honduras was exported to the United States. In Nicaragua beef production increased threefold and beef exports increased five and a half times in the same twenty-year period.[8] By the mid-1980s, Central America had 80 percent more cattle than it had twenty years before, and produced 170 percent more beef.[9]

Many U.S. firms invested heavily in beef production throughout Central America in the 1970s and '80s. They included Borden, United Brands, and International Foods. Indeed, American multinational corporations, including Cargill, Ralston Purina, W. R. Grace, Weyerhauser, Crown Zellerbach, and Fort Dodge Labs, provided a great deal of the technological support structure for the Central American beef industry, from frozen semen to refrigeration equipment, grass seeds, feed, and medicine.

The pattern of forest clearing, land concentration, and displacement of peasant populations is being repeated throughout Latin America in a systematic effort to transform an entire continental landmass into a grazing land to support the rich beef diets of wealthy Latin Americans, Europeans, Americans, and Japanese. In Mexico, 37 million acres of forest have been destroyed since 1987 to provide additional grazing land for cattle. Mexican ecologist Gabriel Quadri summed up the feelings of many of his countrymen when he warned, "We are exporting the future of Mexico for the benefit of a few powerful cattle farmers."[10]

In Colombia, where a World Bank study shows that 70 percent of the agricultural land is owned by rich landlords, the land is frequently used for grazing cattle.[11] When land reforms were proposed, many Colombians fenced their unused land and stocked it with cattle to show occupancy.[12]

Nowhere has the effect of cattle raising been more profound on both land and people than in Brazil. Many Americans first became aware of the Brazilian cattle connection when the media reported on the assassination of Chico Mendez, the Brazilian rubber tapper who was murdered by cattle ranchers in a dispute over the use of the rain forests. Rubber tappers had long enjoyed the use of the rain forests to provide a livelihood for their families. Ranchers, anxious to clear the Amazon for cattle pastures, had been forcing the rubber tappers out of the forest for several years. The protracted battle between the ranchers and rubber tappers came to a head when Mendez, the leader of the Rubber Tappers Union, was shot and killed in 1987.[13]

Mendez's assassination underscored the growing schism between rural peasants and cattle-ranching interests over the conversion of the Amazon rain forests into pastureland. Brazil, like many Latin American countries, is a land of great potential wealth, owned and controlled by a small ruling oligarchy. Today, 4.5 percent of the country's landowners own 81 percent of the nation's farmland, while 70 percent of the rural households are landless.[14]

In 1966 the Brazilian government initiated a program called Operation Amazonia, designed to convert the world's last great tropical rain forest into commercially productive land.[15] The government provided special tax incentives to encourage domestic and foreign corporations to invest in the Amazon region. Overnight, multinational companies flocked to the Brazilian interior, clearing dense forests, in part, for grazing land for cattle. American multinational companies, including Swift, Armour, Dow Chemical, United Brands, W. R. Grace, Gulf & Western, and International Foods, began investing heavily in the Amazon. So did European and Japanese multinational firms, including Volkswagen and Mitsui.[16] All of these global companies rushed to take advantage of the last great land grab on the planet. Companies were given ample assistance from the World Bank, the Inter-American Development Bank, and the United States Agency for International Development (USAID), which were enthusiastic over the commercial prospects of creating a vast pastureland in the Amazon basin.

Between 1966 and 1983, nearly 40,000 square miles of Amazon forest were cleared for commercial development.[17] The Brazilian government estimated that 38 percent of all the rain forest destroyed during that period was attributable to large-scale cattle developments.[18] Today, millions of cattle are grazing on the cleared area of the Amazon. The tragic irony is that the land being cleared and enclosed is poorly suited for grazing. The soil base in a tropical ecosystem is extremely thin and contains very few nutrients. These ancient ecosystems exist in a climax state, quickly recycling energy back from roots to canopy with very little allowed to remain on the forest floor. After just a few years of grazing—generally three to five—the soil is depleted, forcing the cattle ranchers to clear more virgin land.[19]

Under Brazilian law, to gain title to public land in the Amazon the land must first be cleared to demonstrate a serious commitment to settlement.[20] Multinational corporations often wait for peasant farmers to raze and burn forested areas, then purchase the cleared land for a nominal fee to use for commercial pasture. The felled timber is rarely marketed, the colonists finding it more expedient to set it on fire.[21] Astronauts report seeing hundreds of fires twinkling across the Amazon forests on their flybys over the continent.[22] The commercial loss of the timber, though significant, pales in comparison to the ecological cost.

Only 2,000 years ago, the tropical rain forest belt covered 5 billion acres of the earth and took up 12 percent of the earth's land surface. In the intervening period, man has destroyed half the tropical biomass, most of the destruction occurring in the last two centuries of European colonial expansion. Of the remaining forest, 57 percent is located in Latin America, most of it in the Amazon.[23]

The Amazon rain forests cover some 2.7 million square miles, an area roughly the size of the contiguous United States. The Amazon runs through eight other countries besides Brazil. Its rivers and forests stretch to Bolivia in the south, Venezuela in the north, and Peru in the west.[24] The Amazon biomass is so dense that "a monkey could climb into the jungle canopy at the foothills of the Andes and swing through 2,000 miles of continuous 200-foot-high forest before reaching the Atlantic coast."[25]

The Amazon River, the second-largest river in the world, snakes through 4,000 miles of rain forest and is fed by over 10,000 tributaries. If laid end to end, its tributaries would circle the earth's equator two times. The Amazon boasts a volume of water sixty times that of the Nile and eleven times that of the Mississippi. One-fifth of all the river water in the world is disgorged by the Amazon. At some places along its route the river is wider than the English Channel.[26]

The Amazon rain forests, like other tropical rain forests, are richly layered. The vegetation arches up from the forest floor in a grand hierarchy, with small ground plants and shrubs at the base. Vines and epiphytes curl around the tree trunks, wrapping the forest in a snarled maze that is virtually impenetrable in places. The trees create a tiered landscape, with some reaching heights of 50 feet, others rising to 150 feet or more.

Visitors to the Amazon rain forests are often surprised by the stillness. There is very little sign of life on the forest floor. Most of the insects, birds, and mammals live on the various tiers. The floor, the understory, and the canopy are separate habitats, and a species will spend its entire life confined to just one of the levels. The climate varies considerably from canopy to floor. In some places, the forest is so dense that less than 2 percent of the sunlight ever reaches the ground. The understory is more shaded, humid, and colder than the canopy and can vary in temperature up to 8 degrees or more. These ancient climax ecosystems are the most complex and fragile ecological niches on the earth. Relationships between species are so finely tuned that even the slightest perturbation can set in motion a chain reaction that undermines an entire niche.[27]

So complex and so little understood are these tropical ecosystems that "no more than two dozen scientists" in the world are even competent to study their dynamics, according to Dr. Peter Raven, chairman of the National Research Council's Committee on Research Priorities in Tropical Biology.[28] Yet, it is in these ancient forests that upward of 50 percent of all living species dwell.[29] Tropical botanist Ghillean Prance of the New York Botanical Gardens once counted over 350 tree species on just two and a half acres of the Amazon forests.[30] In the tropical rain forest bordering Panama and Costa Rica, Edward O. Wilson of Harvard identified over 500 species of birds in a 300-square-mile area—four times the number of bird species found in all of eastern North America.[31] Panama's remaining rain forests have as many plant species as the whole of the European continent. According to a report prepared by the National Academy of Sciences, a four-square-mile section of rain forest contains

> as many as 1,500 species of flowering plants and as many as 750 species of trees; such a patch also contains 125 mammal species, 400 species of birds, 100 of reptiles, 60 of amphibians, and 150 of butterflies.[32]

Insect species are so prolific, says the National Academy report, that two and a half acres may contain over 42,000 different species.[33] Each tree may be home to over 1,700 insect species. A single square meter of leaf will often house 50 species of ants alone. Researchers have found "three species of beetles, six species of mites, and three species of moth" living in the fur of a single sloth.[34]

Some of the tropical species are so rare that they exist only on a single mountain range, or in a single stretch of forest. Scientists estimate that there could be as many as 15,000 plant species still undiscovered in the tropical rain forests.[35] The rain forests of Latin America are home to millions of species; perhaps as much as a fifth of all the life on earth.

The aesthetic, environmental, and commercial impact of razing and burning millions of acres of ancient rain forests to make room for cattle ranching is beyond human calculation. Without the rich biodiversity found in the Central and South American rain forests —and the other remaining rain forests scattered around the world— future generations would be unable to provide themselves with new foodstuffs, pharmaceutical products, fiber, and energy sources.

Most Americans are so indoctrinated in the marvels of the petrochemical and plastics revolution they are unaware of how much they rely on plants, many of them from the tropical rain forests, to serve their daily needs. Nearly a quarter of all medications and pharmaceuticals are derived from tropical plants.[36] Seventy percent of the plants identified by the National Cancer Institute as having anticancer properties come from the tropical rain forests. Many kinds of surgical procedures depend on the bark of the South American curare liana plants. D-turbo turbocurarine and other alkaloids derived from different species of the *Chondodendron* and *Strychnos* genera are used to relax skeletal muscles during delicate surgical operations. Steroid hormones, like cortisone and diosgenin, the active ingredients in birth-control pills, are derived from tropical species of wild yams found in Guatemala and Mexico.[37]

Natural rubbers, latexes, resins, gums, dyes, waxes, and oils from tropical plants are used in industrial materials and as chemical bases for consumer products ranging from lipstick and deodorant to cellophane and furniture varnish.[38]

Still, despite the enormity of the potential biological losses, multinational corporations, national governments, and local ranchers continue their relentless assault on the rain forest, bulldozing, clear-cutting, and burning acre after acre of the richest biomass in the world, destroying millions of years of evolutionary development.

Throughout Latin America today, Caterpillar tractors are poised to do battle with the ancient forests. Each day they take their toll, pushing farther and farther into the jungle, destroying everything in their path. The sound of powerful motors, revving and idling, pierces the silence of the pristine ecosystems. Frances Moore Lappé describes the process: "Gargantuan 35-ton D-9s mounted with angle plows weighing 2,500 pounds each . . . bulldoze the forests at 2,700 yards an hour uprooting everything in sight."[39]

Mexico and Central America, which used to be covered by 160,000 square miles of tropical rain forest, now have less than 50,000 square miles left, much of the area having been clear-cut and burned to make room for cattle pastures. The remaining forest cover will likely be eliminated within the next twenty-five years.[40]

The United Nations report *On Our Common Future*, the Bruntland Commission study, predicts that if deforestation of the Amazon continues at its present rate until the year 2000, over "15 percent of the plant species would be lost" on earth.[41]

Each of us bears some measure of responsibility for the loss of the world's ancient rain forests. For example, it is estimated that for every quarter-pound hamburger that comes from a steer raised in Central and South America, it is necessary to destroy approximately 75 kilograms (165 pounds) of living matter "including some of twenty to thirty different plant species, perhaps one hundred insect species, and dozens of bird, mammal, and reptile species."[42]

With the costs of clearing forests so cheap, few cattlemen care to ponder the intangibles of biosphere security and genetic diversity. Stewarding a rain forest soil base that is thin and marginal to begin with seems a waste of time and money. The cost of adding petrochemical fertilizer and other energy inputs often exceeds the commercial value of the land. The easier course is to slash, burn, graze, and move on, repeating the cycle over and over again. Geographer Susanna Hecht reports that 90 percent of the new cattle ranches in the Amazon go out of business within less than eight years, their soil base depleted from overgrazing. As the government opens new highways into the interior, the ranchers follow suit. A few years later, says Hecht, a visitor can travel along the state highways and "pass through hundreds of miles of abandoned secondary scrub."[43] An American rancher who owns grazing land in the Amazon described the attitude of the newest cattle colonists:

> You can buy the land out there now for the same price as a couple of bottles of beer per acre. When you've got half a million acres and 20,000 head of cattle, you can leave the lousy place and go live in Paris, Hawaii, Switzerland, or anywhere you choose.[44]

The wasting of the Amazon is not unique. The 4,000-year westward expansion of the cattle culture has been marked by pillage and plunder, as well as a wanton disregard for virgin land, native peoples, and the needs of future generations. While many Americans are quick to condemn the Brazilian government for encouraging the enclosure and commercialization of the Amazon, we are less mindful of our own history on the Great Plains. The cavalier attitude of the Brazilian ranchers is reminiscent of the attitude of American ranchers on the western range. The cry of "free grass" may well be looked back on by future generations as the distinguishing refrain of the Americas, both North and South.

29

Hoofed Locusts

The destructive impact of cattle extends well beyond the rain forests to include vast stretches of the world's rangeland. Cattle are now a major cause of desertification, which the United Nations Environmental Program defines as

> impoverishment of arid, semiarid and subarid ecosystems by the impact of man's activities. This process leads to reduced productivity of desirable plants, alterations in the biomass and in the diversity of life forms, accelerated soil degradation, and increased hazards for human occupancy.[1]

Desertification is caused by the overgrazing of livestock; over-cultivation of the land; deforestation; and improper irrigation techniques. Cattle production is a primary factor in all four causes of desertification. The United Nations estimates that 29 percent of the earth's landmass now suffers "slight, moderate or severe desertification."[2] Nearly 13 million square miles of the semiarid and arid land of the world, an area four times the size of the United States, is now classified as "moderately" desertified—land that has lost a quarter of its potential productivity.[3] Another 6 million square miles of land is severely desertified, having lost over half of its natural productivity. Some 850 million human beings live on land threatened by desertification.[4] Over 230 million people live on land so severely desertified that they are unable to sustain their existence and face the prospect of imminent starvation.[5]

Each year nearly 1.5 million acres of land around the world are virtually lost to the desertification process. An additional 52 million acres become so eroded that they can no longer be grazed or cultivated.[6] The spreading man-made deserts are trapping millions of families in a deadly downward spiral. Unable to eke out a subsistence living on the eroded land, millions of people have begun a mass exodus from the countryside to squalid urban centers. Desertification of the world's rangeland, forests, and fields has helped spawn the greatest mass migration in world history. By the turn of the century, over half of humanity will live in urban areas.

The human toll of spreading desertification is beyond calculation: tens of millions of dispossessed and displaced human beings wandering across eroded fields, parched deserts, and denuded forest clearings, in search of a safe haven, finding only crowded urban slums, shanty towns, and sidewalk encampments at the end of their futile journeys. The United Nations Environmental Program paints a bleak picture.

> Throughout the Third World, land degradation has been the main factor in the migration of subsistence farmers into the slums and shanty towns of major cities, producing desperate populations vulnerable to disease and natural disasters and prone to participate in crime and civil strife. . . . such exodus exacerbates the already dire urban problems . . . and at the same time, it has delayed efforts to rehabilitate and develop rural areas—through the lack of manpower and the increased negligence of land.[7]

Not surprisingly, the regions most affected by desertification are all cattle-producing areas and include the western half of the United States, Central and South America, Australia, and sub-Saharan Africa.

Today, the billion or more cattle on the planet are overgrazing and trampling native and artificial grasses, stripping much of the vegetative cover from the earth's remaining grasslands. Without flora to anchor the soil, absorb water, and recycle nutrients, the land becomes increasingly vulnerable to wind and water erosion. More than 60 percent of the world's rangeland has been damaged by overgrazing in the course of the last half century.[8]

In addition, millions of acres of cropland are being eroded from overcultivation, as farmers strain the carrying capacity of their soil to produce feed grain for cattle and other livestock and food for a growing human population. The United Nations Environmental Program estimates the annual loss of topsoil worldwide at 25 billion tons.[9] The loss of topsoil has diminished the productivity of the world's croplands by 29 percent or more in recent years.[10] In Australia, says Prime Minister Robert Hawke, soil erosion is the most serious environmental problem facing the country and is affecting "nearly two-thirds of our continent's arable land."[11] In the Soviet Union, India, and the Americas, soil erosion is seriously compromising the productivity of both cropland and rangeland. In Africa, soil loss and spreading desertification is the most important environmental problem facing the continent.

It is estimated that for every inch of topsoil lost to erosion, grain yields are diminished by 6 percent. According to the Worldwatch Institute the loss of 25 billion tons of topsoil worldwide each year has reduced the annual world grain harvest by a comparable 6 percent—a loss of 9 million tons of grain per year.[12] In many countries hard hit by soil erosion, farmers are forced to plow more marginal lands just to keep pace with production needs, further eroding the land. In the wealthier nations the diminished soil base is being artificially enhanced with massive amounts of petrochemical fertilizer. In a very real sense, much of the world's grain is now being grown in an oil base in a desperate attempt to increase production levels to keep pace with the increasing demand for food and feed by humans and livestock.

An inch of topsoil takes between 200 and 1,000 years to form under natural conditions.[13] With the human and cattle population growing at an unprecedented rate, it seems that virtually every available square mile of rangeland and cropland is being exploited, depleted, and eroded with little thought of tomorrow or the needs of future generations.

Soil erosion and spreading desertification have become a serious problem in the United States. Two hundred years ago, most cropland in the United States contained at least twenty-one inches of topsoil.

Today, the country has lost nearly one-third of its prime top soil as a result of overgrazing, overcropping, and deforestation. In some regions of the country, less than six inches of soil remain.[14] Iowa, once considered the greatest agricultural land in the world, has lost over half its topsoil in less than one century.[15] Each year, over 4 billion tons of soil are lost to rain erosion and 3 billion to wind erosion in the United States.[16]

Mathematician Robin Hur estimates that nearly 6 billion of the 7 billion tons of eroded soil in the United States is directly attributable to cattle and feed crop production.[17] Unfortunately, the environmental costs of maintaining a rich beef culture high atop the world's protein ladder are never factored into the price of beef itself. Instead, increased soil erosion and spreading desertification is classified as an "externality," a secondary cost of production that is allowed to accumulate in the form of an environmental debt to be born by future generations. David Pimentel estimates the direct and indirect costs of soil erosion and runoff in the U.S. to exceed $44 billion a year.[18] Every beef-eating American contributes personally to the process. The Worldwatch Institute estimates that each pound of feedlot steak costs about 35 pounds of eroded topsoil.[19]

Parts of the Great Plains and the western range are fast becoming a barren desert. Millions of acres of public lands are being lost each year to the forces of desertification. Ecosystems that once teemed with pronghorn, elk, wild horses, burros, coyotes, wolves, hundreds of species of birds, freshwater fish and aquatic life, prairie wildflowers and grasses, are dying, victims of overgrazing by western cattle ranchers more interested in short-term profit than long-term conservation. The magnitude of the losses and the spread of the deterioration is impressive. Mighty rivers and streams have been reduced to a trickle. Many have dried up altogether, leaving giant mud flats and thousands of miles of cracked and crusted arroyos scarring the landscape. Riparian areas, the oases of the range, have been turned into so many ecological ghost towns. The cottonwoods are long gone in some areas. So too the wildflowers, and rodents. The wildlife that remains dwindles in numbers with each passing day.

Cattle are destroying much of the American west. Between 2 and 3 million cattle are currently grazing on some 306 million acres of public land in the eleven far-western states. Their domain encompasses about 40 percent of the landmass of the American west and

12 percent of the total landmass of the lower forty-eight states.[20] While western beef cattle make up only a small percentage of the beef production in the United States, they are a primary cause of much of the ecological destruction of the western half of the United States.[21]

Let loose on public lands, each animal eats its way through 900 pounds of vegetation every month.[22] They strip the rangeland of its forage of grass and herbage and browse on shrubs and trees, even consuming cactus and tree bark. Their powerful cloven hoofs trample native plants and compact the soil with the pressure of 24 pounds per square inch.[23] The soil compaction reduces the air space between soil particles, reducing the amount of water that can be absorbed.[24] The soil is less able to hold the water from the spring melting of snow and is more prone to erosion from flash floods that run along the surface. In western Colorado alone, grazed watershed areas produce up to 76 percent more sediment than un-grazed areas.[25]

The constant pounding of the soil by cattle hoofs has far more subtle but equally profound impacts on the microworld of life on the rangelands. Billions of organisms—bacteria, protozoa, fungi, algae, nematodes, insects, earthworms, and mites—live in the top two inches of soil, where they play a critical role in maintaining soil fertility and building new soil. The trampling of soil by cattle disrupts and destabilizes these mini-habitats, further weakening the already compromised soil base on the rangelands.[26]

The combination of overgrazing and the relentless pounding of the soil has destabilized the plain biome and devastated native flora and fauna. By eliminating the plant cover, the cattle have left the rest of the animal kingdom—insects, birds, mammals—without adequate food and shelter. By compacting the soil, the cattle have greatly diminished the capacity of the land to both retain water and rebuild soil, further undermining the already precarious vegetative cycle. No longer anchored by plant roots or shaded from the sun, and unable to absorb water, the topsoil is being blown away by wind and carried off by surface floods at an alarming rate. In some areas of the west, over half of the topsoil has already been eroded. As early as the 1950s, an unpublished report prepared by the Bureau of Land Management underscored the dimensions of the erosion problem.

It is estimated that the federal rangelands produce 320 thousand acres-feet of sediment annually—exceeding the combined volume of sediment discharged by the Mississippi and Colorado rivers. Converted to a weight basis, the annual sediment loss is equivalent to nearly 500 million tons of soil. To transport this volume by rail would require 244,846 trains of 50 cars each, with each car carrying a load of 40 tons.[27]

Some studies estimate that the western range produces less than half the biomass it did a hundred years ago, before cattle were allowed to roam at will. The riparian zones are the hardest hit by cattle grazing on the western range. These are the narrow strips of land that run alongside rivers, streams, and ponds, where much of the flora and fauna of the range are concentrated. In states like Nevada, over 80 percent of the 300 terrestrial wildlife species "are directly dependent on riparian habitat" even though these small oases make up less than 1 percent of the landmass.[28] Riparian zones play a central role in regulating and purifying the flow of water on the western range. They serve as a refuge and nesting area for wildlife and provide shade from the summer sun and protection from the winter snow.

Cattle ranchers have taken over the vast majority of riparian zones on the western range, reducing these pristine habitats to watering holes and feeding areas for their herds. The cattle have destroyed the native vegetative cover, compacted the soil, and left these habitats bare and lifeless. "According to the Arizona state park department, over 90 percent of the original riparian zones of Arizona and New Mexico are gone."[29] A 1988 report of the General Accounting Office (GAO) was equally grim, estimating that 90 percent of the 5,300 miles of riparian habitat managed by the Bureau of Land Management in Colorado was in unsatisfactory condition, as was 80 percent of Idaho's riparian zones. The GAO report concluded that "poorly managed livestock grazing is the major cause of degraded riparian habitat on federal rangelands."[30]

The introduction of the Eurasian bovine into a complex and fragile American biome, whose many subtle relationships were forged over thousands of years of evolutionary history, has proved disastrous. Even the most trivial changes have enormous consequences. For example, when the cattle wade in and out of streams, the pressure of their hoofs against the embankments loosens the soil, collapsing large chunks into the rivers. In some areas of Utah, streams are now almost twice as wide where cows have grazed.[31] As the streams become wider and more shallow, the water surface heats up from the greater exposure to sunlight. Higher water temperatures and cattle waste, in turn, diminish the oxygen-carrying capacity of the streams.[32] The warmer water, containing less dissolved oxygen, adversely affects cold-water fish, especially trout. Unable to compete with fish like chubs, carp, and squawfish, which can tolerate warmer water and less oxygen, the trout populations have decreased in number throughout the western range.[33] An ungrazed part of a stream in Montana produced 268 percent more trout than did a grazed part of the same stream. And in Nevada, the Bureau of Indian Affairs has resorted to fencing cattle out of a tributary of Summit Lake to protect the threatened Lahontan cutthroat trout.[34]

Plant species have also fallen victim to the cattle invasion on the western range. According to the GAO, more plant species in the United States are eliminated or threatened by livestock grazing than by any other single factor. Of the five new plants placed on the national registry of endangered species in August and September of 1989, three were "victims of grazing."[35] Perennial bunchgrasses, once the primary plant on the western plains, have been reduced as much as 85 percent in states like Idaho as a result of overgrazing. As mentioned earlier, many of the native grasses have been replaced by Old World species that arrived along with the cattle and successfully invaded and colonized entire niches. Filaree, Russian thistle, and halogeton are among the most prolific of the nonnative plants.

The most successful of the "Old World invaders" is cheatgrass. The plant spread across the plains in less than half a century, becoming the most visible and abundant grass on the spring ranges by the 1930s. A decade later, it was the dominant species on over 4 million acres of rangeland. Cheatgrass is an adequate forage grass but highly flammable after it dies and dries. In fact, cheatgrass is 500 times more likely to burn than any other grass and is responsible for many of the fires that burn out of control on the western range, destroying millions of acres of wildlife habitat.[36]

Cattle grazing has so diminished the carrying capacity of the western rangeland that many native birds have been greatly reduced in number or eliminated altogether. The Montezuma quail has been

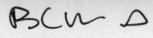

all but eliminated on the Texas range. Wild turkeys have disappeared from parts of Arizona. Sage grouse, lesser prairie chickens, and sharp-tail grouse have all been seriously reduced in numbers as a consequence of overgrazing on public rangelands.[37]

In study after study comparing nesting success on rangelands with little or no cattle to rangelands with heavy herd concentrations, the bird populations were far more prolific in the absence of cattle. This has been especially true for songbirds.

Perhaps the most disturbing impact of overgrazing on public land has been the marked reduction in the number of wild animals. Elk, bighorn sheep, pronghorn and antelope have virtually disappeared from much of the western range. Utah state ecologist Frederic H. Wagner estimates the number of large animal species to be "less than 5 percent of their primeval numbers."[38] Pronghorn have shriveled in numbers from 15 million a century ago to less than 271,000 today. Bighorn sheep, once numbering over 2 million, are now less than 20,000 in number. The elk population has plummeted from 2 million to less than 455,000.[39]

The Bureau of Land Management (BLM) has been partly responsible for the wholesale decline in large animals. From its inception, this government agency has favored cattle when allotting herbage on federally leased land. For example, in the Burns district of Oregon "about 252 million pounds of herbage are allotted to livestock, while less than 8 million pounds are allotted to wildlife."[40] Unable to compete with cattle for limited grass, thousands of big animals are forced to migrate to marginal rangeland, where they face a slow death by starvation. Many die each year entangled in barbed-wire fences. Skeletal remains of big animals are sometimes visible on the western range, enmeshed here and there along the fencing, looking eerily like totems in an ancient funeral mound.

The spraying of herbicides to kill trees and brush has been a major factor in the decline of big animals. The BLM and western ranchers often spray thousands of acres in a single operation to eliminate the shrubs and brush these animals rely on to survive. After clearing large tracts, the government plants monocultures of exotic grasses like crested wheat grass to accommodate cattle. The conversion of wildlife areas into artificial pastures weakens the native habitats even further, leaving the big animal herds defenseless, homeless, and hungry.

Despite the fact that federal lands are supposed to be administered in a fashion that protects both wildlife populations and ranching interests, the reality is that the Bureau of Land Management spends "ten times as much on grazing programs designed to benefit livestock as on wildlife."[41]

From the very beginning of its oversight of the plains, the federal government has made it a policy to rid the western range of its wildlife habitats. Government officials have helped turn hundreds of millions of acres of public land into a giant pasture of grass for cattle to graze on. To ensure cattle near-total hegemony over the plains, the government and western ranchers have engaged in a systematic campaign to rid the rangelands of every conceivable predator that might pose a potential threat to the bovine. The Bureau of Land Management and other government agencies have targeted mountain lions, coyotes, bears, lynx, bobcats, and even eagles for extinction in the past century.

Predators act as a check against the proliferation of prey species and serve as regulators, culling wildlife populations to make sure that animal populations do not exceed the carrying capacity of their environment. The extermination of millions of predator animals on the western range has contributed to the destabilization of the plains ecosystems, making them vulnerable to the force of spreading desertification.

The federal government initiated the first predator control program back in 1915, appropriating $125,000 to eradicate animals on public lands. Today, the Division of Animal Damage Control in the U.S. Department of Agriculture spends millions of dollars every year to eradicate predator species, many of which pose no real threat to the livestock.

The history of government efforts at predator control in the twentieth century is every bit as grim as the government's handling of the buffalo in the nineteenth century. In their book *Sacred Cows at the Public Trough*, wildlife writers Denzel and Nancy Ferguson catalog a century of indiscriminate killing and mass slaughter of predator populations on the plains.

In the beginning of the century, government trappers used metal leg-hold traps, snares, and guns to eliminate tens of thousands of animals. "Denning" became popular at the time, and is still used by government agents. Kerosene is poured into the den and lit, setting the young on fire in their nest. In the 1940s the government turned to a new device, the "coyote getter," a cyanide dispenser powered by a pistol cartridge.[42] Coyotes and other predators are lured to a scented wick which, when tugged, ejects cyanide into the animal's mouth. The animal dies a painful death. Today, government agents rely on a new version of the cyanide gun, the M-44, to kill thousands of coyotes and other predator animals each year.

In the late 1940s the government added still another weapon to its predator control arsenal, a dangerous chemical made up of sodium monofluoroacetate, known by the trade name Compound 1080.[43] The chemical destroys the nervous system of animals and causes cardiac arrest. Between 1961 and 1970 the government engaged in what can be best described as an orgy of killing on the western plains, trapping, gassing, poisoning, shooting, burning, and drowning every predator animal it could find. Over ten years, 141,000 baits containing meat laced with Compound 1080 were placed out on the plains. The bait stations were placed at six-mile intervals in a "gigantic grid" to snare and exterminate coyotes. During the same ten-year span, the federal government scattered more than 7 million tallow pellets containing strychnine across the western range.[44]

The mass killings of millions of predators has resulted in an infestation of "pest" animals on the western plains. Without the predators to check their populations, rabbits, squirrels, kangaroo rats, pocket gophers, and other rodents have periodically proliferated in some areas. Government agents have used air drops of poisoned grain to artificially check the rodent population, rather than attempting to reestablish the historical ecological balance between predator and pest populations.

Overgrazing and the ecological destabilization caused by government programs has also led to an infestation of locusts, grasshoppers, harvester ants, and other insects. Not unexpectedly, the government response has been to spray massive amounts of insecticide, further weakening the ecosystems and making the land still more vulnerable to desertification. In 1989 the Animal Damage Control program (ADC), referred to as the "gopher chokers" by other federal government employees, killed 86,502 coyotes, 7,158 foxes, 236 black bears, 1,220 bobcats, and 80 gray timber wolves.[45] In 1990 the ADC budget totaled $29.4 million. Carol Grunewald, formerly editor of the *Animal Activist Alert* at the Humane Society of the United

States, notes that the cost to the taxpayer of eradicating predator animals exceeds "the losses suffered by farmers and others to wild animals."[46]

The federal government has even taken to rounding up thousands of wild horses and burros, warehousing them and auctioning them off in the misguided belief that these small numbers of animals pose a competitive threat to the millions of cattle grazing on public lands.

The cattle complex on the western range has wreaked great damage on the North American continent. Still, the destruction of pristine wildlife habitats and entire ecosystems has elicited only sporadic murmurs of protest. There has been no widespread public outrage, no hue and cry. For the most part, the ranching interests have been successful at keeping tight control over their domain—millions of acres of public land that have been used, abused, and exploited mercilessly for the sake of the beef industry. Occasionally, a lone voice has risen up to challenge the powers that be. Writer and conservationist Edward Abbey issued a prophetic jeremiad in a speech delivered before cattlemen at the University of Montana in 1985:

> Most of the public lands in the West, and especially the Southwest, are what you might call "cow burnt." Almost anywhere and everywhere you go in the American West you find hordes of [cows]. . . . They are a pest and a plague. They pollute our springs and streams, and rivers. They infest our canyons, valleys, meadows, and forests. They graze off the native bluestems and grama and bunch grasses, leaving behind jungles of prickly pear. They trample down the native forbs and shrubs and cacti. They spread the exotic cheatgrass, the Russian thistle, and the crested wheat grass. Weeds. Even when the cattle are not physically present, you see the dung and the flies and the mud and the dust and the general destruction. If you don't see it, you'll smell it. The whole American West stinks of cattle.[47]

The near extinction of the buffalo, the elimination of large animals, predators, and native flora, and the introduction of "Old World" grasses and cattle have crippled the Great Plains. The enclosure, commodification, and monoculturing of the western range ranks as one of modern man's most ambitious public works projects. In terms of sheer magnitude and scope, its impact on the American landscape is perhaps equaled only by that of the U.S. Interstate Highway Act of the 1950s, which transformed much of America into a suburbanized highway culture.

Today, large sections of the western rangeland lie in ruins, while much of the rest teeters on the edge of ecological collapse. In the 1980s the BLM issued a report entitled *Ailing Rangelands* detailing the extent of the destruction. According to the BLM, over 94,671,893 acres were then in "unsatisfactory condition."[48] A report issued by the National Wildlife Federation and the Natural Resources Defense Council in 1989 blamed "poor livestock grazing practices" for much of the problem.[49] More to the point, the President's Council on Environmental Quality issued a report in the same decade, warning the public that "the overall land area affected by desertification in North America is surprisingly large." The report added that overgrazing "has become the most potent desertification force, in terms of total acreage affected within the United States."[50]

According to a 1991 report prepared for the United Nations, as much as 85 percent of the western rangeland—nearly 685 million acres—is being degraded by overgrazing and other problems. Dr. Harold Dregne, professor of soil science at Texas Tech University, the author of the U.N. study, estimates that 430 million acres in the western part of the United States is suffering a 25 to 50 percent reduction in yield, again primarily because of the overgrazing of cattle.[51]

Despite warnings, even from government agencies, the environmental community and the American public have been slow to react to what may be shaping up as an environmental catastrophe. Writing in the magazine *Audubon*, Philip Fradkin summed up the dimensions of the crisis on our western lands—a crisis that has, up to now, remained among the best-kept environmental secrets in the country.

> The impact of countless hooves and mouths over the years has done more to alter the type of vegetation and land forms of the West than all the water projects, strip mines, power plants, freeways, and subdivision developments combined.[52]

In 1989, on the eve of the centennial celebrations of six western states, *Newsweek* ran a story on the western range, unmasking the long history of ecological and political abuse that has turned the region into the most "exploited and ignored" section of the United States. According to *Newsweek*:

> Decades of federal largesse have relegated the area to near-colonial status. On a per capita basis five of the centennial states are among the top ten recipients of federal spending. Despite such heavy investment, from the New Deal to its descendants—massive water and agricultural subsidies—the region has steadily declined.[53]

Employment opportunities are declining in much of the range country. Up to 60 percent of college graduates now migrate out of the region, and the census figures project a mass migration of young people between the ages of 17 and 24 in the coming decade.[54]

A few planners have suggested that the best way to effectively reverse the desertification process that has fast turned the west into a desolate outback is to reclaim the land by creating a gigantic buffalo commons. Rutgers University professors Frank and Deborah Popper have proposed the creation of a huge national park covering parts of ten western states east of the Rockies. The public reclamation project would include the reintroduction of buffalo and wild animals on an area one-fifth the size of the contiguous United States.[55] Proponents of the plan believe that

> over the next generation the plains will lose almost all of its people. Then a new use for the suddenly empty plains will emerge, one that is, in fact, so old that it predates the American experience.[56]

30
Kicking Up Dust

Nowhere is the problem of overgrazing more severe than in Africa, where millions of acres of rangeland are being swallowed up each year—making desertification the single greatest threat to the ecology of the continent and the survivability of its human population. As noted in Chapter 2, cattle were introduced into the African continent between 5000 and 2300 B.C. by the Middle Eastern empires as well as by the nomadic herdsmen of the Eurasian steppes. Cattle are found throughout Africa. Over 50 percent of the surface area of East Africa is given over to the grazing of some 23 million head of cattle.[1] In this vast region of grasslands and savannahs, "cattle complexes" are the driving force behind the social and economic life of the tribal peoples.

For centuries, nomadic tribes and semipastoral farming populations were able to strike an effective balance between cattle rearing and ecological restraints, using age-old migratory practices and husbandry techniques to ensure that their domestic animals did not overtax the carrying capacity of the land. Colonial rule altered the equation, forcing changes on tribal peoples that inevitably led to the desertification of the continent.

The French, long the dominant European power in the African Sahel—the region stretching from Senegal to Chad—carved up its sphere of influence into a succession of arbitrary nation-states, whose borders were designed more with military considerations and market forces in mind than to accommodate the migratory patterns of indigenous pastoral tribes. Cut off from their traditional migratory routes, nomadic tribes were forced to concentrate their herds on the limited rangeland available to them within the newly established national borders, triggering the process of overgrazing, soil erosion, and desertification. The French compounded the problem by placing a head tax on each nomad. The effect of the tax was far-reaching. African tribal cultures had long maintained subsistence economies, living off barter and exchange. The government-imposed taxes forced the pastoralists into a money economy. For the first time, cattle were sold for cash to pay the government head tax.

Other colonial policies put additional pressure on the herdsmen. French commercial interests began enclosing and commodifying large tracts of former pastureland to grow peanuts and cotton for export to the home market, further diminishing the amount of available grazing land. Other European colonial powers in Africa launched similar efforts, transforming much of the continent from a subsistence to a market economy. Nomadic tribes found themselves trapped between two very different economic systems, one dependent on barter, the other on money. No longer able to survive entirely on barter, the herdsmen began to enlarge their herds, selling off the surplus cattle so that they could pay for necessities.

European colonial rule also brought a demand for beef exports. The lure of the market enticed many tribes to begin raising cattle for the international beef trade. The cattle complex, which for centuries had been the cultural centerpiece of tribal life, was weakened by colonial restraints and market forces.

The end of European colonial rule in the 1950s and 1960s did little to change the political and commercial trends that were undermining tribal life and putting increasing pressure on the carrying capacity of the land. Like their colonial predecessors, the newly liberated nation-states of Africa were anxious to exert control over their populations. The nomadic way of life posed a threat to the orderly administration of government services, including health care, education, military conscription, and taxation. New methods were introduced to encourage herdsmen to adopt a more sedentary existence.

Perhaps the most ill-conceived of the new practices was the introduction of drilled deep-wells across Africa. Foreign development programs, including the United States Agency for International Development (USAID), poured funds and technical skills into the task of drilling thousands of wells. It was believed, at the time, that a reliable and constant flow of water in one place would encourage the pastoralists to end their nomadic migration with the rain cycles and settle down. The herdsmen took the bait, establishing semipermanent encampments around water holes. The seemingly inexhaustible supply of cheap and abundant water encouraged the nomadic tribes to expand their herds. Within a few years, the grazing areas surrounding water holes were stripped bare of vegetation, trampled, compacted, denuded, and exhausted by too many cattle on too little range. Lappé and Collins report that along some water holes in the Sahel, up to 6,000 head of cattle were grazed on land that could feed fewer than 600 animals.[2]

Unmindful of the long-term environmental consequences, governments continued to encourage the concentration of larger and larger cattle populations around well sites, setting up the conditions for widespread desertification of the African continent. In the Sudano-Sahelian region—the band of twenty-one countries stretching from Cape Verde on the Atlantic coast to Somalia on the Indian Ocean—the cattle population increased by 25 percent between 1975 and 1984. In some places the cattle population multiplied six times or more.[3] There are now 186 million cattle grazing on the African continent, or one cow for every three people.[4] This in a region where agricultural production has been unable to keep pace with the demands of a growing human population for close to two decades. In the nine nations of southern Africa, the number of cattle now exceeds the carrying capacity of the land by 50 to 100 percent.[5]

The rising number of cattle and the increasing concentration around man-made wells are devastating the ecology of many parts of Africa. In Sudan alone, an area extending from 12 miles to 25 miles beyond the village water holes has turned to sand. With the addition of each new well on previously ungrazed land, the process begins anew, with ever larger circles of denudation rippling out over the continent. The circular sites have been aptly labeled "sacrifice areas," barren stretches of land that have fallen victim to the modern cattle complex.[6] Today, herdsmen and farmers are fighting each other for the remaining land, continuing to strain the carrying capacity of the soil by overgrazing and overcultivation—all this in a desperate effort to feed more people and survive the whims and caprices of a global market economy over which they have no control.

Many African countries are making a wholesale transition into a modern ranching economy, adopting western technologies and husbandry practices in an attempt to gain an even larger share of the European and international beef market. In Kenya, Swaziland, Zimbabwe, and Botswana, commercial cattle ranching is already becoming a sizable industry. In Botswana, where half the population owns cattle, the government has encouraged commercial ranching operations. To protect the 1.5 million cattle in the country from competition from other wild animals, the ranchers and the government have erected hundreds of miles of wire fences around the herds. The fencing has seriously disrupted the migratory patterns of African wildebeest and other herbivores. In recent dry seasons, tens of thousands of wild animals have died of dehydration and starvation, some bleeding to death entangled in wire mesh, in a frantic effort to reach water and forage on the other side.[7] In some African countries "a significant percent of the indigenous wild animals have disappeared forever," according to Dr. Michael Fox of the Humane Society of the United States.[8] Overgrazing and desertification are the major contributing factors in almost every instance.

Conditions in North Africa appear little better. According to the Worldwatch Institute, the human and cattle populations "have exceeded the carrying capacity of arid lands in Algeria, Egypt, Libya, Morocco, and Tunisia." In Algeria, north of the Saharan Atlas Mountains, the United Nations Environmental Program (UNEP) reports that "large settlements and cultivated lands are threatened by shifting sand dunes and sand drifts."[9] In Morocco, the desertification process is exacting an equally harsh toll.

The Sahara desert has been moving steadily southward at an alarming rate of thirty miles per year, engulfing once-fertile rangeland along a 3,500-mile frontier.[10] According to UNEP, some 7.7 billion acres of rangeland around the world have already been affected by desertification. Over 25 percent of the desertification is taking place in the twenty-one countries of the Sudano-Sahelian region.[11]

The overgrazing of cattle and periodic droughts have created an ever-widening human crisis. Millions of rural refugees attempting to flee the path of spreading desertification have migrated into

crowded urban areas. The urban population of the Sahel has qua-
drupled in just twenty years.[12] In Mauritania, 20 percent of the rural
population has migrated into the cities. In Burkina Faso, one-sixth
of the country's population has picked up stakes and moved into
urban centers.[13] Entire villages and rural communities have been
deserted along the whole of the Sahel, as impoverished and malnourished populations have sought relief in the cities from the
droughts and spreading desertification that is sweeping the countryside. Some never make it. In the major droughts from 1968 to 1973
and 1982 to 1984, more than 250,000 people died of famine in the
African countryside.[14] Those that made it to the cities were forced
to live on the streets, barely existing with sporadic government rations. In 1974, 200,000 people in Niger were wholly dependent on
government food distribution programs. In Mali, 250,000 people
were aid-dependent.[15]

The United Nations estimates that "by the year 2000, Burkina
Faso, Chad, Mali, Mauritania, Niger, and Senegal will have collective
urban populations of 11.8 million, a 224 percent increase over
1975."[16]

The modern cattle complex is destroying many regions of the
African continent. This rich landmass that just a hundred years ago
was teeming with wildlife, lush vegetation, dense forest, and ancient
savannahs is now turning into one of the world's most desertified
regions. Its land is eroded, and stripped bare of flora and fauna from
overgrazing.[17] Parts of Africa teeter on the verge of an irreversible
ecological collapse trapping millions of people in a downward spiral
whose consequences are barely fathomable. The Sahel is literally
blowing away under the weight and force of tens of millions of
hoofed locusts, relentlessly devouring everything in their path on
their trek across the grassland. Eroded soil from Africa is blowing
onto other continents around the world.[18]

Today millions of African herdsmen find themselves trapped between their tradition-bound cultures, steeped in the ways of the
ancient cattle complexes, and the political and economic restraints
imposed on them by modern nation-states and the international commodity markets. Tugged and pulled by both forces, they find themselves increasingly unable to survive the steady barrage of economic
and environmental assaults that are fast turning much of the African
continent into a giant wasteland.

31

Quenching Thirst

Now, even the freshwater reserves of the planet are threatened by a combination of droughts, overcultivation and overgrazing. Water tables are dipping so low in East Africa that six out of seven countries in the region are expected to experience severe shortages by the end of the current decade. All five North African countries along the Mediterranean are likely to experience the same stress before the turn of the century.[1] Water tables in Mexico and in southern India are also dropping precipitously.[2]

Fresh water, a once seemingly inexhaustible resource, is now becoming scarce in many regions of the world.[3] Between 1940 and 1980, worldwide water use doubled, in large part to meet the needs of a burgeoning human population. Seventy percent of all the water consumed goes to agriculture—to grow food and feed.[4] Today 15 percent of the world's cropland is under irrigation, or some 670 million acres, requiring almost 4 trillion cubic yards of water per year.[5] By the year 2000, forecasters predict that an additional 25 to 30 percent more water will be needed to keep pace with the increase in agricultural land under irrigation.[6] Water shortages in the United States, especially in the western states, have now reached critical levels, with overdrafts now exceeding replenishments by 25 percent.[7] Although Americans are becoming aware of the water shortages in the western part of the country, they are unaware that cattle and other livestock play a role in the decline in water tables.

Nearly half the water consumed in the United States now goes to grow feed for cattle and other livestock. To produce just a pound of grain-fed steak requires hundreds of gallons of water to irrigate feed crops consumed by the steer. Food economist Frances Moore Lappé notes that "the water used to produce just 10 pounds of steak equals the household consumption of [her] family for an entire year." *Newsweek* is even more graphic, observing that "the water that goes into a 1,000-pound steer would float a destroyer." According to David Pimentel, producing a pound of beef protein often requires up to fifteen times more water than producing an equivalent amount of plant protein.[8] Today, much of the available fresh water in North America is being used to grow feed for cattle. The result is that water tables in the midwest and Great Plains states are fast being depleted, and shortages are beginning to fundamentally alter water-use patterns in the industrial, commercial, and residential sectors. Already, western cities and suburbs have been forced to ration water, limiting both household and commercial uses. Rarely, if ever, are consumers advised that prohibitions on watering lawns, washing automobiles, and other uses are attributable, in part, to the amount of water being siphoned off to raise grain for cattle and other livestock.

Nearly half the grain-fed cattle in the United States are raised in midwestern or western states that rely on a single underground aquifer. The Ogallala aquifer is one of the world's great underground reserves. It stretches from northwestern Texas to South Dakota, crossing through eight states. The Ogallala spans an area three times the size of New York State. Farmers are now withdrawing more water from the Ogallala each year than the annual flow of the Colorado river.[9] Much of the water is being pumped into the grain states to grow feed for the millions of cattle on the western range and the midwestern feedlots. In the last forty years, 120 cubic miles of water have been taken from this essentially nonrenewable reserve. Hydrologists estimate that the aquifer is already half depleted in Kansas, Texas, and New Mexico.[10] In Texas, a quarter of the groundwater has already been used up and many wells are running dry across the northern part of the state as water has been used to grow a range of crops including sorghum for the expanding cattle feedlots. The water tables have become so low that the U.S. Department of Agriculture predicts that in less than forty years, the irrigated areas of the Great Plains will "have shrunk by 30 percent."[11]

In California, where 42 percent of the irrigation water goes to produce feed grain or drinking water for cattle and other livestock, water tables have dropped so low that the earth itself is sinking under the vacuum. Some 5,000 square miles of the San Joaquin Valley have sunk, in some places by as much as twenty-nine feet.[12] Aquifers in the San Joaquin Valley are being pumped "at a rate that exceeds recharge by more than 500 billion gallons annually."[13]

Western cattle ranches have long enjoyed privileged access to local water resources. Early on, cattlemen made sure to set up their operations near streams and rivers so they could meet their water needs first. Control over "water rights" helped provide cattlemen with the necessary economic and political clout to dictate rangeland use. Now, many of the streams and rivers that cross cattle country have dried up altogether, or flow only intermittently, as a result of overgrazing, soil erosion, and desertification.

Unfortunately, existing federal tax laws encourage ranchers and farmers to pump more and more water from underground aquifers. In New Mexico, Kansas, and Texas, landowners are allowed a depletion allowance on the groundwater to "compensate for the fact that their pumping costs rise as the ground water mining lowers the water table."[14] Even the cost of purchasing drilling equipment and sinking wells is tax-deductible. Over half the cost of providing irrigation facilities in the United States has been borne by the federal government, in effect subsidizing ranchers and farmers from public funds.

In the past ninety years, the federal government has sponsored "thirty-two irrigation projects in seventeen western states where 20 percent of the acreage is now irrigated with the help of government subsidies."[15] Lappé reports on one project near Pueblo, Colorado, where the federal government financed a $500 million irrigation plan to help farmers grow sorghum, corn, and alfalfa for livestock feed. The GAO calculated the cost of delivering the water to be around 54 cents per acre-foot even though the farmers were only charged 7 cents per acre-foot.[16] In Utah, farmers pay $18 per acre-foot for water from the Bonneville Water Project while the federal government pays $306 per acre-foot to deliver the water.[17] Often, according to the government study, the market value of the feed is less than the cost incurred by the federal government in providing the water to grow it.

Many ranchers and farmers have made fortunes taking advantage of federally subsidized irrigation programs. Today, according to Lappé, one-quarter of the federally subsidized irrigated land is owned by only 2 percent of the landholders.[18] The U.S. Congress estimates federal subsidies of $2.2 billion go to western water projects. Between $500 million and $1 billion of the total "goes to feed and fodder growers." In California alone, more than 1.5 million acres of federally subsidized water is illegally controlled by powerful corporate and family concerns. Surveying the impact of water subsidies to livestock producers in the western states, Cornell University economist David Fields voiced the concerns of many critics:

> Reports by the General Accounting Office, the Rand Corporation, and the Water Resources Council have made it clear that irrigation water subsidies to livestock producers are economically counterproductive. . . . current water use practices now threaten to undermine the economies of every state in the region.[19]

Cattle are also the source of yet another water-related environmental problem. Cattle produce nearly 1 billion tons of organic waste each year, much of which in the United States, is running off into the groundwater and surface water, contaminating wells, rivers, streams, and lakes throughout the nation.[20] Food geographer Georg Borgstrom estimates that cattle and other livestock account for twice the amount of pollutants as comes from all U.S. industrial sources.[21]

Cattle feedlots have become a dangerous source of organic pollutants, accounting for more than half the toxic organic pollutants found in fresh water.[22] The average feedlot steer produces over 47 pounds of manure every twenty-four hours. On a standard feedlot containing 10,000 head, nearly 500,000 pounds of manure are produced daily.[23] To place the problem in perspective, the organic waste generated by a typical 10,000-head feedlot is equivalent to the human waste generated in a city of 110,000 people.[24] The nitrogen from the cattle waste is converted into ammonia and nitrates and leaches into ground and surface water, where it pollutes wells, rivers, and streams, contaminating drinking water and killing aquatic life.

As the demand for grain-fed beef continues to rise among the well-to-do consumers of the "developed" nations, the world's supply of clean fresh water is likely to dwindle, in some places to a trickle. Already, water shortages and the contamination of lakes, rivers, and streams are creating political unrest between countries that share a common waterway, as well as social unrest inside national borders as groups and classes struggle with one another to secure a share of a diminishing resource.

32

Warming Up the Planet

It was 4,000 years ago that Egyptian priests envisioned the heavens as a giant cow whose legs stretch to the four corners of the earth. Today the image of the bovine stretches across the sky once again, this time in the form of the spent energies of the modern age. Global warming is fast becoming the greatest environmental and human threat in history. The world cattle complex is contributing to the greenhouse gases that are migrating up into the atmosphere, blocking the escape of the sun's heat from the earth.

Although much has been written about the atmospheric impact of burning fossil fuels to run our automobiles and factories and to power our communication grids, homes, and offices, very little has been said about the impact that modern cattle raising is having on the greenhouse effect. The fact is, the grain-fed cattle complex is now a significant factor in the emission of three of the four global warming gases—methane, carbon dioxide, and nitrous oxides—and is likely to play an even larger role in the coming decades. Cattle, once regarded as a sacred symbol of generativeness, and more recently the symbol of mobile capital, are now polluting our atmosphere and earthly environs, transforming the biosphere itself into a wasteland of deadly gases.

A thick blanket of greenhouse gases has existed in the earth's atmosphere for as long as there has been life. The gases allow solar radiation to enter the earth's atmosphere. The earth's surface absorbs much of the solar energy, converting it to infrared energy, or heat. The heat then rises from the earth's surface and bombards the gaseous molecules in the atmosphere, forcing the molecules to vibrate. The gas molecules act as reflectors, sending some of the heat back toward the surface of the earth, creating a warming effect. The greenhouse phenomenon is an essential feature of the earth's atmosphere, providing a warm temperature band conducive to the emergence of life on the planet. The greenhouse cover has remained relatively constant over the long period of evolutionary history.

In the industrial age, massive amounts of coal, oil, and natural gas have been burned to propel the machine culture. The carbon dioxide released into the atmosphere has increased rapidly, blocking the release of heat from the planet. In 1750, the earth's atmosphere contained approximately 288 ppm (parts per million) of carbon dioxide. Today, the atmosphere contains over 350 ppm.[1] From the outset of the American Civil War until today, the industrial nations have released more than 185 billion tons of carbon into the atmosphere from burning massive amounts of fossil fuel.[2] Many scientists predict that the CO_2 content of the atmosphere will likely double by the middle part of the next century, with temperatures rising beyond any levels we've experienced in recorded history.[3]

The burning of fossil fuels accounted for nearly two-thirds of the 8.5 billion tons of CO_2 added to the atmosphere in 1987.[4] The other one-third came from the increased burning of the earth's biomass.[5] Plants take in and store CO_2 in the process of photosynthesis. When they die or are burned, they release the stored-up carbon—often accumulated over hundreds of years—back into the atmosphere.[6] The amount of carbon contained in the biomass and soil humus of the world's forests exceeds the amount of carbon in the atmosphere by 1.3 and 4 times respectively.[7] The Amazon forest alone stores some 75 billion tons of carbon in its trees.[8] When the trees are cleared and burned to make room for cattle pastures, they emit a massive volume of CO_2 into the atmosphere.

About 1.2 billion tons of carbon dioxide were released into the atmosphere from clearing and burning the forests of the Amazon in the peak year of 1987, as wealthy landowners rushed to take advantage of the final months of tax advantages provided by Brazilian law.[9] In that year, the deforestation of the Amazon rain forest contributed 9 percent of the total worldwide contribution to global warming from all sources.[10] Additional greenhouse gases are released from the annual burning of grasslands and agricultural waste.

Much of the biomass being burned in the world today is done specifically to promote the worldwide cattle-ranching industry. Millions of acres of tropical forests are being burned, vast stretches of grazing lands are being charred, and large tracts of agricultural wastes from feed crops are being set afire every year, releasing millions of tons of carbon into the heavens, all to secure the grain-fed beef complex.

Still, the burning of biomass is only part of the story. Commercial cattle ranching contributes to global warming in other ways. Our highly mechanized agricultural sector uses up a sizable amount of fossil fuel energy. With 70 percent of all U.S. grain production now devoted to livestock feed, primarily for cattle, the energy burned just to produce the feed represents a significant addition to CO_2 emissions.[11]

It now takes the equivalent of a gallon of gasoline to produce a pound of grain-fed beef in the United States.[12] To sustain the yearly beef requirements of an average family of four people requires the consumption of over 260 gallons of fossil fuel. When that fuel is burned it releases 2.5 tons of additional carbon dioxide into the atmosphere—as much CO_2 as the average car emits in six months of normal operation.[13]

Moreover, to produce the feed crops for grain-fed cattle requires the use of petrochemical fertilizers, which emit nitrous oxide, another of the greenhouse gases. In the past forty years, the use of chemical fertilizers has increased dramatically from 14 million tons in 1950 to 143 million tons in 1989.[14] Nitrous oxide released from fertilizer and other sources now accounts for 6 percent of the global warming effect.[15]

Finally, cattle emit methane, a potent greenhouse gas. While methane is also emitted from peat bogs, rice paddies, and landfills, the increase in the cattle and termite population and the burning of forests and grasslands account for much of the increase in methane emissions over the past several decades. Methane emissions are responsible for 18 percent of the global warming trend.[16]

Methane levels in the atmosphere remained relatively constant for nearly 10,000 years prior to the industrial era. In the past 300 years, however, the methane concentration in the atmosphere has nearly doubled.[17] Because a methane molecule is able to trap twenty-five times as much heat from the sun as a molecule of CO_2, scientists like Ralph Cicerone of the United State's National Center for At-mospheric Research predict that methane may become the primary global warming gas in the next fifty years.[18] Already, scientists es-timate that more than 500 million tons of methane may be released into the air each year.[19] The world's 1.3 billion cattle emit approx-imately 60 million tons of the total, or 12 percent of all of the methane released into the atmosphere.[20]

These figures, while impressive, reveal only part of the problem. When tropical forests are cleared and burned to provide pastureland for cattle, they emit methane as well as CO_2. The burning of forests, grasslands, and agricultural waste worldwide releases an additional 50 to 100 million tons of methane into the atmosphere.[21] Even more methane is released by the growing numbers of termites that feed on the felled timber of the tropical rain forests once they've been razed for grazing land. Live trees produce substances such as alkaloids and terpenes that help check the growth of the termite population. When the trees are cut down, the termites are able to feed off the dead wood chips without being killed by the chemical secretions. The termite population often increases by a factor of ten in cleared forests. With queens laying up to 80,000 eggs per day, some ento-mologists now estimate that there are 1,500 pounds of termites for every human being on the planet. The ever-expanding termite pop-ulation is suspected of contributing millions of additional tons of methane to the atmosphere each year.[22]

The worldwide cattle culture, which already dominates so much of the earth's geosphere, is now making its presence felt even on the biosphere. The environmental and economic price of maintaining an artificial protein ladder, with grain-fed beef atop the world's food chain, may be the most costly in history. Today, millions of Amer-icans, Europeans, and Japanese are consuming countless hamburgers, steaks and roasts, oblivious to the impact their dietary habits are having on the biosphere and the very survivability of life on earth. Every pound of grain-fed flesh is secured at the expense of a burned forest, an eroded rangeland, a barren field, a dried-up river or stream, and the release of millions of tons of carbon dioxide, nitrous oxide, and methane into the skies.

To grasp the enormity of the crisis, it is necessary to understand the self-regulating nature of the earth's temperature range. Just as every species lives within a narrow temperature band, so does the planet. The earth's mean temperature has not varied more than 3.6 degrees Fahrenheit since the last Ice Age, 18,000 years ago. Many scientists now predict a 4- to 9-degree rise in the earth's surface temperature over the next fifty years as we continue to spew carbon dioxide, methane, nitrous oxide, and chlorofluorocarbons into the atmosphere, blocking solar heat from escaping the planet. A temperature change of this magnitude is likely to plunge the world's ecosystems and human civilization into the throes of an unprecedented crisis. A rise of 4 to 9 degrees Fahrenheit will mean that the earth could experience the passage of an entire geological epoch in less than one human lifetime, forcing ecosystems and social systems to make radical adjustments in an evolutionary moment. The potential for wreaking havoc on the delicate web of environmental and economic relationships that have emerged since the dawn of recorded history is almost inconceivable.

By the year 2030, North American cities like New York and Boston may have the tropical climate of Miami. The midwest farm belt could well be experiencing droughts, and in some regions complete desertification, threatening both the domestic food supply and the export of foodstuffs to the hundreds of millions of people abroad who rely on the American breadbasket to sustain them. Great rivers like the Mississippi may turn into giant mud flats during the summer months, preventing commercial navigation for the first time. Super-hurricanes, as much as 50 percent greater in intensity, are likely to batter coastal regions each year, devastating port cities like Galveston, Norfolk, and Baltimore.

The worldwide consequences of global warming are likely to be equally severe. Scientists predict a three- to five-foot rise in seawater level by the year 2050 as a result of thermal heat expansion of the oceans. If the polar icecaps melt, the rise in water level could be even higher. Salt water will inundate coastal regions, infiltrating fresh-water rivers and lakes, contaminating already scarce drinking water for millions of people. The rising wall of water will likely destroy many low-lying island nations. The Maldives off India, the Marshall Islands in the Pacific, and the Caribbean islands may well be submerged under the great oceans. Like the mythical Atlantis, they may cease to exist, except in the collective memory of the human race. The submerging of landmasses will create a new kind of refugee. Millions of people will be without a homeland, because for the first time in recorded history, whole landmasses will disappear from the face of the earth.

Low-lying nations will have to spend billions of dollars building dikes and shoring up coastal areas if they are to stave off the onslaught. Even then, scientists predict that Egypt could lose 15 percent of its arable land along the Nile Delta, displacing one-seventh of its population. A loss of this magnitude is expected to lower the GNP of Egypt by as much as 14 percent or more.[23] The Environmental Protection Agency (EPA) predicts that a five-foot rise in sea level would destroy up to 90 percent of America's remaining wetlands.[24] Countries like the Netherlands are likely to exhaust much of their capital building massive dikes to hold off the rising water levels.

Global warming will also fundamentally alter rainfall patterns around the planet. As rainfall shifts location and changes in concentration, existing lakes, rivers, and streams will begin to evaporate and in some cases dry up altogether. It is predicted that the upper Colorado River Basin will lose 40 percent of its water.[25] Some climatologists predict a similar decline of 40 percent in the rainfall in the American midwest.[26] The worldwide shift in rainfall is going to force a wholesale rebuilding of dams and irrigation systems. It is estimated that the cost of retooling U.S. dams and irrigation systems could range between $7 billion and $23 billion.[27] Worldwide, over 18 percent of all agricultural land is currently irrigated. The cost of massive restructuring could exceed $200 billion.[28]

The dramatic rise in planetary temperature will have its biggest impact on regional ecosystems. According to the Bellagio Report, a study undertaken by some of the world's leading climatologists in 1987, the greenhouse effect is likely to result in massive forest dieback before the end of the first decade of the twenty-first century. Forests will not be able to migrate fast enough to keep up with the shift in their temperature range. Writing in the journal *Science*, Richard Akerr points out, "Each 1 degree centigrade of warming pushes climatic zones 100 to 150 km [60–95 miles] northward." Consider the impact on one ecosystem alone. Within sixty years, the climate that sustains Yellowstone National Park will have shifted well into Canada. Trees are not capable of migrating at the speed set by the greenhouse phenomenon.[29] In every region of the globe, entire ecosystems—trees, insects, microbes, animals—will be trapped by these rapid shifts in climate and die.

Economic systems, because they are highly dependent on ecosystems, are going to find it difficult, if not impossible, to adjust to the rapid shift in climate and the wild fluctuations in rainfall patterns and other environmental variables. The subsequent disruptions in the world's market economy are likely to be unprecedented and incalculable.

Virtually every nation in the world is currently making economic decisions and future development plans based on the false expectation that the climatic environment their ancestors have experienced for thousands of years will continue to exist fifty years from now. At the conclusion of the World Climate Program in 1985, scientists from twenty-five industrialized and developing nations warned:

> Many economic and social decisions are being made today on long-term projects such as irrigation and hydro power, drought relief, agriculture, land use, structural designs, coastal engineering projects, and energy planning based on the assumption that past climactic data are a reliable guide to the future. This is no longer a good assumption since the increasing concentration of greenhouse gases is expected to cause a significant warming of the global climate in the next century.[30]

Even the most mundane economic activities, which we generally take for granted, are likely to be disrupted. For example, consider the design process of our society's infrastructure. Present-day buildings, bridges, dams, roads, sewer systems, canals, and machinery of all kinds are designed for climatic stress tolerances that will no longer be applicable fifty to one hundred years from now. Jesse Ansubel, of the National Academy of Engineering, expresses the feelings of deep anxiety emerging within the development community when he asks, "What do you do when the past is no longer a guide to the future?"[31]

Global warming is the inverse side of the Age of Progress. It represents the millions of tons of spent energy of the modern era. The biosphere has served as a kind of giant cosmic ledger, recording the minutest details of our profligate consumption during the whole of the industrial era. The modern cattle complex figures prominently in that ledger, its saga imprinted in the countless molecules of carbon dioxide, nitrous oxide, and methane that have migrated up into the heavens in the course of bringing beef to market. Now the biosphere itself may have the final word on the 6,000-year trek westward of the great cattle cultures of the Eurasian world. Altered climate, shorter growing seasons, changing rainfall patterns, eroding range-land, and spreading deserts may well sound the death knell for the cattle complex and the artificial protein ladder that has been erected to support a grain-fed beef culture.

Part Six

THE CONSCIOUSNESS OF BEEF-EATING CULTURES

33

The Psychology of Beef

Before the modern age, our ancestors turned to the gods and spirits to help them expropriate and eat the "stuff" of life. They relied on ritual, the reenactment of sacred myth and animal and human sacrifice to secure life's bounty. Today we turn to science and new and more powerful technologies to effect the same end. Our tools help us ensnare and expropriate the life force around us so that we may live and flourish.

Human beings have always felt ambivalent about their most basic drive. The hero in Anatole France's novel *Histoire Contemporaine*, M. Bergeret, laments the bedrock reality of our existence:

> I would rather think that organic life is an illness peculiar to our unlovely planet. It would be intolerable to believe that throughout the infinite universe there was nothing but eating and being eaten.[1]

Eating the world is both agonizing and pleasurable. Denying life to another so that we too may live is a painful experience. Still, consuming the fruits of conquest is deeply satisfying, and fills us with a sense of our own aliveness. Cultural historian Elias Canetti once remarked that each of us is a king in a field of corpses. If we were to stop for a moment and reflect on the number of creatures

233

and earth's resources, and the materials we have expropriated and consumed in our lifetime, we would be appalled at the carnage and depletion that has been required to secure our existence.

Eating is as much concerned with *eros* as with *thanatos*, with life as with death. Chekhov, overjoyed with life, once blurted out: "What a luxurious thing nature is! I could just take her and eat her up. . . . I feel I could eat everything, the steppe, the foreign countries." Echoing Chekhov's feelings of exuberance, Robert Browning said that he so loved the flowers and leaves that he wanted to "bite them to bits."[2]

The act of consuming the world is filled with the unrequited tension of love and loss, the exuberance of life and the terrifying specter of death. That is why the exercise of power over nature fills us with excitement and passion on the one hand and repulsion and disgust on the other.

Eating, more than any other single experience, brings us into a full relationship to the natural world. The act itself calls forth the full embodiment of our senses—taste, smell, touch, hearing, and sight. We know nature largely by the various ways we consume it. Eating establishes the most primordial of all human bonds with the environment, and that is why in most cultures the experience is celebrated as a sacred act and a communion as well as an act of survival and replenishment. Eating, then, is the bridge that connects culture with nature, the social order with the natural order. Anne Murcott argues that "food is an especially appropriate 'mediator' because when we eat we establish, in a literal sense, a direct identity between ourselves (culture) and our food (nature)."[3]

The late Austrian psychologist Bruno Bettelheim believed that "eating experiences condition our entire attitude toward the world."[4] French anthropologist and philosopher Roland Barthes says that the manner in which a culture expropriates living creatures, the types of creatures it consumes, and the way they are prepared and served are a highly orchestrated form of communication, conveying the values, beliefs, and operational principles that underlie the entire culture.[5] He writes:

> For what is food? It is not only a collection of products that can be used. . . . It is also, and at the same time, a system of communication, a body of images, a protocol of usages, situations, and behavior.[6]

The rules and regulations, compensations and dispensations that a culture establishes for the "eating of nature" both fashion and reflect its worldview. It has been said that "the history of man is only intelligible in the context of the history of food." Nowhere is this more evident than in beef-eating cultures. The influence of beef mythologies, rituals, and practices has been pervasive, affecting and shaping questions of gender and class differentiation, national identity, colonial policies, and even race theory. Even today, the modern cattle complex continues to influence the psychology, life style, and values of peoples throughout the world, making it a formidable cultural force in human affairs.

34

Meat and Gender Hierarchies

Despite the vast differences in context and consciousness that exist between various cattle cultures, most share certain core values. An examination of those values can shed some much-needed light on what needs to be done to move beyond the beef culture in the coming century.

Joseph Campbell describes the essential characteristics that distinguish cultivator cultures from hunting cultures. The former are concerned with growth and regeneration, the latter with slaughter and death.[1] These very different approaches to "eating the earth" require very different worldviews.

The cultivation of plants necessitates tending and nurturing as opposed to stalking and sequestering. Plants are viewed less as prey and property and more as an endowment or gift bestowed from the living earth. Generativity is a prevailing ethos in a strictly agricultural society. While the plant world provides food, clothing, and shelter for people just as the animal world does, the relationship between human beings and their source of food stems from a different cosmological model, one based on the great cycle of nature—what anthropologist Mircea Eliade calls "the eternal return." Because agricultural societies are wedded to the life cycle of nature, regeneration—the life instinct—is always at the cosmological core of their worldview.

Premodern cultures that rely primarily on meat to supply their dietary needs, clothing, and building materials are always closer to the act of killing than cereal grain cultures. In beef-eating cultures, says Joseph Campbell:

> The paramount object of experience is the beast. Killed and slaughtered it yields to people its flesh to become our substance, teeth to become our ornaments, hides for clothing and tents, sinews for ropes, bones for tools. The animal life is translated into human life entirely through the medium of death, slaughter, and the arts of cooking, tanning, sewing.[2]

Bloodletting permeates these societies. Few boundaries exist between nature and culture. Nowhere is this more apparent than in the cooking of food.

French anthropologist Claude Lévi-Strauss points out that cooking is the primary mediator between culture and nature. Only the human species cooks its meat, creating an essential boundary between civilization and the natural world. Cooking is also the universal means "by which nature is transformed into culture, and categories of cooking are always appropriate for use as symbols of differentiation."

Food, says Lévi-Strauss, can be separated into three categories, the raw, the cooked, and the rotten.[3] Cooking transforms the raw into a food, temporarily holding at bay the natural process of decay. The manner in which the meat is cooked, in turn, provides a useful clue to the nature of the people, their values, institutions, and worldviews. Beef-oriented cultures prefer "roasting" over "boiling," as it is closer to the rawness of slaughter. Mixed agricultural societies that both herd and plant also both roast and boil meat. Plant-based cultures rarely prepare meat and boil much of their plant food.

Lévi-Strauss explains the psychological difference between roasting and boiling. He points out that roasting is closer to raw, the meat being exposed directly to the fire. Boiled food, on the other hand, requires a twofold process of mediation. It is placed in a pot of water, and then placed over a fire. The receptacle and the water mediate between the meat and the fire, creating greater boundaries between the culture and nature.[4] Roasting, says Levi-Strauss, maintains only a thin wall between civilization and the natural world. The meat is usually burned on the outside and red or even blood-raw on the inside, making the food as close to raw as to cooked. "Roast meat which is burned on one side and raw on the other, or grilled on the outside and red inside, embodies the ambiguity of the raw and the cooked, of nature and culture." Among many American Indian tribes and other hunter-gatherer societies, roasting is a male-dominated activity while boiling is given over to the females. Roasting is associated with masculinity, prowess, the hunt, and the cult of the warrior.

Boiling, Strauss points out, is more economical and less wasteful than roasting:

> Boiling provides a method of preserving all the meats and its juices, whereas roasting involves destruction or loss. . . . Boiled food is life, roast food death. . . . One suggests economy, the other waste; the second is aristocratic, the first plebeian.[5]

Roasting has always been associated with power, privilege, and celebration, while boiling has always been associated with curative and regenerative values and frugality. In medieval Europe, the roasting of an ox and other animals was commonplace among the warlords and feudal aristocracy, whereas the boiling of meat was standard among the peasants, farmers, and freemen of the cities. Roasting, in most cultures, is reserved for special occasions—Sunday dinner, feast days, banquets, and weddings. Stewing is more routine and mundane, conferring little status and arousing less anticipation and excitement. Roasting is associated with the robust, with valor and virility. By contrast, Edwardian cookery books recommend "steamed and coddled foods as appropriately bland for the sick."[6]

It is not surprising that the dominant beef-eating cultures of Europe, the Americas, and Australia have preferred roasting to boiling. The warlords of medieval Europe, the landed gentry of early modern times, the explorers and discoverers of new worlds, the frontiersmen of the Appalachian Trail, the cowboys of the great plains—all used roasting to mediate their relationship to their prey. One never thinks of cowboys and boiled beef. Even today, in postindustrial America, the image of the cattle culture, with its scenes of cowboys roasting beef over an open fire, is reenacted in countless suburban backyards on summer weekends, as the "man" of the household lights up the charcoal and slaps the raw beef patties on the sizzling metal grill.

Of all foods, beef confers the most status. In virtually every meat-eating culture, red meat, especially beef, is ensconced atop the food pyramid, followed in descending order by chicken and fish and then by animal products—eggs and cheese.[7] Red meat and beef are especially prized because of the qualities ascribed to them. It has long been held in myth and tradition that the blood flowing through red meat confers "strength, aggression, passion and sexuality," all virtues coveted among beef-eating people.[8]

Blood is the vital "living force" of the animal.[9] It is imbued with spirit or manna. The mounted horsemen of the Eurasian steppes, often unable to stop long enough to kill and roast a steer, would cut a small incision in the animal and use a thin hollow reed to suck out its blood to gain nourishment and strength, especially during long and protracted military campaigns. Today, in parts of southern Spain, it is still common for women to go to the local butcher shop after a bullfight to "buy a steak from the bravest bull for her husband's supper, thus ensuring his continued strength and manliness."[10]

Blood is also viewed in traditional cultures as the carrier of inheritance. Bloodlines have been the most convenient way of establishing social hierarchies. As we have already noted, the British aristocracy was obsessed with the breeding of superior stock and took every effort to maintain "pure bloodlines" in their herds. By consuming their "aristocratic" beasts, they ensured that the animal's pedigreed bloodline would meld with their own, keeping them strong in body and pure in spirit.

The blood flowing through red meat has been thought of as conferring passion. Blood conjures up notions of aggression and violence—valued emotions among warriors, sportsmen, and lovers. Soldiers have always been favored with beef before battle. So too have athletes before entering the arena. Consuming blood-rare beef has long been thought to excite the sexual passions. John Newton, the captain of a slave ship, wrote how he gave up meat on one voyage after having a religious conversion experience. He hoped that his change in diet would prevent him from "lusting after the female slaves."[11] In the nineteenth century, educators often recommended eliminating red meat for adolescent males and substituting a vegetarian diet as the "greatest aid we can give boys in the fight against self-abuse."[12]

Red meats, especially beef, have been associated with maleness and male qualities while the "bloodless" white meats have been associated with femaleness and feminine qualities. During the Victorian era and in the early years of the twentieth century, health journals "often suggested a reduction in [red] meat intake for pregnant and lactating women, putting the emphasis instead on delicate, light dishes like chicken, fish or eggs. The prescribed dishes not only mirrored the women's own delicate 'feminine' condition but avoided any of the stimulation of those qualities of red-bloodedness that seemed inappropriate to those fulfilling the nurturing role."[13] Invalids were treated in a similar way, "being fed on the classic 'low' diets of steamed fish, boiled chicken, poached eggs."[14] Red meat was even considered "too strong" to be consumed by the more bookish types, men of letters, accountants, and clerks.[15]

A meat hierarchy exists in virtually every meat-eating culture, separating people by gender. In this respect, meat cultures differ fundamentally from many traditional plant-based agricultural societies. The latter seldom develop a highly stratified food hierarchy. While gender hierarchies exist in plant-based cultures like India and China, the rigid food pyramids so characteristic of meat-eating societies are less in evidence.

In a survey of over a hundred nontechnological cultures, anthropologist Peggy Sanday found, not unexpectedly, that animal-based economies were male-dominated and male-driven while plant-based economies were more oriented toward the feminine pole. The animal-based economies were characterized by male gods, patrilineality, and a gender hierarchy with men at the top of the social pyramid. Women performed the lion's share of the work and virtually all of the "less valued" menial tasks. By contrast, in plant-based cultures, characterized by female deities and matrilineality, the economies were "more likely to be egalitarian."[16] Because women performed the critical role of food gathering, they were able to achieve relative equality with men in their social relationships. Sanday also found that contrary to animal-based cultures in which meat was almost always used as a means of separating the genders and establishing rank and hierarchy, in plant-based cultures "women do not discriminate as a consequence of distributing the staple."[17]

Even in our modern world of high technology and post-industrial sensibilities, the primordial divisions between animal and plant, male and female, continue to haunt the body politic. The ancient cattle complexes of Western civilization have imprinted a near indelible stamp on the consciousness of much of our species. Hegel once remarked that

> the difference between men and women is like that between animals and plants. Men correspond to animals, while women correspond to plants because their development is more placid.[18]

The same system of stratification that places men and meat atop the social pyramid continues to place women and plants on the bottom. In her book *The Sexual Politics of Meat*, Carol J. Adams reminds us of how far these ancient food and gender biases have penetrated the psychological landscape. Meat, for example, has come to signify far more than a food. So coveted is meat in Western culture, that we now use the term metaphorically to represent the essence of something. "Thus we have the 'meat of the matter,' 'a meaty question.' To 'beef up' something is to improve it."[19]

Vegetables, on the other hand, have come to represent dullness. In our highly transient society, where success is equated with speed and mobility, we disparage those who seem to lead a vegetative existence. When a person has been declared brain-dead, we refer to him or her as a vegetable. Plants conjure up the notion of passivity in most people's minds, a value little regarded in an aggressive market-driven society that rewards initiative and risk-taking. In the past century, women have described men as "hunks," "beefcakes," or "animals," and men have referred to women as "hot tomatoes," "shrinking violets," or "wallflowers." By often equating men with meat and women with plants, the social order is able to perpetuate a system of social stratification in which the food hierarchy continually reinforces the gender hierarchy and vice versa.

Despite the inroads made by the modern feminist movement, the ancient biases and practices surrounding the beef culture continue to reinforce food and gender discrimination. The French anthropologist Bourdieu says that among Frenchmen the beef and gender myth still prevails:

> It behooves a man to eat and drink strong things. . . . [Men] leave
> the tidbits to the children and the women. . . . The charcuterie is
> more for the men . . . whereas the crudités (raw vegetables) are
> more for the women, like the salad. . . .[20]

The subtleties that bind men and meat together atop the food chain
and the social order are varied and complex. For example, in the
beef-eating cultures, men come to believe that eating red meat, especially beef, is inherently more manly and masculine than eating
white meats, especially fish. Again, according to Bourdieu:

> Fish tends to be regarded as an unsuitable food for men, not only
> because it is a light food, insufficiently "filling" . . . but also because
> like fruit it is one of the "fiddly" things which a man's hands cannot
> cope with and which make him appear childlike. . . . Above all, it
> is because fish has to be eaten in a way which totally contradicts the
> masculine way of eating, that is, with restraint, in small mouthfuls,
> chewed gently, with the front of the mouth, on the tips of the teeth
> (because of the bones). . . . The whole masculine identity—what is
> called virility—is involved in these two ways of eating, nibbling
> and picking as befits women or with wholehearted male gulps.[21]

Bourdieu concludes that "[red] meat, the nourishing food par
excellence, strong and strong-making, giving vigor, blood, and
health, is the dish for men."[22]

Men have long used meat as a weapon of social control, a means
of conditioning women to accept a subservient status in society. In
Indonesia, for example,

> flesh food is viewed as the property of the men. At feasts . . . it is
> distributed to households according to the men in them. . . . The
> system of distribution thus reinforces the prestige of the men in
> society.[23]

Nowhere is the meat hierarchy more apparent than in England.
In the first national survey of British dietary habits, conducted in
1863, investigators were told that in rural communities the women
and children "eat the potatoes and look at the meat."[24] Among the
urban working class and poor, women reported that they "saved"
the meat for their husbands, believing that the men had to have it
to properly perform their role as provider. According to the survey,

women ate meat on the order of once a week while men consumed meat "almost daily."[25]

Little has changed in the dietary habits of the rural poor and urban working class over the past one hundred or so years. Where meat is too costly or scarce, it is almost always apportioned first to the male head of the household. In a survey conducted in the late 1970s of over 200 working-class women in a small town in northern England, researchers found that the male "breadwinners" were always favored with the most meat and the choicest cuts.[26] Of all the meats, the highest status

> was attributed primarily to a joint of meat but also extended to steak and chops. Mince dishes and stews and casseroles occupied an intermediate position with meats like liver and bacon.[27]

Interestingly enough, researchers discovered that when the male head of the household lost his job, he also was "less likely to be privileged in food consumption."[28] His ration of meat was often reduced in proportion to his loss of income-producing capability, no doubt partially to save on expenses, but also to let him know, in no uncertain terms, that he was no longer worthy of his formerly privileged position in the family hierarchy. Reviewing the data, Marion Kerr and Nicola Charles conclude that "meat undoubtedly provides the most striking instances of adult male privilege."[29]

Even in countries like the United States, where beef has been abundant and cheap, the prevailing norm has always favored men atop the food hierarchy. Adams conducted a random survey of American cookbooks and found the authors reinforcing many, if not most, of the ancient biases and myths. Readers are told to include London broil on the menu for Father's Day because "a steak dinner has unfailing popularity with fathers." In one chapter of a popular cookbook entitled "Feminine Hospitality," women were advised "to serve vegetables, salads, and soups" when hosting ladies' luncheons.[30]

Ironically, but perhaps understandably, as our modern high-tech culture becomes further removed from the kind of bodily labor and pursuits that placed a premium on brute strength and physicality, many men seem more determined than ever to perpetuate the male meat myth. Nutritionist Jean Mayer suggests that the reason may have something to do with the fact that "the more men sit at their desks all day, the more they want to be reassured about their maleness in eating those large slabs of bleeding meat which are the last symbol of machismo."[31]

If there were any lingering doubt as to the powerful symbolism Western cultures still attach to meat and machismo, the statistics linking domestic violence and quarrels over beef are both revealing and compelling. Authorities report that many men use "the absence of meat as a pretext for violence against women." Believing that they are being denied their maleness by being denied their meat, husbands often lash out at their spouses. Their rage is sometimes violent and uncontrollable. Said one battered wife, "It would start off with him being angry over a trivial little thing like cheese instead of meat on a sandwich."[32] Another woman reported,

> A month ago, he threw scalding water over me, leaving a scar on my right arm, all because I gave him a pie with potatoes and vegetables for his dinner, instead of fresh meat.[33]

The identification of raw meat with power, male dominance, and privilege is among the oldest and most archaic cultural symbols still visible in contemporary civilization. The fact that meat, and especially beef, is still widely used as a tool of gender discrimination is a testimonial to the tenacity of prehistoric dietary practices and myths and the influence that food and diet have on the politics of society.

35

Beef, Class,
and Nationalism

While beef consumption has long been used as a powerful conditioning agent, protecting the interests of a male-dominated social order, it has also been used as a class marker, dividing the rich and well off from the working poor and destitute. In the modern era, says Leslie Gofton, "food consumption . . . is a vehicle for social differentiation, an embodiment of class inequality."[1]

Certainly, the American experience bears witness to the symbolic power of beef in establishing clear-cut boundaries of status, success, and achievement. For the waves of European immigrants, who had little occasion or opportunity to eat beef in their native lands, where it was reserved for the tables of the aristocracy and merchant class, "the sizzling beefsteak, the juicy chop, the cut off the joint were . . . every bit as much a token of wealth as a starched collar, a broadcloth coat, or a top hat."[2] It was common, among the better-off laborers of nineteenth-century America—the "labor aristocrats" —to invest a large portion of their newly attained wealth in beef-steaks. In some of the trades, immigrant laborers used to flaunt their newly elevated status as "American working men" by eating a "steak breakfast every day." Railway navvies and construction workers would fry up their steaks "on red-hot shovels over the blacksmith's forge fire."[3]

So anxious were many immigrant groups to Americanize their eating habits by way of initiation into the beef culture that they refused to listen to social reformers of the day, who urged them to eat more stews as a way of economizing. Instead, they continued to sacrifice other needs for beef "in their conviction that one of the marks of success in America was eating a roast beef or a steak."[4] Beef in the nineteenth and early twentieth centuries evoked a powerful image of success and status, not unlike the symbolic role played by automobile ownership today. Entrance into the beef culture was viewed by many immigrants as an essential rite of passage into the American middle class, the most coveted of all goals. Being able to afford a steady diet of steaks and roasts provided a kind of psychic insurance, an acknowledgment that one had indeed arrived and become a part of the "good life." One German immigrant marveled, "Where in the old country do you find a workman who can have meat on his table three times a day?" Commenting on the failure of European socialism to gain a significant foothold in America, the German economist Werner Sombart blamed the problem on the fact that American laborers enjoyed three times the amount of beef as German workers. He wrote, "On the shoals of roast beef and apple pie, all socialistic utopias founder."[5]

Beef consumption in the modern era has affected national aspirations as well as class aspirations. Beef consumption became a powerful symbol of nationalism in the eighteenth and nineteenth centuries. We've already drawn attention to the English identification with roast beef. The French were equally attached to their steak, which they viewed as the symbol of French prestige in the world. Roland Barthes sings its praises:

> The prestige of steak . . . derives from its quasi-rawness. In it, blood is visible, natural, dense, at once compact and sectile. One can well imagine the ambrosia of the Ancients as this kind of heavy substance which dwindles under one's teeth in such a way as to make one keenly aware at the same time of its original strength and of its aptitude to flow into the blood of man. Full-bloodedness is the raison d'être of steak.[6]

For a Frenchman, says Barthes, consuming a steak is a communion, a patriotic act that joins the individual to the state.[7]

[Steak] . . . is a French possession. As in the case of wine, there is no alimentary constraint which does not make the Frenchman dream of steak. Hardly abroad, he feels nostalgia for it. . . . Being part of the nation, it follows the index of patriotic values: it helps them to rise in wartime, it is the very flesh of the French soldier, the inalienable property which cannot go over to the enemy except by treason.[8]

Not surprisingly, the beef psychology has also figured prominently in the fashioning of race theory and has been used to justify colonial policies and the subjugation of foreign peoples. Many intellectuals of the nineteenth century believed that the food hierarchy stretching from plants to red meat paralleled an evolutionary hierarchy stretching from the more "savage" and "brute-like" races of color to the "civilized" white races of Europe. George Beard, a prominent and influential nineteenth-century physician, was the first to advance the notion that the superior races of human beings were naturally disposed to eat higher up on the world's food chain by dint of their more evolved nature and deportment.[9] Beard argued that

as man grows sensitive through civilization or through disease, he should diminish the quantity of cereals and fruits, which are far below him on the scale of evolution, and increase the quantity of animal food, which is nearly related to him in the scale of evolution, and therefore more easily assimilated.[10]

Beard concocted an elaborate racial theory, mixing popular biological and social ideas of the day with ancient European myths about the superiority of meat-eating peoples. Again, as was the case with gender and class distinction, the association of meat with superiority and plants with inferiority was used to create still another boundary, this one separating the white colonial powers from the black, brown, red, and yellow native peoples.

Why is it that savages and semi-savages are able to live on forms of food which, according to the theory of evolution, must be far below them in the scale of development? . . . [Because savages are] little removed from the common animal stock from which they are derived. They are much nearer to the forms of life from which they feed than are the highly civilized brain-workers, and can therefore subsist on forms of life which would be most poisonous to us.[11]

Beard, like many of his contemporaries, believed that British military and commercial superiority in the world was at least partially attributable to its beef-eating ways. Because beef eaters were "by nature" higher on the evolutionary chain, and therefore more fit and able to survive over their competitors, they must inevitably triumph in their struggles with inferior peoples:

> The rice-eating Hindu and Chinese and the potato-eating Irish peasant are kept in subjection by the well-fed English. Of the various causes that contributed to the defeat of Napoleon at Waterloo, one of the chief was that for the first time he was brought face to face with the nation of beef-eaters, who stood still until they were killed.[12]

The beef myth continued to give impetus to race theory and colonial practices until well into the current century. Celebrating the virtues of the American cowboy, the popular Western writer Emerson Hough informed his readers that "the beef herders and the beef eaters of history have been winning peoples"—not the "vegetarian nations."

The attempt to equate beef eating with evolutionary superiority and racial dominance was not without its critics. Many intellectuals of the nineteenth century took exception to the very notion of killing animals for their meat, thinking it to be a sign of savage brutality and regression rather than an evolutionary step forward. Yet so compelling were Darwin's arguments on the "survival of the fittest" that many despaired of advancing ethical arguments that flew in the face of "objective" science and "the natural order of things." Many agreed with Lord Chesterfield's lament. Anguished over the thought of civilized peoples killing and eating other animals, Chesterfield nonetheless capitulated to the biological theories of the day, which quite conveniently saw forces at work in nature that were remarkably compatible with the social and economic forces that were promoting colonial expansion and racial superiority:

> Upon serious reflection, I became convinced of its legality [meat eating], from the general order of nature, who has instituted the universal preying upon the weaker as one of her first principles.[13]

Erasmus Darwin perhaps best articulated the thinking of his day when he described nature as "one great slaughterhouse."[14] His description of nature mirrored the very real slaughter taking place at the time in the Americas, Africa, and Asia as the European colonial powers enslaved and murdered indigenous peoples and ravaged and expropriated native lands.

During World War II, the United States War Department provided every American GI with over 130 grams of animal protein a day, or two and a half times the civilian consumption of meat,[15] based on the still widely held belief that beef-eating warriors are superior fighting men and more likely to prevail in a life-and-death struggle than those who eat lower down on the world's food chain. The military effort to "beef up" every soldier, sailor, and airman took on all of the trappings of a dietary crusade. So effective was the immersion and conversion that social satirist Russell Baker later referred to the effort as "beef madness . . . when richly fatted beef was force-fed into every putative American warrior."[16]

36

Cattle and the Frontier Mentality

In 1806, explorer and adventurer Zebulon M. Pike made his way over America's great western plains. As he surveyed the expanse of grass that stretched westward to the Rockies and beyond, his thoughts turned to "the numerous herds of domestic cattle which [are] no doubt destined to crown with joy these happy plains."[1] Pike sensed that America's destiny lay, in part, with the sea of grass and the rugged Texas longhorn steer. It also rested, however, on a unique amalgam of two great philosophical traditions, one dating back to the early years of the Christian era, the other molded in the intellectual fervor of the eighteenth-century European Enlightenment. The American cattle complex, is, in many ways, a direct beneficiary of this novel blending of philosophical currents and for that reason can only be properly understood within the larger intellectual framework that helped nourish it.

From the very beginning, America has been the land of John Winthrop and Ben Franklin, two historical figures wedded to very different traditions. Winthrop's America was a wilderness populated by evil forces, a fallen nature that needed to be subdued and reclaimed for God's glory. The pilgrims and their descendants were to be the chosen people. Their mission was to be as "a city on a hill." They saw themselves as triumphant foot soldiers of the coming millennial reign, who by dint of faith and fortitude would tame a wilderness and create an Eden—a promised land that would flow with milk and honey.

Franklin's America was to be a land of opportunity, a vast continent of riches that could be tapped and exploited for the material betterment of mankind. His America would be a secular mecca, a magnet attracting the best scientific knowledge and mechanical ingenuity of the European Enlightenment. The Americans would be the world's great experimenters, using a continent as a grand laboratory to tinker with new inventions and innovations. Franklin preferred the utilitarian to the sacred and dreamed of cornucopic visions rather than eternal salvation. His America would be populated by an industrious people grounded in the practical arts.

The American experience came out of these two great European traditions. The first focused on the heavens and eternal redemption, the second on the forces of nature and the pull of the market. This unique melding together of religious fervor and "down home" utilitarianism was captured in the frontier mentality.

Many of the early pioneers who trekked west over the Alleghenies saw themselves less as refugees and more as a chosen people. They were Israelites in the desert, escaping from the tyranny of the Old World, braving the vicissitudes of the wilderness in search of a promised land.

The American environment was viewed, in turn, as a fallen world, a chaotic wilderness that needed to be beaten back, tamed, and harnessed. The conquest of the American frontier took on all the trappings of an ancient morality play, with the forces of light battling against the dark satanic underworld. The slaughter of the American buffalo and the genocidal assault on the native population were recast in millennial terms as a life-and-death struggle against evil itself, a battle of epochal proportions in which Christian faith, favored by God's grace, would inevitably triumph. In his book *Wilderness and the American Mind*, Roderick Nash writes:

> Wilderness not only frustrated the pioneers physically, but also acquired significance as a dark and sinister symbol. They shared the long western tradition of imagining wild country as a moral vacuum, a cursed and chaotic wasteland. As a consequence, frontiersmen acutely sensed that they battled wild country not only for

personal survival but in the name of God. Civilizing the new world meant enlightening darkness, ordering chaos, and changing evil into good. In the westward expansion wilderness was the villain, and the pioneer, as hero, relished its destruction.[2]

The notion of a chosen people, distinguishing themselves on the field of battle, offered both succor and a convenient rationale for the conquest of a continent. That thousands of innocents would perish, whole species would be exterminated, and pristine land defiled was of little consequence in the cosmic battle to secure eternal salvation. In their actions, many western pioneers believed that they were, indeed, fighting the powers and principalities and serving as "Christ's soldiers."

Zebulon Pike's vision of cattle grazing bucolically on the western plains fit the millennial image of a fallen nature resurrected and reconsecrated as an earthly Eden in service to the Lord. The cattlization of the continent represented a visible token, a first beachhead for civilization. Recall the surprise and joy of Spanish explorers in the southwest upon coming across stray cattle left by earlier explorers on the remote frontier. Cattle, one of the first of the domesticated species, a symbol of European power, and a form of capital and wealth for "civilized people" through the long sweep of western history, were like a blessed sign. Cattle represented domestication, pastoralism, civilization, and the force of good in the world. Everywhere cattle were seeded, they were "as a beacon," an outpost of civilization and a sign of the coming of the kingdom.

The devil's terrain was transformed overnight into God's earthly garden. The wild buffalo was replaced with the domesticated steer, the native grasses of the prairies were replaced with the familiar grasses of Europe, and the Indian "savage" was replaced with the "civilized" cowboy, the errant knight of the new Christian order. The winning of the west was viewed by many historians and moralists of the day as a victory for Christianity.

If Winthrop offered "salvation," it was Benjamin Franklin and his philosophical heirs who offered "betterment." It came in the form of the operating principles of the European Enlightenment. Making God's garden fruitful required a new form of husbandry, one grounded in the utilitarian framework. For every act of revelation, the pioneers were administered a dose of utilitarian rationality, making Americans, at one and the same time, the most fervently religious and aggressively pragmatic of the western peoples—a status they retain to this day.

European theologians had prepared the ground for Enlightenment thought with their emphasis on a "man-centered" vision of the created order.[3] In Judeo-Christian theology, man is created in God's image and given "dominion" over the rest of God's handiwork. After the flood, God says to Noah:

> The fear of you and the dread of you shall be upon every beast of the earth, and upon every fowl of the air, upon all that moveth upon the earth, and upon all the fishes of the sea; into your hands are they delivered.[4]

Enlightenment thinkers were convinced that the world around them was designed by God in a rational manner to serve the utilitarian ends of humankind. Francis Bacon, a pre-Enlightenment thinker and the father of modern science, wrote:

> Man, if we look for final causes, may be regarded as the center of the world, insomuch that if man were taken away from the world, the rest would seem to be all astray, without aim or purpose.[5]

Bacon believed it possible to use man's rational faculties to gain "objective knowledge" of God's order and by using that knowledge "enlarge the bounds of human empire to the effecting of all things possible."[6] Using the scientific method, Bacon argued that nature could be "forced out of her natural state and squeezed and molded."[7] Sharing Bacon's enthusiasm, Enlightenment thinkers turned their attention and their considerable intellects to the task of prying open nature's many useful secrets, believing that once nature was known, "it may be mastered, managed and used in the service of human life."[8] Centuries of Christian dogma extolling man's privileged position in the created order provided the theological justification for the "rational" conquest of nature. Subduing nature, said Bacon, "never burdened a conscience with remorse."[9]

The utilitarian spirit of the Enlightenment led to a wholesale denaturing of creation. René Descartes, a mathematician by trade, advanced the radical new idea of nature as a machine. In Descartes's new utilitarian world, God, the benevolent and caring shepherd of Christendom, was replaced with God, the remote and cold technician, who created and set in motion a machinelike universe that was orderly, predictable, and self-perpetuating. Descartes stripped nature of its aliveness, reducing both the creation and the creatures to mathematical and mechanical analogues. He even described animals as "soulless automata" whose movements were little different from those of the automated puppetry that danced upon the Strasbourg clock.[10]

Intellectuals of the day were quickly won over by Descartes's vision. Scientists anxious to learn of the mechanical workings of nature's "living" machines often engaged in barbaric experiments.

> [They] administered beatings to dogs with perfect indifference, and made fun of those that pitied the creatures as if they felt pain. They said the animals were clocks; that the cries they emitted when struck were only the noise of a little spring that had been touched, but that the whole body was without feeling. They nailed poor animals upon boards by their four paws to vivisect them and see the circulation of the blood which was a great subject of conversation.[11]

Descartes acknowledged the utilitarian benefits of describing the creation in mechanistic terms. After all, if other creatures were, in fact, mere machines without souls, then men could be absolved "from the suspicion of crime when they eat or kill animals."[12]

The mechanistic utilitarianism of the Enlightenment helped ease the burden of guilt of European farmers, pastoralists, merchants, and landed gentry busily engaged in draining lowland marshes, clearing forests, shooting "game," slaughtering livestock, and enclosing commonly held lands in the early modern era.

Enlightenment thinkers became far more interested in making nature productive than in restoring a fallen nature. The wilderness was less and less viewed as an evil terrain that needed to be redeemed and more as an unproductive resource that needed to be harnessed for the material benefit of mankind. John Locke, the political philosopher of the Enlightenment, argued that "land . . . left wholly to nature, is called as indeed it is waste."[13] He believed that the living creatures and inanimate materials that make up the earth have no intrinsic value, only utility value. Earthly phenomena become valuable only after human labor and machine technology transforms them into useful materials, products, goods, and services. Like many of his contemporaries, Locke believed in transforming all of nature into a vast store of productive wealth. "The negation of nature," he wrote, "is the way to happiness."[14]

In Europe, the utilitarian thinking of the Enlightenment outgrew its theological roots, transforming the culture of a continent from a spiritual to a secular order in less than 200 years. In the United States, however, Christian millennial thinking continued to inspire the passions of newly arrived immigrant groups, many of whom were fleeing the religious oppression and secularism of Europe. The new spirit of utilitarianism also found a welcome home in America as immigrants set about the task of taming a continent, transforming a wilderness into a productive resource. The combination of Christian evangelical fervor and utilitarian ardor proved a powerful force on the American frontier.

The American west was the new Eden, the boundless cornucopia that Enlightenment thinkers had envisioned, a treasure trove of pristine resources that human beings might harness for the betterment of present and future generations. To Europeans and Americans alike, the west was the land of opportunity, the field of dreams upon which "man" could build his age of progress.

Though conditions were harsh on the plains, they did not dampen the unbridled enthusiasm of young southern migrants anxious to start anew after the destruction of their native soil during the Civil War. Nor were the dangers enough to quell the hopes and aspirations of waves of European immigrants—German, Swedish, Irish, Scotch—in search of a better way of life in the New World.

Surveying the western expanse, the first pioneers—cowboys, ranchers, railroadmen—were no doubt impressed by the great potential that lay stretched out before them, though aware of the enormity of the task that lay ahead. The words of the French aristocrat and Enlightenment thinker the Marquis de Condorcet provided an appropriate refrain for the new consciousness being born on the prairie. A hundred years earlier, in the midst of the French Revolution, he wrote passionately of a new Age of Progress rising like a phoenix from the ashes of the old medieval order:

No bounds have been fixed to the improvement of the human faculties. . . . The perfectibility of man is absolutely indefinite. . . . The progress of their perfectibility, henceforth, above the control of every power that would impede it, has no other limit than the duration of the globe upon which nature has placed us.[15]

The American west represented "unlimited free land," and free land represented unlimited opportunity and progress.[16] Upon official notice of the closing of the American frontier in 1890, historian Frederic Jackson Turner wrote:

Up to our own day American history has been in a large degree the history of the colonization of the Great West. The existence of an area of free land, its continuous recession, and the advance of American settlement westward, explain American development. . . . Since the days when the fleet of Columbus sailed into the waters of the new world, America has been another name for opportunity and the people of the United States have taken their tone from incessant expansion which has not only been open but has been forced upon them.[17]

Turner's thesis in *The Frontier in American History* captured the psychology of a people caught between Old World restraints and New World possibilities. The Americans, he said, are a restless people, anxious to leave tradition behind in search of ever new opportunities. Turner viewed the frontier as "the meeting point between savagery and civilization" and argued that it served as a cleansing ground for the continuous renewal of a people. Americans, he said, are "continually beginning over again on the frontier," their sights always fixed on the immediate future.[18]

This perennial rebirth, this fluidity of American life, this expansion westward with its new opportunities, its continuous touch with the simplicity of primitive society, furnish the forces dominating the American character.[19]

Less anchored to the past than their European ancestors, and far more concerned with the immediate advantages that lie just over the horizon, the Americans adopted a wholly new time orientation, becoming a kind of temporal nomad, living only for the morrow. Their future-directed temporal orientation played well against the spatial

realities of the American west. The American frontiersman learned
to use time to the best advantage on the open plains. Opportunities
needed to be seized, situations quickly grasped and exploited, to
survive and prosper on the prairies. Men and women needed to be
inventive, quick-witted, and manipulative in the taming of a continent. Here was a new man and woman in the making, unfettered
by tradition or sentiment, unresponsive to past allegiances and obligations, cued to the utilitarian needs of the moment.

> The result is that to the frontier the American intellect owes its
> striking characteristics. That coarseness and strength combined with
> acuteness and inquisitiveness; that practical, inventive turn of mind,
> quick to find expedients; that masterful grasp of material things,
> lacking in the artistic but powerful to effect great ends; that restless,
> nervous energy; that dominant individualism, working for good
> and for evil, and with all that buoyancy and exuberance which comes
> with freedom—these are traits of the frontier.[20]

The character traits of the frontier man and woman reflected the
Enlightenment view of the world, with its emphasis on material
acquisition, naked self-interest, autonomy, rationality, entrepreneu-
rialism, scientific prowess, mechanization, market efficiency, and social mobility.

The emerging cattle complex incorporated all of these values and
more, making it the dominant social and political force in the west
and, for a time, in the country. The cowboy was romanticized for
his individualism and his ability to fend for himself. Ranchers were
praised for their wiliness and ingenuity, and above all their inven-
tiveness. Eliminating the Indians' commissary—the buffalo—to
make room for the longhorn steer, linking northern and eastern
markets to southern and western cattle country by way of the railroad, enclosing and commodifying western rangeland with mile
upon mile of barbed-wire fences, inventing sophisticated refrigeration storage technologies to ferry American beef to European markets, and restructuring agriculture to feed surplus grain to cattle were
all part of an elaborate rationalizing process designed to make optimum commercial use of a vast subcontinent of natural resources.

Then too, it was the slaughterhouses of Chicago, we need recall,
that were the first to employ the principles of scientific management,

applying engineering principles to the processing of beef. Mass production, division of labor, specialization, assembly-line production, and efficiency standards were tried and tested in the packinghouses of Chicago decades before they became commonplace in the rest of American industry.

If the cattle complex was viewed by some as the first outpost of civilization on the frontier and a vanguard of the Christian millennial reign, for others it was a powerful vehicle to exploit the riches of a subcontinent. So effective was the combination of Christian evangelism and Enlightenment utilitarianism on the frontier that in the thirty-three years separating the peace at Appomattox from the first shots of the Spanish-American War, the American cattle complex was able to subdue, enclose, and commodify one of the world's great ecosystems, transforming it into a commercial resource to be exploited in the international marketplace.

By the 1890s the frontier was gone, but the frontier mythology continued to live on, embellished and reworked from time to time, to suit the psychosocial needs of successive generations determined to hold on to the core values that formed the American character. For a nation unused to limits or restraints of any kind, the frontier image continues to be the most powerful and evocative of our national symbols, helping us to maintain our belief in unlimited material progress and the future perfectibility of the human race.

37

The Hamburger and the Highway Culture

In the twentieth century the idea of frontier shifted from the wilderness to the emergent suburbs. The end of the westward migration signaled the beginning of a new migration, this one from city to countryside. Where the old frontier had been viewed by Frederick Jackson Turner as the meeting place between savagery and civilization, the new suburban frontier was viewed as the meeting place between an urban and rural way of life. The struggle between civilization and savagery was replaced with a new struggle between progressive and old-fashioned ways of living. The suburban existence has become the new vaunted image of progress, the vision of unlimited material advance and earthly salvation toward which most Americans strive. As was the case on the western frontier, the cattle complex played a significant role in the taming of the new suburban frontier.

The suburbanization of the American countryside was made possible, in large part, by the invention of the automobile and the creation of a highway culture. The new high-speed form of individual transportation helped spawn a massive shift in population out of the cities and into the surrounding countryside. Today, 60 percent of all metropolitan residents live in suburbs.[1] The new suburban way of life brought with it a basic change in work habits and life-styles. The nomadic restiveness characteristic of the pioneering community on the western frontier continued to manifest itself in the highly mobile highway culture. To be a suburbanite was to be constantly on the road, ferrying back and forth between downtown offices and suburban schools, shopping centers, and neighborhoods. Indeed, the quality of always being "on the go," an American trait first observed by de Tocqueville, was as much a part of the new suburban way of life as it was a century earlier among pioneers picking up stakes and moving west. Even today, 18 percent of all Americans change residence every year.[2]

The new suburban frontier changed the eating habits of the nation as effectively as it changed the spatial and temporal orientation of the country. The suburban life-style required convenience, efficiency, and predictability in its food preparation and consumption to accommodate the new fast-paced, highly mobile life-styles of the highway culture. The beef industry responded, making the hamburger and the fast-food restaurant chains synonymous with the new suburban way of life. The story of how the hamburger was used to tame the suburban frontier is a poignant reminder of the influence the American cattle complex still exerts over the affairs of the nation even in this postindustrial period.

The psychological and cultural impact of the hamburger has been impressive and extensive. As a symbol of America, the hamburger has surpassed even the American automobile in the eyes of the rest of the world, becoming the quintessential symbol of the American dream and life-style. Today, people line up in Stockholm and Tokyo waiting to file under the "golden arches" of McDonald's and become part of "the American experience."

Every second, 200 Americans purchase one or more hamburgers at a fast-food outlet, resulting in billions of dollars of revenue for American restaurant chains. Each American consumes, on the average, between 26 and 29 pounds of ground beef per year.[3] Nearly 40 percent of all the beef consumed is now ground beef, most of it in the form of hamburger.[4]

The story of the American hamburger—its origin and development—provides a mirror of the values and sensibilities of the current century. By becoming part of the hamburger culture, Americans and now other people throughout the world buy far more than a quarter pound of beef. With every purchase, the consumer secures a lien on the American worldview, its operating principles, vision, and goals. It was this worldview, more than simply two fried patties on a sesame bun, that sparked near-riots in Moscow when McDonald's first opened its doors to a people hungry to taste the American way of life.

Chopped beef dates back to the Eurasian steppes, the birthplace of the Euro-American cattle cultures. The medieval Tartars were the first to eat a primitive form of the hamburger, raw beef seasoned with salt, pepper, and onion juice, later known as steak tartar. German merchants brought the recipe to Hamburg, where they tailored it to local taste—making it into patties and broiling it before serving. German immigrants brought the "hamburger" to America in the nineteenth century; according to legend, it was first put between two pieces of bread at an Ohio county fair in 1892.[5] The hamburger came to national attention, say other food authorities, at the St. Louis World's Fair in 1904.[6] The sandwich proved immensely popular with the throngs of fairgoers because it could be prepared quickly and could be eaten on the run, without utensils. It was, in short, fast, efficient, and convenient, qualities that were fast becoming the trademark of twentieth-century American life.

The hamburger owes much of its success to the coming of the auto age. The new form of transportation and the new way of eating went hand in hand, each reinforcing the success of the other and both reflecting the new worldview that was reorienting waves of immigrants to the fast-paced American way of doing things.

The automobile seemed a welcome surrogate for a restless people suddenly confronted by the official closing of their own western frontier. One city official gushed that the automobile would be "the magic carpet of transportation for all mankind."[7] The automobile put Americans back on the trail once again, creating a renewed sense of movement, the one temporal value that had so distinguished the American experience since its inception.

The westward movement was replaced by the highway culture in the twentieth century. The first paved highway was laid between Detroit and the Wayne County Fair Grounds in 1909. By 1925, Henry Ford was turning out 9,000 cars a day, and paved highways were being laid out across the country.[8] Two years later, over 26 million automobiles were scurrying back and forth on freshly laid cement corridors. The first automobile expressway, the Bronx River Parkway, was already in use, shuttling commuters between New York City and White Plains, New York, and several other high-speed expressways were under construction.

Automobile production and highway expansion were put on hold during World War II, only to be resurrected with a missionary zeal in the postwar era. In 1956, President Dwight Eisenhower signed into law the Interstate Highway Act, providing for the construction of a network of superhighways, stretching some 41,000 miles and connecting every region of the country into a single unified transportation grid. The federal government was to pay 90 percent of the cost of construction in what was to be the most expensive and ambitious public works project in the history of the world.[9] Less than thirty years later, at a cost of $350 billion, the U.S. Interstate Highway System was completed. Its construction paved the way for the "highway culture," a wholesale change in living arrangements, work patterns, and life-styles that transformed the American cultural landscape.

The U.S. highway system helped spawn a neo-nomadic culture. The average American now travels some 9,600 miles per year in his or her automobile. With 140 million automobiles now in use, Americans can justly claim the distinction of being the most traveled people of any culture in history.

Today Americans are continually on the go. Our fast-paced, mobile life-style requires changes not only in spatial and temporal arrangements but in eating habits as well. The answer came in the form of the hamburger, a food product that embodied many of the same values and features as the new form of transportation that was reorienting the life-style of the American public. The first glimmer of a potential relationship came in the early 1920s when White Castle opened up its first hamburger outlet in Wichita, Kansas.[10] The firm catered to the new clock-conscious urban commuters, providing uniformly prepared hamburgers that could be purchased and eaten in a matter of minutes. Many customers ordered their burgers to go, preferring to wolf down a sackful of the tiny fried beef treats in their cars as they drove to and from their daily rounds.

In 1925, Howard Johnson opened up the first of its Georgian-style restaurants in New England, providing roadside fare for weary travelers.[11] Small diners became popular about the same time. Many of the early diners were converted trolley cars. By the 1930s, companies like P. J. Tierney & Sons began constructing fully modernized diners, designed to look like first-class railroad diners. Sporting names like the Fenway Flyer and Rocket Diner, these mobile-looking restaurants begin popping up along streets and highways, especially along the Atlantic seaboard and in New England. With their sleek appearance, easy access, and fast service, they cornered much of the highway market.[12]

In the opening decades of the century, virtually every industry seemed intent on copying the lead of the automotive industry, each attempting to streamline its activities, to create a fast-paced service and products as uniform, predictable, and inexpensive as the cars Henry Ford was turning out on his Detroit assembly lines.

It was one of Ford's major competitors, Charles Mott, the founder of General Motors, who opined that "it would be hard to name a branch of human activity . . . not made to function more smoothly and more effectively in the service of humanity because of the . . . automobile."[13] Certainly the restaurant trade was already well along the way to turning the act of eating into something akin to an assembly-line process. The cafeteria was invented in Chicago near the turn of the century, and by World War II was a staple in cities across the country. Customers pushed their trays down a metal counter, picking up already prepared dishes along the way, like so many automatons. Joseph V. Horn and F. Hardart introduced the first automat in Philadelphia in 1902. By the time FDR took office in 1932, thousands of hungry Americans in cities like New York were busy opening up countless little glass compartments in search of a quick meal.[14]

Fast service required fast food. The hamburger proved to be the ideal choice for the new auto age. It was not only cheap and easy to prepare, but also highly manipulable. It could be molded, made uniform, and mass-produced. Hamburger patties were eminently manageable.

The hamburger "took off" after World War II. By the mid-1950s it had become a near-craze, eclipsing apple pie as the food most identified with America. The hamburger's ultimate ascendance came in the 1950s as millions of suburbanites took to the backyard barbecue. Although hamburgers had made a slow gain in popularity during the first half of the century, it was not until the new suburbanites of the 1950s began barbecuing in backyards on weekends that hamburgers became an indispensable part of the American diet.

It was on the backyard grills that beef finally triumphed over its nearest competitor and longtime rival, pork. For over 200 years, beef and pork producers had competed with each other for the taste buds of the American consumer. In New England, beef had always been the preferred meat, whereas in the southeast, pork had ruled supreme. In the middle Atlantic and the midwestern states, the cow and the pig were about evenly matched, while in the southwestern states, plains states, and western states, beef was king. The outdoor barbecue grill helped give beef the advantage and, in the process, helped propel the hamburger into the national limelight.

Pork patties could not be effectively cooked on the new outdoor grills. They would crumble and fall through the grate onto the charcoal, ruining many a meal. Equally important, says anthropologist Marvin Harris, pork patties had to be cooked much longer than beef patties because of the very real danger of trichinosis.[15] Harris points out that the USDA does not inspect pork for trichinosis. The procedure would be far too costly and time-consuming, requiring that each cut of meat be put under a microscope for detailed examination. Because pork is not inspected, says Harris, "About 4 percent of Americans have trichinella worms in their muscles and mistake their trichinosis flare-ups for mild cases of the flu."[16]

To address the potential health dangers of eating pork, the USDA, the Surgeon General, and the American Medical Association launched an ambitious public education campaign in the 1930s designed to educate housewives on the precautionary need to cook pork thoroughly until it turns "from pink to gray." Says Harris, "these warnings ruled out the grilling of pork chops, which upon turning gray through and through, also turned tough and dry through and through."[17] Barbecued spareribs provided a possible alternative and have been cooked on backyard grills. Because they are well soaked in sauce, they maintain their juiciness, but, as Harris points out, they are too messy, offer less meat, and can't be put between a bun. In all of these particulars, beef patties proved more convenient than pork.

Hamburgers triumphed for still another reason—the beef industry's influence in Washington. The story of the hamburger's ascendance has as much to do with government regulation and market forces as personal taste and convenience. Harris explains how an obscure code of federal regulations adopted in 1946 virtually guaranteed the hamburger unchallenged market dominance in the postwar era. The USDA Code defines the hamburger as "a ground meat patty which contains no meat or fat other than beef or beef fat." If a hamburger contains even "a smidgeon of pork or pork fat," it cannot be classified as a "hamburger."[18] Equally important, because the government regulations allow up to 30 percent of the patty to be derived from beef fat, the packinghouses can mix beef and beef fat from "entirely different animals."[19] These two provisions ensured the beef industry a lock on the meat trade in the second half of the twentieth century.

As Harris points out, the cheapest beef is grass-fed cattle. Because range meat is not laced with marbled fat, if it is ground up into hamburger meat and made into patties, it will crumble on the grill, just like pork patties. To ensure firmness, the beef has to be mixed with fat. Any fat, animal or vegetable, would bind the beef, but because USDA regulation requires that only beef fat be used, the beef industry has been able to monopolize the market. The impact of this single regulation has been far-reaching. Says Harris, "Let hamburger be made of pork with beef fat, or beef with pork fat, or prevent hamburgers from being made of beef fat from one animal plus beef from another, and the entire beef industry would collapse overnight." By monopolizing the ingredients and being able to mix beef and beef fat from different animals, the beef industry was able to create an international beef patty that was cheap and affordable, achieving precisely the edge it needed to overcome the "pig's natural superiority as a converter of grain to flesh."[20]

The beef companies import cheap range-fed beef from Central America, Australia, New Zealand, and other countries and grind it up along with the waste fat from grain-fed cattle in the United States to make the American hamburger. In fact, a percentage of many "American" hamburgers is imported beef.[21] Over the past thirty years, the hamburger has risen to national prominence, partially at the expense of native people in other countries, especially Central America. Much of their land, as noted earlier, has been confiscated and commercially enclosed to provide cheap range-fed cattle for the American market. In his book *Beyond the Myths of Culture*, Eric Ross summed up the intimate connection that exists between the all-American hamburger and the exploitation of other lands and peoples:

> Much of the postwar rise in beef consumption resulted from the mass availability of hamburger. . . . Beef burgers had much greater potential for market expansion since their producers could appropriate grassland in Latin America to modulate prices, while domestic pork and beef, based on increasingly expensive grain, become more costly. . . . Thus, the most dramatic rise in United States beef consumption since 1960 coincided . . . with the rapid rise in U.S. beef imports that began in the early 1960s. . . . American beef consumption continues to rest upon the availability of grassland—but, now, as part of a process of international capitalist underdevelopment in which arable land is actually being converted to cattle pasture and being withdrawn from local subsistence production.[22]

The entire process, says Ross, is strikingly reminiscent of the English expropriation of Irish grassland in the eighteenth and nineteenth centuries:

> Clearly what has emerged is a direct descendant of the paradigmatic colonial relationship between England and Ireland where Irish tenant farmers were reduced to a marginal consumption while they produced . . . cattle for export to England.[23]

Both cheap and convenient, the hamburger helped usher in a new dietary regime—fast foods. The American life-style changed dramatically in the aftermath of World War II. More women were entering the work force, many assuming jobs in the new white-collar and service industries. With less time available to cook in the suburban home, families turned to already-prepared foods for the first time. Frozen TV dinners made their debut in the 1950s. Snacks like potato chips and individually packaged pies and cakes became popular. Frozen hamburger patties became the all-purpose dinner staple, something that could be cooked up at the last moment after both working parents arrived home, tired and exhausted from a long workday and from battling rush-hour traffic.

With both parents working, dining out became a regular feature of daily life, whereas before it had been reserved for special occasions or weekend entertainment. Between 1948 and 1985 "the share of total food dollars spent away from home increased from 24 to 43 percent."[24] Most of that increase has occurred in the fast-food industry.

Today, going out to eat has become synonymous with taking the family for a hamburger at one of the country's ubiquitous fast-food chain restaurants. Between 1948 and 1982, the fast-food industry grew from an 8 percent to a 30 percent share of the away-from-home food market.[25] There are now over 583,000 food service outlets across the country, feeding 100 million Americans every day. Over 42 percent of the total United States population now eats out at least once a day.[26] In a twelve-month period, America's food service industry serves over 78 billion meals and is responsible for the sale of 40 percent of all the meat consumed in the country. Its revenues exceed $207 billion and it employs over 8 million people, making it the largest employer of any industry in the United States.[27]

If credit can be extended to a single person for the success of the hamburger and the fast-food industry, then certainly the distinction is due Ray Kroc, the indefatigable founder of the McDonald's restaurant chain. Kroc revolutionized American eating habits during the postwar era. Today the chain he built boasts 11,000 restaurants in fifty-two countries employing 600,000 people with an annual sales revenue of $17 billion.[28] Over half of the population of the United States lives within a three-minute drive of a McDonald's restaurant. The chain now controls over 10 percent of the "away from home" food business.[29] McDonald's purchases over 1 percent of all the beef wholesaled in the United States. Every month, tens of thousands of head of cattle have to be fattened, slaughtered, and ground into patties to provide millions of hamburgers to hungry customers.[30]

Kroc changed American eating habits as effectively as Henry Ford changed the way Americans traveled. And he did so using many of the same operating principles and values that put the nation on wheels. Kroc realized, early on, the vast potential that lay along the interchanges of the United States highway system. The highway culture had spawned a new way of life with its suburban tracts, shopping malls, and office parks tucked away just off the nation's interstates. Kroc was determined to bring the auto culture, the suburbs, and the fast-food hamburger together in a single complex, and he set about the task with an almost missionary zeal.

In the early 1960s, Kroc began crisscrossing the country in his company's plane. From on high, he looked down with binoculars, pinpointing traffic intersections, suburban developments, and shopping centers, all nexus points for the fast-growing highway culture. Like a general pinning flags on a war map, Kroc placed a McDonald's restaurant at every strategic location, McDonaldizing much of the suburban landscape in less than a generation.[31] His entrepreneurial fervor bordered on the messianic, as he himself noted in his own memoirs. Kroc once remarked:

> I speak of faith in McDonald's as if it were a religion. And without meaning any offense to the Holy Trinity, the Koran, or the Torah, that's exactly the way I think of it. I've often said that I believe in God, family, and McDonald's—and in the office, that order is reversed.[32]

It is interesting to note that church steeples played a prominent role in Kroc's strategic planning. He consciously placed his restaurants near suburban churches, believing that the pure, wholesome image of his restaurant and the neighboring church would shine as a beacon of light on each other. Not surprisingly, Kroc had early on targeted the suburban churchgoing families as his prime market audience.[33] Even his golden arches, say some social commentators, bore a striking resemblance to pictorial images of the gates of heaven.

Kroc hoped to create the image of a sanctuary, a place his hungry flock could retreat to, away from the din and roar of an unpredictable and chaotic world. Pilgrims could rest and be refreshed, knowing that everything would be orderly, predictable, and above all efficient, the secular catechism of the new suburban spirituality.

Kroc offered a new kind of "peace of mind," one nurtured in the soil of high technology and machine performance. He replaced "good works" with "efficiency" and eternal salvation with "a break today" at McDonald's. His call to the faithful was heard in suburban neighborhoods around the country. By 1991, millions of people had converted to the McDonald's liturgy. Today more people eat at McDonald's in a month than attend the churches and synagogues of the country.[34]

While Kroc's zeal is legendary, it was his organizing style that made the hamburger and fast foods an integral part of American life and a symbol of the new mobile life-style of late-twentieth-century America.

Kroc successfully integrated engineering standards into the preparation and marketing of hamburgers just as the meat-packers had in their industry half a century earlier. Quality controls, predictability of outcome, quantifiable standards of analysis, efficiency, and utility were to become the modus operandi of McDonald's, as well as of the scores of fast-food imitators that popped up around the country in the postwar period.

Uniformity and speed were the critical factors in McDonald's formula for success. To advance these goals, Kroc relied on the same principles of "scientific management" that efficiency expert Frederick Taylor had employed in other industries earlier in the century. Every process at McDonald's is broken down into its component parts, with precise written instructions given to its largely unskilled employees on how to carry out each task assigned to them. Nothing is left to personal initiative or guesswork. Instead, a 385-page operating manual, McDonald's in-house bible, prescribes every single procedure in meticulous detail.[35] Deviation from the market plan is not tolerated by management.

The McDonald's process began with the standardization and uniformity of the beef patties themselves.

> This basic machine-cut hamburger patty weighed 1.6 ounces, measured 3.875 inches in diameter, and contained no lungs, heart, cereal, or soybeans. In each pound of meat there were ten hamburgers, that were to contain no more than 19 percent fat. Everything was calculated down to the exact size of the bun (3.5 inches wide) and the amount of onions that went on it (one-fourth of an ounce). In addition, the bun had to have a higher-than-normal sugar content for faster browning.[36]

Kroc left nothing to chance. In his memoirs he reminisced over the care and attention paid to the tiniest details, even the choice of wax paper to separate the layers of patties and the procedure for stacking the patties.

> It had to have enough wax on it so that the patty would pop off without sticking when you slapped it onto the griddle. But it couldn't be too stiff or the patties would slide and refuse to stack

up. There was also a science in stacking the patties. If you made the stack too high, the ones on the bottom would be misshapen and dried out. So we arrived at the optimum stack, and that determined the height of our meat suppliers' packages.[37]

At McDonald's, as at the other fast-food franchises that followed, the cook is eliminated altogether, his or her role replaced by auto-mated high-tech machines that tell their unskilled attendants exactly what to do and when to do it. On the McDonald's grills, "blinking lights" even tell the counterman when to flip the burgers.[38]

Kroc was impressed with what the young Ford had achieved with his Model T. He remembered Ford saying, "I don't care what color they want as long as it's black." Kroc applied the same principle of standardization to his hamburger. Each was identical to the one be-fore. Customers were not allowed to garnish their burger according to their individual taste. To do so would slow up the line, reduce efficiency, and increase the expense of production. Kroc was adamant on this point: "The minute you get into customizing, you're on an individual basis. The cost of the product is exactly the same, but the labor triples. We can't do that."[39]

Kroc allocated a mere fifty seconds to serve a McDonald's ham-burger, shake, and french fries.[40] By the later 1970s, he was churning out billions of burgers on his assembly lines and had already taken his place alongside Ford as one of the great innovators of twentieth-century production processes.

While the early meat-packing giants were the first to use assem-bly-line production to slaughter cattle and package beef, Kroc succeeded in enclosing the remainder of the process, applying in-dustrial-design techniques to the preparation of the final product. Harvard Business School professor Theodore Levitt described Kroc's great accomplishments:

A McDonald's retail outlet is a machine that produces a highly polished product. Through painstaking attention to total design and facilities planning, everything is built integrally into the machine itself, into the technology of the system. The only choice available to the attendant is to operate it exactly as the designers intended. McDonald's is a supreme example of the application of manufac-turing and technological brilliance to problems that must ultimately be viewed as marketing problems.[41]

Today the process of eating has been reduced to the same set of Enlightenment assumptions that governs much of the rest of contemporary society. As in the past, the beef industry played a prominent role in helping to shape and define the current culture. Now even the ultimate consumer of beef has been reconditioned in his or her eating habits to the principles of rational organization, the science of mechanization, quality controls, quantifiable standards, predictable outcomes, and the efficient and utilitarian use of time.

The same technological criteria used to manipulate cattle on the factory farm feedlot and slaughterhouse disassembly lines have been used effectively to manage workers' performance on the kill floors of the nation's abattoirs and to reorient consumers' eating habits in the waiting lines at the nation's fast-food outlets. Each element in the modern cattle complex—cattle, workers, consumers—is now viewed as a unit of production and consumption in a profit-driven, utilitarian framework.

Still the American experience is viewed with anticipation and longing by millions of people in other countries in search of "the good life." Many continue to view membership in the exclusive beef club as a sign of having arrived, of being part of the chosen few. For that reason, they line up at McDonald's in cities around the world, the utilitarian spirit of the age drowning out any reservations they might entertain about the Faustian bargain they are entering into. Den Fujita, the chief of McDonald's Japanese operations, captured the power of the new beef icon when he exclaimed, "If we eat hamburgers for a thousand years, we will become blond. And when we become blond we can conquer the world."[42]

38

The Deconstruction of Modern Meat

The cow is among the most placid of animals. In temperament, she seems peaceful, contented. She sees the world dimly, lacking the yellow spot on the retina (macula lutea) that helps bring objects in the environment into sharp focus. Her sense of smell and taste are highly developed and sensitive to the slightest changes. She grazes in an almost somnambulant state, as if withdrawn and preoccupied. She seems to exist in another world, a haven far removed from the fits and starts that jar the sensibilities of other animals.

The bull radiates strength. His mass is concentrated in the front of his body. He has a powerful neck. His hindquarters are slender and seem barely able to support his broad frame.[1] His gait is determined, alert, the full thrust of his body always ready to lunge forward. The bull is territorial. His eyes are intense, his gaze baleful. His being appears uncompromising and dignified.

Modern meat is a testimonial to the utilitarian ethos. The spirit of the animal is ruthlessly repressed and deadened shortly after birth. Cattle are castrated, injected with hormones and antibiotics, sprayed with insecticides, placed on a cement slab, and fed grains, sawdust, sludge, and sewage until they reach the appropriate weight. The animals are transported by truck to automated slaughterhouses, where they are killed, disassembled into their constituent parts, mixed, molded, shaped, and reconstituted into useful products and by-products that are far removed from the sentient creatures from which they were derived.

Children of the industrial world have little relationship to or understanding of the animals they incorporate into their bodies three or more times a week. Youngsters are often shocked on coming upon a beef carcass hanging in a butcher shop. They have grown up to think of meat as "a thing," a piece of material produced by the same processes that provide them with toys, clothes, and other such things.

The rank utilitarianism of the modern era has merged with the rational production processes of industrial technology, transforming cattle into so much manipulative matter whose worth is measured exclusively in market terms. The modern cattle complex, in both its organization and goals, is reflective of the state of mind of the modern age. Like nature itself, cattle have been stripped of their intrinsic value, reduced to a resource and then to a commodity, further reduced into an array of commercial products to be consumed and discarded back into the environment in various stages of entropic decay.

In modern cattle production a 1,000-pound steer "dresses out" to approximately 620 pounds of carcass after being disassembled on the slaughterhouse floor. The carcass yields about 540 pounds of retail meat products.[2] Cuts of beef include round steak, top round, bottom round, rolled rump, rump roast, sirloin steak, porterhouse steak, T-bone steak, club steak, flank steak, rolled flank, hind flank, standing rib roast, rib steak, pot roast, ground beef, beef brisket, corned beef, and short ribs.

Beef is made up of "lean muscle, fatty and connective tissue, bones, and skin. In addition, there are blood vessels, lymphatic vessels, glands, and nerve tissue."[3] Fat is found under the skin and between the muscles. The muscles themselves are made up of cells that are tubular in shape. The muscle cells are bound together by a "network of connective tissue." Connective tissue is concentrated at the end of the muscles to form tendons which "affix the muscle to the bone." Lean muscle may contain up to 75 percent water. The remainder is approximately 20 percent meat protein, 3 percent fat, 1 percent mineral matter, glycogen, and other organic substances.

Cattle bones contain 30 to 40 percent water, 15 to 20 percent fat, and 15 to 20 percent protein. The rest is mineral matter.[4]

The glycogen in the muscle tissue produces a preservative, lactic acid, after the death of an animal. If the animal is frightened or physically abused just before slaughter, it is likely to use up its glycogen reserve. "Excited, frightened, and overheated animals will not bleed fully, and their dead flesh will be pink or fiery, making them unattractive carcasses."[5] A variety of procedures are used to tenderize meat. Chemical methods are common. Aging methods, controlled temperature environments, and mechanical stimulation are also used to tenderize the meat.

In recent years, the beef-packing industry has turned to "formed, fabricated, and restructured" meat products.[6] New production technologies now allow producers to break down meat and restructure it into simulated versions of high-quality cuts. Simulated steaks are often indistinguishable in texture and taste from the real cuts and easier to maintain quality controls over during the production and packaging process.

> Formed or molded meat products are achieved by applying mechanical work, or energy, to chunks of uncooked whole meat, either fresh or cured, using methods such as mechanical mixing, churning, pounding, tumbling, or massaging, in such a way that the chunks of meat become soft and pliable, and develop a creamy, tacky exudate on their surfaces. In addition . . . formed products also provide a better uniformity of color, texture, and fat distribution.[7]

In an earlier chapter, we discussed the new process of vacuum-wrapped boxed beef that has become standard in the packing industry. By customizing beef into portion-controlled individual cuts, packers are able to recycle trimmed fat, bones, and other waste parts from the carcass for use in a range of cattle by-products. Boxed beef saves retailers warehouse space and the cost of employing full-time butchers.

Only around 54 percent of a slaughtered steer is actually used as beef products for human and pet consumption. More than 40 percent of the animal—fat, bones, viscera, hide—is converted by renderers into a range of substances, materials, and products used in the preparation of other foods, household products, pharmaceuticals, and industrial products.[8] Collagen, an element of the connective tissues, is used in glue and in sausage casings. Collagen-based adhesives are also used in wallpaper, glues, bandages, emery boards, and plasterboard. Gelatin is used in ice cream, candies, yogurt, mayonnaise, and other foods, as well as in photographic film and phonograph records. Beef fat and fatty acids are used in shoe cream, crayons, floor wax, oleomargarine, cosmetics, deodorants, detergents, soaps, perfumes, insecticides, linoleum, insulation, and freon. The hoofs and horns are used in combs, piano keys, and imitation ivory. The hides are used in leather goods, upholstery, shoes, and luggage. The hair is used in paintbrushes. Insulin from the pancreas is used to treat diabetes. Glucagon from the pancreas is used to treat hypoglycemia. Trypsin and chymotrypsin are used to treat burns and wounds. Pancreatin is used as an aid in digestion. Cattle blood plasma is used to treat hemophilia and anemia. Thrombin is a blood coagulant. Bone marrow is used to treat people with blood disorders and soft cartilage is even used in plastic surgery. The intestines are used as medical sutures. ACTH from the pituitary gland is used to alleviate arthritis and allergies. Cattle by-products are also used as binders for asphalt paving and as cutting oils and industrial lubricants. It is said in the beef industry that they use everything but the moo.[9]

Of course, the bovine has long been the object of human use. From time immemorial, human beings have relied on cattle and other animals for food, clothing, shelter, traction, fuel, and other necessities. The primary difference between ancient cultures and our modern society is the substitution of a technologically mediated relationship with the animal for a personal one.

In ancient cultures, an intimate relationship existed between man and beast. Human beings lived in close contact with other animals, be they domestic or wild. Because the human and animal worlds were so closely linked, people identified strongly with their prey, often to the point of taking on their attributes or projecting their own sensibilities onto the animals. Animals were very much a part of the human world and the social order. In hunting cultures, much of the social life of the community, including its rituals, revolved around a relationship to the wild beasts. In herding cultures, human beings and their domesticated animals coexisted, sharing their daily rounds.

Early on, human beings realized that the other animals were not all that different from themselves. They shared similar physical and behavioral characteristics. They could think and act, show affection and love, look out for their self-interests, protect their young, and provide for their futures. The similarities were enough to trouble people about killing and consuming other animals.

To resolve ambivalent feelings about killing and eating other sentient creatures, premodern meat-eating cultures developed an array of ritual acts to atone for their taking of other life. In some cultures, hunters begged the animal's forgiveness for having killed it and beseeched it not to seek revenge from the grave. Some hunting tribes collected the bones after eating the flesh from them and reassembled them back into their original order, even providing them with a formal burial to show their respect and to express their sense of indebtedness and gratitude.[10]

As we noted earlier, the palace priests served as the butchers in the first great civilizations of the Middle East and Mediterranean. Their temples were both places of worship and elaborate abattoirs.[11] Cattle and other livestock were transported to the temple, where they were slaughtered in ritual ceremonies, with some of their parts offered up to the gods as sacrifices, the rest distributed to those of rank in the palace hierarchy. Walter Burkert describes the process of sacrifice in Greek society in his book *Homo Necans*.

First, the priests purified themselves by bathing and donning clean ceremonial gowns. They generally abstained from sexual activity for an appropriate period before the sacrifice. The animal, usually a cow, was cleaned, groomed, and adorned with ornaments, then led to the altar in a ceremonial procession. At the foot of the sacred altar, the beast's head was sprinkled with holy water, which encouraged it to shake its head. The shaking was interpreted as a signal of assent, "a sign that the beast concurred with its own slaughter." The priests then thrust a knife deep into her neck. As the animal's blood flowed over the altar "the women signaled the emotional climax of the event by uttering long wailing screams."[12] The carcass was then cut up. The beating heart was placed on the altar while the rest of the animal was roasted on an open fire and distributed to the participants. The bones and a few symbolic morsels of flesh were burned as "an offering to the gods."[13] The symbolic sacrifice helped alleviate the participants' sense of guilt, providing a means of atonement for the taking of an animal's life. By securing the animal's assent, they were able to wash their hands of a murder and became merely accomplice and executioner in a sacred act willed by the gods and entered into freely by the animal. According to an ancient Babylonian text, the head priest would lean down and whisper into the ear of the dead animal, "This deed was done by all the gods; I did not do it."[14]

Judaism and later Christianity did away with the sacrificial aspects of animal slaughter. While man was no longer required to atone for the taking of another creature's life or make sacrifices to the gods, he was given a new means of justifying the consumption of animal flesh. By casting man in God's image and making him overseer of the creation, the Judeo-Christian theologians provided him with a rationale for the killing of animals and the eating of their flesh. Later, Enlightenment thinkers provided a biological justification, suggesting that all of nature existed to serve the utilitarian needs of human beings. Darwinian enthusiasts added that the sole purpose of evolution was to promote the survival of the most fit in the competitive struggle in nature. Since human beings were the most highly evolved of the creatures, they would only be performing their proper evolutionary role by expropriating and metabolizing as much as humanly possible of the flesh of other creatures.

Despite the elaborate religious and biological rationales created over the centuries to justify the slaughter and consumption of other creatures, they have not been sufficient to quiet the anxieties of Western men and women, who continue to empathize with and feel ambivalent toward the beasts they eat. Premodern cultures, with their emphasis on sacrifice, atonement, indebtedness, and placation, appear to have successfully mediated the tensions inherent in the human-animal relationship. By contrast, the anthropomorphic rationalizations of Judeo-Christian theology and the utilitarian spirit of the Enlightenment, while intellectually sophisticated, were far too abstract to assuage the intense, visceral response people had to the spilling of another creature's blood.

To ease their consciences, modern men and women have erected a series of barriers designed to distance themselves as much as possible from the animals they eat. By removing themselves from an intimate relationship with their prey, they have been able to suppress deep-seated emotional connections and the fear, shame, disgust, and regret that often accompany the killing of a fellow creature.

We have already alluded to the way in which Enlightenment

thinkers objectified nature, transforming it into a resource and commodity, even endowing it with machinelike attributes in order to
justify ruthless technological manipulation and commercial expropriation. The beef-eating cultures have further separated themselves
from the animals they eat by shifting blame for their deaths, con-
cealing the act of slaughter, misrepresenting the process of dismemberment, and disguising the identity of the animal during food
preparation.

Shifting blame is not a new phenomenon. In ancient Athens,
palace priests "fled from the altar in mock panic" after the ritual
slaying of a bull. After the sacrifice, a trial was held, in which the
sacrificial knife was found guilty of committing the act, and punished
by being destroyed.[15] In the later medieval and early modern era,
blame was shifted to the town butchers. Where palace priests had
been held in awe and the act of killing viewed as a sacrifice, by the
medieval age, local butchers were regarded with contempt and
loathing and the act of killing was viewed as slaughter.

In a dictionary reference of 1657, butchers were described as
"greasy, bloody, slaughtering, merciless, pitiless, crude, rude, grim,
harsh, stern . . . surly."[16] Butchers were considered so mean-spirited
and callous that they were made ineligible for jury service in cases
of capital punishment in England because of their "inherently" cruel
inclination.[17] In 1716, poet John Gay admonished Londoners "to
shun the surly butcher's greasy tray, butchers, whose hands are dy'd
with blood's foul stain, and always foremost in the hangman's
train."[18]

Stripped of its sacred quality, the slaughter of cattle and other
livestock was viewed with repugnance by a growing number of
people in Europe and in the Americas. The Reverend S. Barnett, a
London minister, urged the authorities to remove the slaughterhouse
from public visibility, arguing that seeing them tends to "brutalize
a thickly crowded population, and to debase the children."[19] Of
particular concern was the stench of death emanating from the abattoirs and the refuse dumped into open sewers along public streets.
French social philosopher Alain Corbin describes the conditions:

> In butchers' narrow courtyards odors of dung, fresh refuse, and
> organic remains combined with foul-smelling gases escaping from
> intestines. Blood trickled out in the open air, ran down the streets,

coated the paving stones with brownish glazes, and decomposed in the gaps. . . . The malodorous vapors that impregnated roadways and traders' stalls were some of the deadliest and most revolting; they make the whole body susceptible to putridity. Often the stifling odors of melting tallow added to this foul-smelling potpourri.[20]

Today, cattle and other livestock are tucked away, out of sight of the public, until they are purchased in the form of prepacked cuts of beef at the local supermarket. Ranchers have sequestered the nation's beef cattle in rural enclaves cordoned off from public view like so many industrial parks. The feedlots are now so highly automated that there is little if any direct contact between the "caretaker" and the animals. Even the daily allotment of food is often managed and maintained by computer. "At this level of detachment," says James Serpell, "the animal becomes a mere cipher, a unit of production, abstracted out of existence in the pursuit of higher yields."[21]

The nation's slaughterhouses, once located in the urban heart of busy midwestern cities like Cincinnati and Chicago, are now to be found on the outskirts of small midwestern towns where the activity inside on the kill floors has little or no impact on the sparsely settled human communities on the outside. Upton Sinclair's description of the hidden nature of slaughterhouses is even more appropriate today than at the turn of the century. In *The Jungle* the young worker Jurgis tells of his feelings upon being ushered onto the kill floor for the first time: "[It] was like some horrible crime committed in a dungeon, all unseen and unheeded, buried out of sight and of memory."[22]

Along with shifting blame and concealment, modern man has attempted to misrepresent the process of slaughtering beef and other livestock, reducing the act of killing to a rational process suggestive of machine production. In a recent issue of the British *Meat Trades Journal*, the editors proposed that the term "butcher" and "slaughter" be replaced with the terms "meat plant" and "meat factory" to accommodate the sensibilities of an increasingly squeamish consuming public.[23] Today the United States Department of Agriculture describes cattle as "grain-consuming animal units," demonstrating forcefully that the mechanistic and utilitarian thinking of the Enlightenment still holds considerable sway over the contemporary use of language.[24]

The beef-packing industry and the consuming public would no

doubt be more than a little disturbed if beef were marketed as a "slaughtered animal" or the "partly cremated portions of dead animals." Even the terms "beef," "veal," "pork," "venison," and "mutton" are euphemisms, conjuring up an image of food devoid of any relationship with the animals from which they came.[25] Few people would feel comfortable ordering part of a cow, a small calf, a pig, a deer, or a sheep on a restaurant menu.

Modern culture has distanced itself from the animals it eats in still another important way—the preparation of meat for consumption. In the great halls of medieval castles, large sections of oxen and whole pigs were often roasted on spits in view of the guests. On the Lord's day, an entire lamb might be prepared. In medieval households it was common practice to place the whole animal or a large portion of it on the dining table. Whole roasted birds with their feathers stuck back in to look alive were served up, as were whole rabbits, quarters of calves, and the like.

Beginning in the early modern era, much of the food preparation was removed from public scrutiny and fussed over behind the scenes in the kitchen and scullery. The newly urbanized societies, especially in France and Germany, became increasingly uncomfortable at the sight of whole animals served up at the table. Serving a whole dead animal was too forceful a reminder of killing and death and the thin line that separated humans from their prey; only beasts tear into a whole animal. The new culinary standards began to stress disguise. More and more of the carving was done away from the dining table, in the kitchens by the cooks. Heads were removed from animals, fowl, and fish, and meat was increasingly divided into small portions, filleted out of sight of the diners, and then served to eliminate any identification with the animal that was being eaten. English critic William Hazlitt wrote in 1826:

> Animals that are made use of as food, should either be so small as to be imperceptible, or else we should . . . not leave the form standing to reproach us with our gluttony and cruelty. I hate to see a rabbit trussed, or a hare brought to the table in the form which it occupied while living.[26]

The ubiquitous hamburger represents the final deconstruction of modern meat. The bovine has been disassembled into indistinguishable matter, and made manipulatable and reshapable by the highly mechanized production process. The steer has been "forced out of its natural state and squeezed and molded" by the same scientific methods that Bacon first employed to deconstruct and reshape the rest of nature. The cow has been dismembered, disemboweled, reconstituted, and flattened into round, orderly, easily packagable units that can be fast-frozen, transported, stacked, grilled, and consumed with a minimum of inconvenience. The process by which cattle are raised, fattened, slaughtered, and packaged is highly rational, utilitarian, and expedient. The entire process is automated, with a minimum of human involvement.

39

Cattle and Cold Evil

The modern cattle complex is pervasive. Its activities have had a major effect on the deterioration of the world's environment. Yet the impact of cattle upon the world community has been little discussed. The silence surrounding the modern cattle complex and modern meat is all the more troubling given its role in helping to create the most inequitable pattern of food production and distribution in world history. The modern cattle complex spearheaded an unprecedented worldwide campaign in this century to transform the world's grain harvest from food to feed, denying millions of people their fair share of the world's endowment.

In Chapter 9 we learned that a third of the world's grain harvest is now being fed to cattle and other livestock while nearly a billion human beings go to bed malnourished. Today Europeans, Americans, and Japanese eat atop an artificial food chain, laced with marbled beef, gorging themselves on animal fat.

The human toll exacted by the modern cattle complex has been impressive. Millions of people in "developing" countries have been displaced from their ancestral land to make room for cattle grazing. Most have been forced to migrate to squalid urban sprawls where they survive by scavenging. Chronically hungry, they succumb to a range of diet-deficiency diseases. In many third world countries, one out of ten infants never makes it to a first birthday. For those who survive, life is little more than a slow death at the hands of environmental assaults and parasitic and opportunistic diseases that ravage their already compromised immune systems.

The rich and well-to-do consumers of the first world enjoy the fruits of a grain-fed diet, but die a different kind of death by dint of eating high up on an artificial protein chain. Their bodies clogged with cholesterol, their arteries and organs choked with animal fat, they fall victim to the "diseases of affluence," often dying in excruciating pain from heart disease, colon and breast cancer, and diabetes.

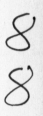

The modern cattle complex represents a new kind of malevolent force in the world. In a civilization that still measures evil in very personal terms, institutional evil born of rational detachment and pursued with cold calculating methods of technological expropriation has yet to be assigned an appropriate rung on the moral ladder.

Moral outrage still follows individual acts of wrongdoing. When a member of society commits violence, takes another's life, or robs another of property or freedom, the individual and the act are universally condemned. The evil is apparent, visible, direct, and amenable to judgment. The modern world recognizes personal evil that inflicts direct bodily harm on another. It has yet to recognize the emergence of a new and far more dangerous form of evil, one spawned by technological premises, institutional imperatives, and market objectives. While our contemporary society continues to guard against the commission of personal evil, it has largely failed to incorporate into its moral framework a sense of righteous indignation and moral repulsion against institutionally certified violence.

Although it is true that some limited examples of institutionally directed violence are singled out for punishment, the crimes are generally of a personal nature—a corporate or government official punished for embezzlement, discrimination, or negligence of some kind. But what of the other kind of wrongdoing, the kind that emerges from the inherent nature of the premises that drive the institutions? The church gives some faint lip service to the idea of fighting "the earthly powers and principalities," but even here recognizes only traditional concepts of morality inspired by the Ten Commandments. What of evil born of rationalized methods of discourse, scientific objectivity, mechanistic reductionism, utilitarianism, and market efficiency? The evil inflicted upon the modern world by the cattle complex is of this nature. To be sure, greed, defilement, and exploitation have accompanied the cattle complex throughout its westward sojourn. A new dimension of evil, however, has been incorporated into the modern cattle complex—a cold evil that flows from the very Enlightenment principles that animate much of the modern worldview.

Cold evil is evil inflicted from a distance; evil concealed by layer upon layer of technological and institutional garb; evil whose ultimate beneficiaries are so far removed in time or place from the people who have been victimized by the process that no causal relationship is suspected or experienced. It is evil that cannot be felt because of its impersonal nature. To suggest that a person is committing an evil act by growing feed for cattle or consuming a hamburger might appear strange, even ludicrous, to most people. Even if the facts were to be made explicit and incontrovertible, the trail of evil mapped out with painstaking detail, it is unlikely that many in society could muster up the same passionate sense of outrage that they might extend to incidences of hot evil—an armed robbery, a rape, the deliberate torture of a neighborhood dog.

Chances are that the supermarket manager who stocks the grain-fed beef will never personally experience the anguish of the victims of poverty, those millions of families thrown off their land so that it can be used to grow livestock feed for export. Teenagers gobbling down cheeseburgers at a fast-food restaurant will likely be unaware that a wide swath of tropical rain forest had to be felled and burned to bring them their meal. Consumers buying prepackaged cuts of steak will never know of the pain and discomfort experienced by the animals in high-tech automated feedlots.

In a civilization so steeped in the Enlightenment assumptions of mechanization and market efficiency, the very idea that those same set of assumptions are a source of potential evil is anathema. Most of the governing relationships in modern society are mediated by rational discourse, by objective detachment, by utilitarian consid-erations, by technological intervention, by efficient pursuit. The modern cattle complex, as we have learned, was among the first of the institutional forces to embrace the assumptions of Enlightenment thinkers, to incorporate the engineering standards of the modern worldview into every aspect of its operations.

It is these assumptions and standards that have been used so effectively in the modern era to sever the bonds of intimate relationship with the rest of nature. It is the motivating principles of the Enlightenment that have stripped nature of its aliveness and robbed other creatures of their essential nature and intrinsic worth.

In the cold calculating domain of the modern world, we have substituted material self-interest for eternal salvation, expediency for renewal, and production quotas for generativeness. We have flattened the organic richness of existence, turning the world around us into abstract mathematical equations, statistics, and bottom-line performance standards. Cold evil is perpetuated by institutions and individuals bound by rational organizing principles, with only market forces and utilitarian goals to guide their choices and decisions. In such a world, there is little opportunity to honor the creation, empathize with our fellow creatures, steward the environment, and protect the rights of future generations.

The environmental and human effects of the modern way of thinking and structuring of relationships has been near-catastrophic, weakening ecosystems, and undermining the stability and sustainability of human communities. The great challenge that lies ahead of us is to come to grips with the dark side of the modern worldview—to address the cold evil that comes of reducing all of nature and life to commercial resources that can be technologically mediated, manipulated, and reconstructed to suit the narrow objectives of utilitarianism and market efficiency.

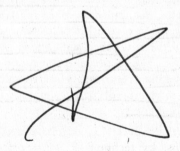

40

Beyond Beef

Awakening the conscience and consciousness of the world's communities to the ravages of cattle and cold evil is a daunting task. In the name of progress and profit, the modern cattle complex has destroyed natural ecosystems and transformed parts of the planet into a semibarren wasteland unfit for human, animal, or plant habitation. In the name of rationality and objectivity, the modern cattle complex has reduced nature, even human labor, to a commercial resource, manipulatable and exchangeable in the open marketplace. In the name of market efficiency, the modern cattle complex has turned the cow, the packinghouse worker, and the consumer into ciphers of production and consumption, utilities and targets stripped of any kind of intrinsic or sacred value; empty shells choreographed to fit the tempo of high-technology feedlots, disassembly lines, and fast-food counters.

The beef mythology has been used over and over again to perpetuate male dominance, foster class divisions, and promote the interests of nationalism and colonialism. It has perpetuated social inequality and economic disenfranchisement on a worldwide scale.

The story of humanity's long relationship to cattle is the story of our changing relationship to our own generativeness. The bull and the cow, the ancient icons of our own virility and fertility, have been desacralized and denatured, stripped of their aliveness, and turned into machines of production. They have been robbed of their being, deconstructed into sheer matter for manipulation, and made into things. In a world steeped in utility, grounded in expediency, with only the market to give direction and meaning, the cow continues to be an ideal mirror to our own evolving consciousness—a stark reflection of how we have transformed and remade ourselves in the modern world. We have substituted mechanism for organism, utilitarianism for spiritualism, and market values for community standards, turning ourselves from beings to resources.

Reconsecrating our relationship to the bovine is a gesture of great historical significance. By making a personal and collective choice to go beyond beef, we strike at the heart of the modern notion of economics with its near-exclusive emphasis on "industrial productivity," a concept that has come to replace the ancient idea of generativeness.

The cattle complex has been among our most important training grounds in the art of modern economics. Today cattle are brought into the world through artificial insemination, embryo transfers, and cloning techniques. Bred for market efficiency rather than species fitness, they are force-fed, injected with chemicals, monitored by machines, constrained and controlled, squeezed and molded to meet the prerequisites of factory farming. They are treated as industrial products from birth to slaughter. Although they contain more fat, weigh more, and mature faster than feral cattle, they are far less hearty, often less able to reproduce, and riddled with opportunistic and parasitic diseases, and they require an array of sophisticated technological and pharmaceutical supports to survive. Their increased productivity is at the expense of their diminished generativity. As long as industrial productivity remains the sole measure of our relationship to the bovine and the other animal and plant species, we will be unable to develop an economic ethic that is truly compatible with the rules and rhythms that govern sustainability.

In nature, generativeness, not productivity, is the measure of sustainability. Generativeness is a life-affirming force. Its essence is organic. Its teleology is regenerative. Industrial production is often a death force. Its essence is manipulatable matter. Its teleology is consumption. Our changing relationship to the bovine, from one of revered generativeness to one of controlled productivity, mirrors the changing consciousness of Western civilization as it has struggled to define itself and its relationship to both the natural order and the cosmic scheme.

In the first stage of our relationship to the bovine, our ancient ancestors worshiped a "generative force" to which they were beholden and over which they had little or no control. While their relationship to cattle was both sacred and intimate, it was based on fear and dependency. They paid homage to the bovine in order to curry favor with the gods, to secure the blessings of a fecund and bountiful existence. Their rituals and practices were designed to manipulate the cosmic forces to their advantage, so that they might prosper. They ate beef to incorporate the divine spirit of generativeness into their being, so that they might participate in the great cycle of eternal rebirth.

In the second stage of our relationship to the bovine, we substituted ourselves for the gods and transformed the bovine into a productive resource to be manipulated. We gained control over cattle and by extension the generativeness of nature, making both dependent on our rational will. We grew out of our dependency on nature, but in the process we lost a sense of the sacred and intimate companionship with the rest of the created order. We consumed beef to gain power over nature and our fellow human beings.

Today the third stage of the human-bovine saga beckons. By choosing not to eat the flesh of cattle, we serve notice of our willingness to enter into a new covenant with this creature, a relationship that transcends the imperatives of the market and profligate consumption. Freeing the bovine from the pain and indignities suffered on the modern mega-feedlots and in the slaughterhouses is a humane act of great symbolic and practical import. Liberating these creatures from the process of dehorning, castration, and estrus-blocking, from forced hormone injections, massive doses of antibiotics, insecticide showers, and an ignoble death on an automated assembly-line kill floor, is an act of contrition. It is an acknowledgment of the damage we moderns have inflicted on the whole of the creation in pursuit of unrestrained power over the forces of nature.

To go beyond beef is to transform our very thinking about appropriate behavior toward nature. In the new world in the making, human activity is cued as much to the intrinsic generativeness of nature as to the artificial dictates of the marketplace. We come to appreciate the source of our sustenance, the divinely inspired creation that deserves nurture and requires stewardship. Nature is no longer viewed as an enemy to be subdued and tamed, but rather the primordial community in which we dwell. Other creatures are no longer treated as victims or objects, but rather as partners and participants in the larger community of life that makes up nature and the biosphere.

Our changing relationship to the bovine—the ancient symbol of generativeness—will be a sign of the new world in the making. The benefits of moving beyond beef will be immediate and visible, providing tangible evidence of the life-affirming future that awaits our children's generation.

Reducing the cattle population to ecologically sustainable numbers will help facilitate an ecological restoration of nature on every continent. America's western range will slowly come to life again. Ancient rivers will flow, their waters bathing and healing thousands of damaged riparian zones across the great plains. Native wildflowers and perennial bunchgrasses will sprout and bloom, spreading a verdant carpet across the western landscape. Cottonwood trees will shade the prairie once again, providing refuge for thousands of native birds. Streams and springs will come to life, bringing back freshwater trout and other native fish. The large mammals of the plains—elk, moose, pronghorn, antelope, bighorn sheep—will repopulate the western range once again, their numbers spreading out to fill the millions of acres of restored grassland. Predator species will thrive. Coyotes, wolves, bobcats, mountain lions, and lynx will steal their way back onto the great western range, performing their traditional role of culling big animal herds to ensure that native species do not exceed the carrying capacity of the plains ecosystems.

In Central and South America, the dissolution of the cattle complex will help idle tractors and bulldozers and diminish the familiar drone of thousands of machine saws cutting their way through the thicket of ancient forest ecosystems. Countless species of plants, insects, and animals will be granted a reprieve from what once appeared to be a sure death at the hands of cattle ranchers and multinational corporations. Millions of creatures, many of whom have inhabited this earth for millennia, will be given a chance to regroup, reproduce, and repopulate the forests. Future generations will have the opportunity to know, interact with, and appreciate these many diverse life forms; this multitude of wild and exotic creatures that creep, crawl, dart, fly over, swing through, and stalk the ancient forests, all fellow travelers in the unfolding evolutionary saga.

In Africa, the spreading desert will be slowed, allowing nature time to regenerate. Wildlife, once abundant in the sub-Sahara, will slowly return. So too will the rich native flora. Wildebeest, elephants, zebras, rhinos, and lions will roam again over the open savannas, repopulating ancient habitats.

In Australia, New Zealand, and parts of Asia, the dissolution of the global cattle complex will foster a similar restoration of ancient forests and grasslands, as well as native flora and fauna.

Fewer cattle will lessen the strain on the world's remaining freshwater reserves and decrease the emission of global warming gases into the atmosphere. While the biosphere will still be choked with carbon dioxide from the burning of fossil fuels and the emission of man-made chlorofluorocarbons, the worldwide reduction in cattle will significantly reduce methane emissions as well as carbon dioxide emissions resulting from the burning of forests and other biomass to provide pastureland.

As millions of Americans, Europeans, Japanese, and others make personal choices to reduce their beef consumption, the artificial protein ladder, erected during this century, will begin to collapse. The societal decision to reduce beef will profoundly affect the economics of human survival in the coming century. In the new world that is coming, millions of human beings will voluntarily choose to eat lower on the food chain so that millions of others may obtain the minimum food calories they need to sustain their lives. This grand redistribution of the earth's bounty, the most far-reaching in history, will unite the human race in a new fraternal bond. A new species awareness will begin where the rich meet the poor on the descending rungs of the world's protein ladder.

The decision to eat further down on the planet's food chain will force a wholesale reassessment of the entire grain-fed meat complex ranging from factory farm chickens to hogs. The collapse of the global cattle complex will likely precipitate a chain reaction, resulting in the elimination of other grain-fed meats from the human diet.

The dissolution of the commercial cattle complex will spare the rich and might help save the poor. Eliminating grain-fed beef and eating lower on the food chain will dramatically reduce the incidence of heart disease, cancer, and diabetes. Millions of human beings will enjoy better health and a longer life span. Billions of dollars in health care costs will be saved.

At the same time, more agricultural land and more grain will be potentially available to the poor. Liberating the land to grow grain for human beings could trigger a large-scale human migration out from the crowded urban shanty towns back to the countryside. Millions of displaced peasants would be able to return to their ancestral lands, where they could take up small-scale subsistence agriculture once again, providing their families with sustenance directly from the earth.

Of course, pressure will have to be put on ruling elites in developing countries to ensure an adequate redistribution of land so that the peasant populations can be self-sustaining. With access to land and grain, children of the poor will be able to survive infancy without falling victim to the range of parasitic and opportunistic diseases that now plague so many. Children will have a chance to grow up with sound bodies and minds capable of experiencing the fullness of human existence.

Moving beyond the beef culture is a revolutionary act, a sign of our willingness to reconstitute ourselves, to make ourselves whole. Restoring nature, resacralizing our relationship to cattle, and renewing our own being are inseparably linked. They are the essential elements of a new postmodern sensibility, the harbingers of a new earth-centered awareness. The dissolution of the modern cattle complex and the elimination of beef from the diet of the human race portends a new chapter in the unfolding of human consciousness. By doing battle with "the world steer," a new generation expresses its sensitivity to the biosphere and its regard for the plight of the poor. By eliminating beef from the human diet, our species takes a significant step toward a new species consciousness, reaching out in a spirit of shared partnership with the bovine and, by extension, other sentient creatures with whom we share the earth.

NOTES

Introduction

1. Cattle numbers come from Food and Agriculture Organization of the United Nations, *Production, 1989 Yearbook*, Vol. 43 (Rome, Italy: FAO, 1990), table 89.
2. Pieter Buringh, "Availability of Agricultural Land for Crop and Livestock Production," in David Pimentel and Carl Hall, eds., *Food and Natural Resources* (San Diego: Academic Press, 1989), 71. Pimentel estimates that a conversion of the present American grass/grain livestock system to a totally grass-fed system would free up in the United States alone about 130 million tons of grain for direct human consumption, enough to feed about 400 million people. David Pimentel, *Food, Energy and the Future of Society* (New York: Wiley, 1979), 26. Today, worldwide, about one-third of the 1.7 billion metric tons of total grain production is fed to livestock, which would suggest, using Pimentel's ratio, that a totally grass-fed livestock system worldwide might free enough grain up to feed over a billion people. U.S. Department of Agriculture, Economic Research Service, *World Agricultural Supply and Demand Estimates*, WASDE-256, July 11, 1991, table 256-6; World Bank, *Poverty and Hunger* (Washington, DC: World Bank, 1986), 24.
3. USDA, Economic Research Service, table 256-6; World Bank, *Poverty and Hunger*, 24.

Part One. CATTLE AND THE
MAKING OF WESTERN CIVILIZATION

1. Sacrifice to Slaughter

1. Jack Randolph Conrad, *The Horn and the Sword* (Westport, Conn.: Greenwood Press, 1973), 76.
2. Ibid., 72–74.
3. Yi-fu Tuan, *Dominance and Affection: The Making of Pets* (New Haven: Yale University Press, 1984), 71.
4. Conrad, 78–79.
5. Ibid., 80.
6. Orville Schell, *Modern Meat* (New York: Random House, 1984), 267.
7. Ibid.
8. Quored in ibid., 270.
9. "Cattle Feeding Concentrates in Fewer, Larger Lots," *Farmline*, June 1990.
10. Jim Mason and Peter Singer, *Animal Factories* (New York: Harmony Books, 1990), 67.
11. Ibid., 51.
12. Jeannine Kenney and Dick Fallert, "Livestock Hormones in the United States," *National Food Review*, July-September 1989, 22–23.
13. Fred Kuchler et al., "Regulating Food Safety: The Case of Animal Growth Hormones," *National Food Review*, July-September 1989, 26.
14. Mason and Singer, Animal Factories, 70; FDA Veterinarian, "Antibiotics in Animal Feeds Risk Assessment," May/June 1989.
15. Mason and Singer, 83-84; National Research Council, Board on Agriculture, *Alternative Agriculture* (Washington, D.C.: National Academy Press, 1989), 49.
16. National Research Council, 44.
17. National Research Council, Board on Agriculture, *Regulating Pesticides in Food* (Washington, D.C.: National Academy Press, 1987), 78, Table 3–20.
18. Ibid, 78-80, Tables 3–20 to 22.
19. Mason and Singer, 51.
20. Schell, 127.
21. Ibid., 129.
22. Ibid.
23. Ibid., 152.
24. Ibid., 155.
25. Jimmy M. Skaggs, *Prime Cut* (College Station: Texas A&M University Press, 1986), 191.
26. Quoted in Ibid.

2. Gods and Goddesses

1. J. J. Barloy, *Man and Animals* (London: Gordon & Cremonesi, 1974), 50.
2. Ibid.; Jack Randolph Conrad, The Horn and the Sword (Westport, Conn.: Greenwood Press, 1973), 20.
3. Erich Isaac, "On the Domestication of Cattle," *Science* 137, July 20, 1962, 196–98.

4. Quoted in A. H. Sayce, "Bull (Semitic)," in *Encyclopedia of Religion and Ethics* (New York: Charles Scribner's Sons, 1911), 2:888.
5. Conrad, 91.
6. Quoted in Theophile Meek, *Hebrew Origins* (New York: Harper & Brothers, 1950), 140. Numbers 23:22, Meek translation.
7. Conrad, 131.
8. Ibid., 146.
9. Quoted in Steven Lonsdale, *Animals and the Origins of Dance* (London: Thames & Hudson, 1982), 81.
10. Conrad, 149.
11. Ibid., 150–51.
12. Quoted in Pennethorne Hughes, *Witchcraft* (London: Longmans, Green, 1952), 91.

3. Neolithic Cowboys

1. Marija Gimbutas, "The First Wave of Eurasian Steppe Pastoralists into Copper Age Europe," *Journal of Indo-European Studies* 5, Winter 1977, 281.
2. Marija Gimbutas, "Old Europe, 7000–3300 B.C.: The Earliest European Civilation Before the Infiltration of the Indo-European Peoples," *Journal of Indo-European Studies* 1, Spring 1973, 12.
3. "The First Wave . . . ," 277.
4. Ward H. Goodenough, "The Evolution of Pastoralism and Indo-European Origins," in George Cardona et al., eds., *Indo-European and Indo-Europeans* (Philadelphia: University of Pennsylvania Press, 1970), 258.
5. Gimbutas, "First Wave," 277.
6. Goodenough, 260.
7. Reay Tannahill, *Food in History* (New York: Stein & Day, 1973), 123.
8. Gimbutas, "First Wave," 280–81.
9. Tannahill, 122.
10. Ibid., 121.
11. Eric Partridge, *Origins: A Short Etymological Dictionary of Modern English* (New York: Greenwich House, 1983), 84.
12. Wilfred Funk, *Word Origins and Their Romantic Stories* (New York: Crown, 1979).
13. James J. Parsons, "The Scourge of Cows," *Whole Earth Review*, Spring 1988, 41.
14. Robert B. Hinman et al., *The Story of Meat* (Chicago: Swift & Company, 1939), 5.
15. Steven Lonsdale, *Animals and the Origins of Dance* (London: Thames & Hudson, 1982), 80.

4. Gifts and Capital

1. Bruce Lincoln, *Priests, Warriors, and Cattle* (Berkeley: University of California Press, 1981), 168.
2. Ibid., 169.
3. Ibid., 96–7.
4. Ibid., 101.
5. Ibid., 170.

5. *Holy Cow*

1. Reay Tannahill, *Food in History* (New York: Stein & Day, 1973), 123.
2. Jack Randolph Conrad, *The Horn and the Sword* (Westport, Conn.: Greenwood Press, 1973), 52.
3. Marvin Harris, *Cannibals and Kings* (New York: Random House, 1977), 143.
4. Ibid., 146.
5. Marvin Harris, *The Sacred Cow and the Abominable Pig* (New York: Touchstone/ Simon & Schuster, 1987), 52.
6. Ibid., 53–54.
7. Quoted in ibid., 55.
8. Ibid.
9. Harris, *Cannibals*, 144.
10. Quincy Wright, *A Study of War* (Chicago: University of Chicago Press, 1942), 1:134.
11. John Reader, "Human Ecology: How Land Shapes Society," *New Scientist*, September 8, 1988, 53.
12. Marvin Harris, *Cows, Pigs, Wars and Witches* (New York: Vintage/Random House, 1974), 6–7.
13. J. J. Barloy, *Man and Animals* (London: Gordon & Cremonesi, 1974), 58.
14. Harris, *Sacred Cow*, 49.
15. Conrad, 65.
16. Harris, *Cows*, 7, 62.
17. Harris, *Sacred Cow*, 49.
18. Harris, *Cows*, 8.
19. Conrad, 65.
20. Barloy, 59.
21. Harris, *Sacred Cow*, 50.
22. Harris, *Cows*, 8–9.
23. Reader, 53–54.
24. Harris, *Cows*, 13–14.
25. Reader, 53.
26. Harris, *Cows*, 19.
27. Harris, *Sacred Cow*, 56.
28. Ibid., 48.
29. Quoted in Barloy, 57.
30. Quoted in Harris, *Sacred Cow*, 65.

6. *Matadors and Machismo*

1. Jack Randolph Conrad, *The Horn and the Sword* (Westport, Conn.: Greenwood Press, 1973), 161–63.
2. Ibid., 183.
3. Pauline S. Powers, *Obesity: The Regulation of Weight* (Baltimore, Md.: William & Wilkins, 1980), 206.
4. Carson I. A. Ritchie, *Food in Civilization: How History Has Been Affected by Human Tastes* (New York: Beaufort Books, 1981), 68–85.
5. Ibid., 78–79.

6. Fernand Braudel, *Capitalism and Material Life, 1400–1800* (Glasgow: Fontana/William Collins, 1975), 129.

7. Ritchie, 79.

8. Braudel, 127–29.

9. Eric B. Ross, "An Overview of Trends in Dietary Variation from Hunter-Gatherer to Modern Capitalist Societies," in Marvin Harris and Eric B. Ross, *Food and Evolution* (Philadelphia: Temple University Press, 1987), 28.

10. Quoted in Ritchie, 80.

11. Ibid., 84.

12. Food and Agriculture Organization of the United Nations, *Production, 1989 Yearbook*, Vol. 43 (Rome, Italy: FAO, 1990), table 89.

13. David Dary, *Cowboy Culture* (New York: Knopf, 1981), 4.

7. Cattlizing the Americas

1. Denzel Ferguson and Nancy Ferguson, *Sacred Cows at the Public Trough* (Bend, Ore.: Maverick Publications, 1983), 11.

2. David Dary, *Cowboy Culture* (New York: Knopf, 1981), 5.

3. Charles Hackett, ed., *Historical Documents Relating to New Mexico, Nueva Vizcaya, and Approaches Thereto, to 1773* (Washington, D.C.: Carnegie Institution, 1923), 1:41.

4. Dary, 6.

5. Quoted in ibid., 8.

6. Ibid., 9.

7. Ibid., 10.

8. Ibid., 13–14.

9. Ibid., 15.

10. Ibid., 25.

11. Ibid., 37–40.

12. Herbert E. Bolton, *The Padre on Horseback* (San Francisco: Sonora Press, 1932), 64.

13. Richard W. Slatta, *Cowboys of the Americas* (New Haven: Yale University Press, 1990), 22.

14. Quoted in Herbert E. Bolton, *Fray Juan Crespi: Missionary Explorer on the Pacific Coast, 1769–1774* (Berkeley: University of California, 1927), 264–65.

15. Slatta, 23.

16. Nora E. Ramirez, "The Vaquero and Ranching in the Southwestern United States, 1600–1970" (Ph.D. diss., Indiana University, 1979), 16, 22.

17. Slatta, 10.

18. Ibid., 13.

19. Carson I. A. Ritchie, *Food in Civilization: How History Has Been Affected by Human Tastes* (New York: Beaufort Books, 1981), 186; Dary, *Cowboy Culture*, 16.

20. John Super and Thomas Wright, *Food, Politics, and Society in Latin America* (Lincoln: University of Nebraska Press, 1985), 5.

21. Quoted in Ritchie, 185.

22. Quoted in Fernand Braudel, *Capitalism and Material Life, 1400–1800* (Glasgow: Fontana/William Collins, 1975), 135.

23. Ritchie, 187.

24. Slatta, 104–5.
25. Ibid., 105.
26. Ibid., 105–6.
27. Ibid., 106.

8. British Beefeaters

1. C. Anne Wilson, *Food and Drink in Britain* (London: Constable, 1973), 69.
2. Ibid., 69–70.
3. Quoted in Keith Thomas, *Man and the Natural World* (New York: Pantheon, 1983), 29.
4. Quoted in Fernand Braudel, *Capitalism and Material Life, 1400–1800* (Glasgow: Fontana/William Collins, 1975), 68.
5. Quoted in Jack Goody, *Cooking, Cuisine, and Class* (Cambridge, England: Cambridge University Press, 1982), 135.
6. Quoted in ibid., 141.
7. Ibid., 141–42.
8. Quoted in Leslie Gofton, "The Rules of the Table: Sociological Factors Influencing Food Choice," in C. Ritson et al., eds., *The Food Consumer* (New York: Wiley, 1986), 139.
9. Keith Thomas, 26.
10. Quoted in ibid.
11. Quoted in Wilson, 98.

9. Let Them Eat Potatoes

1. Eric B. Ross, "An Overview of Trends in Dietary Variation from Hunter-Gatherer to Modern Capitalist Societies," in Marvin Harris and Eric B. Ross, *Food and Evolution* (Philadelphia: Temple University Press, 1987), 29.
2. Quoted in ibid., 30.
3. Quoted in ibid.
4. Ibid., 31–32.
5. U.S. Department of Agriculture, Economic Research Service, *World Agricultural Supply and Demand Estimates*, WASDE-256 (Washington, D.C.: USDA, July 11, 1991), tables 256-23, -19, -16, -6, -7.
6. World Bank, *Poverty and Hunger* (Washington, D.C.: World Bank, 1986), 24.

10. Corpulent Cows and Opulent Englishmen

1. Harriet Ritvo, *The Animal Estate* (Cambridge: Harvard University Press, 1987), 45–50.
2. Ibid., 49.
3. James Dickson, "On the Application of the Points by Which Livestock Are Judged," *Quarterly Review of Agriculture* 6 (1835–36), 269.
4. Ritvo, 59–60.
5. Ibid., 60–62.
6. Quoted in ibid., 79.
7. Ibid., 80.
8. Ibid., 73.
9. Ibid., 67.

Part Two. HOW THE WEST WAS WON

11. Rail Links and Cattle Crossings

1. Quoted in Elizabeth Atwood Lawrence, *Rodeo* (Knoxville: University of Tennessee Press, 1982), 51.
2. Quoted in ibid., 51.
3. Walter Prescott Webb, *The Great Plains* (Boston: Ginn, 1931), 208.
4. Ibid., 210.
5. J. Frank Dobie, *The Longhorns* (New York: Grosset & Dunlap, 1941), 11–12, 27–28.
6. Webb, 211–12.
7. Quoted in Daniel J. Boorstin, *The Americans: The Democratic Experience* (New York: Vintage/Random House, 1974), 6–7.
8. Quoted in Webb, 214.
9. Boorstin, 8.
10. Ibid., 29.
11. Slatta, *Cowboys of the Americas* (New Haven: Yale University Press, 1932), 19.
12. Quoted in Webb, 220.
13. Skaggs, 54.
14. Wilbur S. Shepperson, "The Maverick and the Cowboy," *Nevada Historical Society Quarterly* 30 (Summer 1987), 149.
15. Jimmy M. Skaggs, *Prime Cut* (College Station: Texas A&M University Press, 1986), 56.

12. The Great Bovine Switch

1. Maurice Frink et al., *When Grass Was King* (Boulder: University of Colorado Press, 1956), 22.
2. Edward E. Dale, *Cow Country* (Norman: University of Oklahoma Press, 1943), 8–9.
3. Frink et al., 22.
4. Daniel J. Boorstin, *The Americans: The Democratic Experience* (New York: Vintage/Random House, 1974), 6.
5. Quoted in Mark H. Brown and W. R. Felton, *Before Barbed Wire* (New York: Henry Holt, 1956), 98.
6. Walter Prescott Webb, *The Great Plains* (Boston: Ginn, 1931), 44.
7. W. Hornaday, "The Extermination of the American Bison with a Sketch of Its Discovery and Life History," *Annual Report, Smithsonian Institution*, Part III (Washington, D.C.: U.S. Government Printing Office, 1889), 367–548.
8. Ibid.
9. Eric B. Ross, *Beyond the Myth of Culture* (New York: Academic Press, 1980), 199.
10. Colonel Richard Irving Dodge, *The Hunting Grounds of the Great West* (London: Chattow & Windus, 1877).
11. Quoted in Wayne Gard, *The Great Buffalo Hunt* (New York: Knopf, 1959), 218; Tom McHugh, *The Time of the Buffalo* (New York: Knopf, 1972), 275–76.
12. McHugh, 253–54.
13. Ibid., 258.

14. Quoted in ibid., 259.
15. Quoted in ibid., 263.
16. Colonel Richard Irving Dodge, ibid.
17. Quoted in McHugh, 210, 249.
18. Quoted in Wayne Gard, *The Great Buffalo Hunt* (New York: Knopf, 1959), 210.
19. William F. Cody, *The Life of Hon. William F. Cody: An Autobiography* (Lincoln: University of Nebraska Press, 1978), 173.
20. Quoted in McHugh, 250–51.
21. Ibid., 283.
22. Ross, 199.
23. Quoted in McHugh, 285.
24. Gard, 298.
25. McHugh, 279.
26. Gard, 296.
27. McHugh, 279.
28. Quoted in Gard, 305–6.
29. Ibid., 296, 298–99.
30. McHugh, 285.
31. Ibid., 286–87.
32. Ibid., 288.

13. Cowboys and Indians

1. Edward E. Dale, *Cow Country* (Norman: University of Oklahoma Press, 1943), 5–7.
2. Quoted in Herman J. Viola, *After Columbus: The Smithsonian Chronicle of the North American Indian* (New York: Orion, 1990), 153–54.
3. Quoted in ibid.
4. Michael P. Malone, ed., *Historians and the American West* (Lincoln: University of Nebraska Press, 1983), 183.
5. Dale, 157–58.
6. Maurice Frink et al., *When Grass Was King* (Boulder: University of Colorado Press, 1956), 13.
7. Dale, 82.
8. Ibid., 14.
9. Frink et al., 23.
10. Dale, 157–58.
11. Ibid., 157.
12. Ibid., 159.
13. Ibid., 166.
14. Quoted in ibid., 171.
15. Ibid., 184–85.
16. George Wuerthner, "The Price Is Wrong," *Sierra*, September/October 1990, 38.

14. Grass Is Gold

1. Quoted in Denzel Ferguson and Nancy Ferguson, *Sacred Cows at the Public Trough* (Bend, Ore.: Maverick Publications, 1983), 4.

2. Quoted in Daniel J. Boorstin, *The Americans: The Democratic Experience* (New York: Vintage/Random House, 1974), 8–9.
3. Maurice Frink et al., *When Grass Was King* (Boulder: University of Colorado Press, 1956), 137.
4. Eric B. Ross, *Beyond the Myths of Culture* (New York: Academic Press, 1980), 201.
5. Edward E. Dale, *Cow Country* (Norman: University of Oklahoma Press, 1943), 91–92.
6. Quoted in Frink et al., 140.
7. Dale, 89.
8. Clay, quoted in Frink et al., 135; Marshall W. Fishwick, "The Cowboy: America's Contribution to the World's Mythology," *Western Folklore* 11:2 (April 1952), 80.
9. Frink, 141.
10. Ibid., 144.
11. Ibid., 144–59.
12. Ibid., 265.
13. Dale, 101.
14. Quoted in Richard W. Slatta, *Cowboys of the Americas* (New Haven: Yale University Press, 1990), 109.
15. Frink et al., 227.
16. Quoted in ibid.
17. Quoted in ibid., 198–99.
18. Quoted in ibid., 200.
19. Quoted in ibid., 231, 232.

15. The Politics of "Corned Beef"

1. Eric B. Ross, *Beyond the Myths of Culture* (New York: Academic Press, 1980), 194.
2. Ibid.
3. Walter Prescott Webb, *The Great Plains* (Boston: Ginn, 1931), 231.
4. Ross, 199.
5. Edward E. Dale, *Cow Country* (Norman: University of Oklahoma Press, 1943), 93.
6. Quoted in Ibid.
7. Ibid., 94.
8. Maurice Frink et al., *When Grass Was King* (Boulder: University of Colorado Press, 1956), 235; Eric B. Ross, "An Overview of Trends in Dietary Variation from Hunter-Gatherer to Modern Capitalist Societies," in Marvin Harris and Eric B. Ross, *Food and Evolution* (Philadelphia: Temple University Press, 1987), 38.
9. Frink et al., 235.
10. Ross, "Overview," 36–37.
11. Frink et al., 259.
12. Ross, *Beyond the Myths*, 204.
13. Ibid.
14. Elmer L. Cooper, *Agriscience, Fundamentals and Applications* (Albany: Delmar Publishers, Inc., 1990), 434; Wayne Swanson and George Schultz, *Prime Rip* (Englewood Cliffs, N.J.: Prentice-Hall, 1982), 19.

15. Swanson and Schultz, 19–20.
16. Quoted in Ross, *Beyond the Myths*, 205.
17. Jimmy M. Skaggs, *Prime Cut* (College Station: Texas A&M University Press, 1976), 178–79.
18. Ross, *Beyond the Myths*, 207.
19. Quoted in ibid.
20. Ibid.
21. "Cattle Feeding Concentrates in Fewer, Larger Lots," *Farmline*, June 1990, 2.
22. Skaggs, 181.
23. Rue Jensen and Donald R. Mackey, *Diseases of Feedlot Cattle* (Philadelphia: Lea and Febiger, 1965), 49–55.
24. U.S. Department of Agriculture, Economic Research Service, *World Agricultural Supply and Demand Estimates*, WASDE-256, July 11, 1991, table 256-16.
25. Ibid., tables 256-16, 6.
26. Lester Brown et al., *State of the World 1990* (Washington, D.C.: Worldwatch Institute; New York: W. W. Norton, 1990), 12.
27. See note 2 in Introduction.

16. Barbed Wire and Land Scams

1. Walter Prescott Webb, *The Great Plains* (New York: Ginn, 1931), 229–30.
2. David Dary, *Cowboy Culture* (New York: Knopf, 1981), 312.
3. Ibid., 308.
4. Maurice Frink et al., *When Grass Was King* (Boulder: University of Colorado Press, 1956), 57–58.
5. Quoted in Dary, 319.
6. Webb, 238.
7. Dary, 320.
8. Jimmy M. Skaggs, *Prime Cut* (College Station: Texas A&M University Press, 1976), 62; Denzel Ferguson and Nancy Ferguson, *Sacred Cows at the Public Trough* (Bend, Ore.: Maverick Publications, 1983), 24–25.
9. Quoted in Dary, 321.
10. Ibid., 324.
11. Quoted in Frink et al., 228.
12. Quoted in ibid., 230–31.
13. Quoted in Skaggs, 62.
14. Quoted in ibid., 63.
15. Quoted in ibid., 79.
16. Ferguson and Ferguson, 36.
17. Quoted in Frink et al., 232.
18. Ferguson and Ferguson, 36; public grazing figures from Free Our Public Lands, P.O. Box 5764, Tucson, Ariz. 85703.
19. Keith Schneider, "Come What May, Congress Stays True to the Critters," *New York Times*, May 6, 1990, Sec. 4, 4.
20. George Wuerthner, "The Price Is Wrong," *Sierra*, September/October 1990, 38.
21. Jon R. Luoma, "Discouraging Words," *Audubon* 88, September 1986, 98.
22. Ferguson and Ferguson, 41.
23. Ibid.
24. Wuerthner, 38.

25. Ibid.
26. Luoma, 98.

Part Three. THE INDUSTRIALIZATION OF BEEF

17. *The Beef Trust*

1. Jimmy M. Skaggs, *Prime Cut* (College Station: Texas A&M University Press, 1976) 90.
2. Ibid., 91–94.
3. Ibid., 96–99.
4. U.S. Federal Trade Commission, *Report on the Meat Packing Industry*, 6 vols. (Washington, D.C.: U.S. Government Printing Office, 1919), 46–47.
5. Quoted in Skaggs, 100–1.
6. Quoted in ibid.
7. Ibid., 105.
8. Ibid., 102–3.
9. Eric B. Ross, *Beyond the Myths of Culture* (New York: Academic Press, 1980), 208.
10. Ibid., 209.

18. *The Disassembly Line*

1. James R. Barrett, *Work and Community in the Jungle: Chicago's Packinghouse Workers* (Urbana: University of Illinois Press, 1987), 56.
2. Siegfried Giedion, *Mechanization Takes Command* (New York: W. W. Norton, 1969), 212.
3. Upton Sinclair, *The Jungle*, with Introduction and Notes by James R. Barrett (Urbana: University of Illinois Press, 1988), 32.
4. Quoted in Carol J. Adams, *The Sexual Politics of Meat* (New York: Continuum, 1990), 52.
5. Barrett, 24.
6. Henry Ford, *My Life and Work* (1922), 81, quoted in Allan Nevins, *Ford: The Times, the Man, the Company* (New York: Charles Scribner's Sons, 1954), 471–72.
7. Giedion, 246.
8. Jimmy M. Skaggs, *Prime Cut* (College Station: Texas A&M University Press, 1976), 110.
9. John R. Commons, ed., "Labor Conditions in Slaughtering and Meat Packing," in *Trade Unionism and Labor Problems* (Boston: Ginn & Co., 1905), 224.
10. Paul Aldrich, ed., *The Packers' Encyclopedia* (Chicago: National Provisioner, 1922), 20, quoted in James R. Grossman, "A Dream Deferred: Black Migration to Chicago, 1916–1921," Ph.D. diss. (University of California, Berkeley, 1982), 254.
11. *National Provisioner* 39, October 17, 1908, and Dec. 5, 1908.
12. Sinclair, 39.
13. Skaggs, 112.
14. Ibid., 115.
15. Ibid., 116-18.
16. Ibid., 160; Barrett, 256-59.

17. Quoted in Barrett, 259.
18. Ibid, 263.

19. Modern Meat

1. Jimmy M. Skaggs, *Prime Cut* (College Station: Texas A&M University Press, 1986), 9.
2. Quoted in ibid., 190–91.
3. A. V. Krebs, *Heading Towards the Last Roundup: The Big Three's Prime Cut* (Des Moines: Prairie Fire Rural Action, June 1990), 48.
4. Ibid., 48, 53–4.
5. Quoted in ibid., 60.
6. Ibid., 51.
7. Peggy Hillman, "Speeches" in Lewis G. Anderson, *Solidarity: An Injury to One Is an Injury to All*. General Report of the 1986 National Packinghouse Strategy and Policy Conference, United Food and Commercial Workers International Union, AFL-CIO, Section Two, 18–28.
8. Krebs, 61; Bruce Ingersoll, "Worker Injuries Highest in Meat Packing," *Los Angeles Times*, October 18, 1978; Christopher Drew, "Meatpackers Pay the Price," *Chicago Tribune*, October 23, 1988, Sec. 1.
9. Government Accountability Project, Comments on Proposed Rule on Streamlined Inspection System to Linda Carey, May 15, 1989, USDA Docket No. 83-008P, 27.
10. Quoted in Ingersoll.
11. Robert D. Hersey, "Meatpacker Fined a Record Amount on Plant Injuries," *New York Times*, October 29, 1988; Krebs, 62.
12. Hillman, 18-28.
13. Krebs, 23.
14. Quoted in Jonathan Kwitny, *Vicious Cycles: The Mafia in the Marketplace* (New York: W. W. Norton, 1979), 252–53.
15. Quoted in ibid.
16. Skaggs, 195.
17. Quoted in Frances Moore Lappé, *Diet for a Small Planet* (New York: Ballantine, 1982), 44.
18. Skaggs, 198.
19. Bartell Nyberg, "ConAgra Exercising Option to Buy SIPCO," *Denver Post*, July 25, 1989.
20. "Concentration in Meat Packing," *CRA Newsletter* (Center for Rural Affairs), August 1987.
21. Bruce Marion, "Restructuring of Meat Packing Industries: Implications for Farmers and Consumers," presented at hearings held by the House Agricultural Committee of the Iowa State Legislature, Des Moines, Iowa, December 7, 1988; Dale Kasler, "IBP Keeps Tight Grip on Market," *Des Moines Register*, Sept. 24, 1988.

20. The Automated Jungle

1. Upton Sinclair, *The Jungle*, with an Introduction and Notes by James R. Barrett (Urbana: University of Illinois Press, 1988), 131.
2. Quoted in Jimmy M. Skaggs, *Prime Cut* (College Station: Texas A&M University Press, 1986), 124.

3. Ibid., 209.

4. Ibid., 209–10.

5. Quoted in commentary from Carol Foreman to Linda Carey, May 15, 1989, U.S. Department of Agriculture, Food Safety and Inspection Service, Public Docket No. 83-008P, 53 *Federal Register* 48262, November 30, 1988, Public Comments on Food Safety and Inspection Service Proposed Rule on Streamlined Inspection System for Meat Safety, 5.

6. Government Accountability Project, Fact Sheet on Streamlined Inspection System, August 16, 1989, 1.

7. Commentary from Bill Detlefsen to Linda Carey, April 23, 1989, USDA Docket No. 83-008P.

8. Commentary from Stephen Cockerham to Linda Carey, January 13, 1989, USDA Docket No. 83-008P.

9. Government Accountability Project, Comments on Proposed Rule on Streamlined Inspection System to Linda Carey, May 15, 1989, USDA Docket No. 83-008P, 14.

10. Government Accountability Project, Summary of 1990 Whistleblowing Disclosures on USDA's Proposed Streamlined Inspection System (Washington, D.C.: GAP, 1990), 5.

11. Commentary from Gregory Harstick to Linda Carey, January 13, 1989, USDA Docket No. 83-008P, 2.

12. Commentary, Foreman to Carey, 4.

13. Ibid.

14. Government Accountability Project to Carey, 3.

15. Ibid., 4.

16. Commentary from Jim Dekker to Linda Carey, January 13, 1989, USDA Docket No. 83-008P.

17. Government Accountability Project, Summary 6, "To Carey," 15.

18. Government Accountability Project to Carey, 15.

19. Commentary, Foreman to Carey, 12.

20. Commentary, Dekker to Carey.

21. Government Accountability Project to Carey, 22.

22. Government Accountability Project, Summary, 7.

23. Ibid., 8.

24. Commentary from Dora Fries to Linda Carey, Jan. 18, 1989, USDA Docket No. 83-008P, 1.

25. Government Accountability Project, Summary, 1.

26. Ibid., 2.

27. Ibid.

28. Ibid.

29. Ibid.

30. Ibid.

31. Ibid., 3.

32. Commentary, Foreman to Carey, 3.

33. Ibid.

34. Government Accountability Project, *Summary*, 3.

35. Commentary, Foreman to Carey, 4.

36. Government Accountability Project to Carey, 10.

37. Commentary, Harstick to Carey, 2.

38. Commentary, Foreman to Carey, 19.

39. Government Accountability Project to Carey, 11.
40. Foreman to Carey, 19.
41. Government Accountability Project to Carey, 10.
42. Commentary, Cockerham to Carey, 9; Commentary from Michael Anderson to Linda Carey, January 30, 1989, USDA Docket No. 83-008P, 5.
43. Commentary, Anderson to Carey, 5.
44. Government Accountability Project, Summary, 4.
45. Ibid., 4.
46. Government Accountability Project, Commentary from John Krusinski to Linda Carey, May 2, 1989, USDA Docket No. 83-008P, 2.
47. Ibid., 3.
48. Ibid., 2.
49. Ibid., 1.
50. Stephanie Pain, "Mad Cows and Ministers Lose Their Heads," *New Scientist*, August 11, 1968, 27; Sheila Rule, "Fatal Illness in Cows Leads to British Inquiry," *New York Times*, May 20, 1990; Joe Vansickle, "Mad Cow Disease Baffles British," *Beef*, August 1990.
51. Foundation on Economic Trends, Jeremy Rifkin, Petition to USDA, Center for Disease Control, and NIH on Bovine Immunodeficiency Virus. August 3, 1987; James Wyngaarden, B (NIH) and Bert Hawkins (USDA). Letter to Jeremy Rifkin, Foundation on Economic Trends, Washington, D.C., September 23, 1987. Foundation on Economic Trends, Petition to Dr. Bernadine Healy, NIH, Edward Madigan, USDA, and James Glosser, APHIS, USDA on BIV, BLV and Retroviruses of American Cattle, Washington, D.C.: Foundation on Economic Trends, May 31, 1991.
    Response by Dr. Bernadine Healy, NIH, July 18, 1991.
52. Ibid.
53. Response to Freedom of Information Request of March 18, 1991, to Foundation on Economic Trends, Van Der Maaten, M.J. and C.A. Whetstone, Bovine Lentivirus, USDA Agricultural Research Service, Ames, Iowa; Keith Schneider, "AIDS-Like Cow Virus Found at Unexpectedly High Rate," *New York Times*, June 1, 1991.

21. *The World Steer*

1. Eric B. Ross, "An Overview of Trends in Dietary Variation from Hunter-Gatherer to Modern Capitalist Societies," in Marvin Harris and Eric B. Ross, eds., *Food and Evolution* (Philadelphia: Temple University Press, 1987), 33.
2. Quoted in Ross, 33.
3. Arnold Strickton, "The Euro-American Ranching Complex," in Anthony Leeds and Andrew P. Vayda, *Man, Culture, and Animals* (Washington, D.C.: American Association for the Advancement of Science, 1965), 235.
4. Ross, 33–34.
5. Office of Technology Assessment, Technologies to Sustain Tropical Forest Resources, U.S. Congress, OTA-F-214, March 1984, Forest Resources, 96–97.
6. Steven E. Sanderson, "The Emergence of the World Steer . . . ," in F. Lamond Tullis and W. Ladd Hollist, eds., *Food, State, and International Political Economy* (Lincoln: University of Nebraska, 1986), 124.
7. Ibid.

8. Ibid., 147.

9. Quotes from Sanderson, 135, 139; telephone communication with Linda Bailey, Economic Research Service, USDA, Washington, D.C.; meat shipments are from USDA, Foreign Agriculture Service, as summarized by Scott Lewis, *The Hamburger Connection Revisited: The Status of Tropical Deforestation and Conservation in Central America and Southern Mexico* (San Francisco: Rainforest Action Network, 1991).

10. Associacão Promotora de Estudos da Économica, A Economica Brasil-eira e Suas Perspectives, Apecao XXIX, 1990 (Rio de Janeiro: APEC, 1990), 5. FAO of the United Nations, *Trade, Commerce, Commercio, 1989 Yearbook* (Rome, Italy: FAO, 1990), vol. 43, 29; Fernando Homen de Melo, "Unbalanced Technological Change and Income Disparity in a Semi-Open Economy: The Case of Brazil," in Tullis and Hollist, 262-75.

11. David Barkin and Billie R. Dewalt, "Sorghum, the Internationalization of Capital and the Mexican Food Crisis," paper presented at the American Anthropological Association Meeting, Denver, 16 November 1984, 16; acreage figures from Scott Lewis, "The Hamburger Connection Revisited . . ."; grain figures from Barkin and Dewalt, p. 16; and Steven Sanderson, *The Transformation of Mexican Agriculture* (Princeton: Princeton University Press, 1986).

12. Sanderson, 134.

13. Ibid., 139.

14. Catherine Caulfield, "A Reporter at Large: The Rain Forests," *New Yorker*, Jan. 14, 1985, 80.

Part Four. FEEDING CATTLE AND STARVING PEOPLE

22. Cattle Everywhere

1. Food and Agricultural Organization of the United Nations, *Production, 1989 Yearbook*, Vol 43 (Rome, Italy: FAO, 1990), table 89.

2. Paul Ehrlich and Anne Ehrlich, *The Population Explosion* (New York: Simon & Schuster, 1990), 35.

3. David Pimentel and Carl Hall, eds., *Food and Natural Resources* (San Diego: Academic Press, 1989), 80.

4. World Resources Institute et al., *World Resources 1990–91* (New York: Oxford University Press, 1990), table 18.3, 282–83.

5. Ibid.

6. Ibid.; U.S. Department of Commerce, Bureau of the Census, *Statistical Abstract of the United States 1990*, table 1162.

7. M. E. Ensminger, *Animal Science* (Danville, Ill.: Interstate Publishers, 1991), 22.

8. Lynn Jacobs, "Amazing Graze: How the Livestock Industry Is Ruining the American West," in *Desertification Control Bulletin, No. 17* (Nairobi, Kenya: United Nations Environmental Program, 1988); Free Our Public Lands, P.O. Box 5784, Tucson, Ariz. 85703, *Public Lands Ranching Statistics 1990*.

9. World Resources Institute and International Institute for Environment and Development, *World Resources, 1988–89* (New York: Basic Books, 1988), 78; Edward C. Wolf, "Maintaining Rangelands," in Lester Brown et al., *The State of the World 1986* (New York: W. W. Norton, 1986), 64.

10. FAO, *Production*, table 92.
11. Ibid.
12. Ibid.
13. Ibid.
14. Beef cattle sales figures come from Bureau of the Census, *Statistical Abstract 1990*, table 1123. Supermarket sales come from C. David Coats, *Old Macdonald's Factory Farm* (New York: Continuum, 1989), 69.
15. "Cattle Feeding Concentrates in Fewer, Larger Lots," *Farmline*, June 1990.
16. FAO, *Production*, table 92.
17. Marvin Harris, *The Sacred Cow and the Abominable Pig* (New York: Touchstone/ Simon & Schuster, 1987), 109.
18. Jim Riley, "Where Are Beef's Potential Markets," *Beef*, July 1989, 30.
19. FAO, *Production*, table 92; Bureau of the Census, *Statistical Abstract 1990*, table 1161.
20. Judith Jones Putnam, "Food Consumption," *National Food Review* 13:3 (November 20, 1990).
21. Max Boas and Steve Chain, *Big Mac* (New York: Dutton, 1976), 118.
22. Marvin Harris, "The Revolutionary Hamburger," *Psychology Today*, October 1983, 6.
23. Based on 65 pounds of meat a year and 659 pounds of dressed meat per 1,105-pound steer. M. E. Ensminger, *Animal Science*, 468, table 19-6.
24. Norman Meyers, *The Primary Source* (New York: W. W. Norton, 1983), 135; Bureau of the Census, *Statistical Abstract 1990*, table 1451.
25. *Choices*, Fourth Quarter 1989, 26.
26. Joe Vansickle, "A Tripling by Century's End," *Beef*, August 1990.
27. Jay Richter, "Washington Report," *Beef*, July 1989, 15.
28. Frances Moore Lappé, *Diet for a Small Planet* (New York: Ballantine Books, 1982), 90; Vansickle, *Beef*, August 1990, 30. David Blandford, "The Food People Eat," in C. Ritson et al., *The Food Consumer* (New York: Wiley, 1986), 29.
29. Blandford, 28-9.
30. Ibid.
31. Harris, *Sacred Cow*, 25.
32. Ibid.

23. Malthus and Meat

1. Thomas Robert Malthus, *Population: The First Essay* (Ann Arbor: Ann Arbor Paperbacks/University of Michigan Press, 1959), 5.
2. Ibid., 6.
3. Lester R. Brown et al., *State of the World 1990* (Washington, D.C.: Worldwatch Institute; New York: W. W. Norton, 1990), 3-4.
4. Ibid., 4.
5. Ibid.; World Resources Institute et al., *World Resources 1990–91*, 86.
6. Brown et al., *State of the World 1990*, 10.
7. Ibid., 5.
8. Lester Brown et al. *State of the World 1989* (Washington, D.C.: Worldwatch Institute; New York: W. W. Norton, 1989), 55.
9. Paul Ehrlich and Ann Ehrlich, *Population Explosion* (New York: Simon & Schuster, 1990), 66–87; Brown et al., *State of the World 1989*, 43–46.

10. World Resources Institute et al., *World Resources 1990–91*, 254, table 16.1; Ehrlich and Ehrlich, 14.

11. Paul and Anne Ehrlich, 18; statement released September 3, 1988, at the Pugwash Conference on Global Problems and Common Security, at Dagomys, near Sochi, USSR.

12. G. Tyler Miller, *Energetics, Kinetics and Life* (Belmont, Calif.: Wadsworth, 1971), 291.

13. U.S. Department of Agriculture, Economic Research Service, *World Agricultural Supply and Demand Estimates*, WASDE-256, (Washington D.C.: USDA, July 11, 1991), tables 256-6, -7, -16, -19, -23.

14. M. E. Ensminger, *Animal Science* (Danville, Ill.: Interstate Publishers, 1991), 23.

15. Ibid., fig. 1-25, 20.

16. David Pimentel and Marcia Pimentel, *Food, Energy and Society* (New York: Wiley, 1979), 58.

17. Ensminger, 23: "Assuming a feeding period of 140 days and a gain of 450 lb in the lot, the total market weight (1050 lb) would represent 2.57 lb of feed grain expended for each pound of gain (450 × 6 = 2,700 . . .)."

18. USDA, Economic Research Service, WASDE–256, ibid. David Pimentel et al., "Energy and Land Constraints in Food Protein Production," *Science* 190 (1975), 756.

19. Frances Moore Lappé, *Diet for a Small Planet* (New York: Ballantine Books, 1982), 69.

20. Ibid., 71.

21. World Commission on Environment and Development, *Our Common Future: The Bruntland Commission Report* (Oxford: Oxford University Press, 1987), 120.

22. Quoted in Doyle, *Altered Harvest* (New York: Viking Penguin, 1985), 287.

23. "Climbing the Protein Ladder," *Farm Journal*, December 1978, 52.

24. USDA, Economic Research Service, WASDE-256, tables WASDE 256-6, -16.

25. Frances Moore Lappé and Joseph Collins, *Food First: Beyond the Myth of Scarcity* (New York: Ballantine Books, 1982), 166.

26. Lappé, 92.

27. Marvin Harris, *The Sacred Cow and the Abominable Pig* (New York: Touchstone/ Simon & Schuster, 1987), 24.

28. A. Moyes, *Common Ground* (Boston: Oxfam, 1985).

29. Paul Ehrlich et al., *Ecoscience: Population, Resources, Environment* (San Francisco: W. H. Freeman, 1977), 315; Ensminger, 20, 22.

30. Pimentel et al., "Energy Land Constraints," 754.

31. David Pimentel and Carl W. Hall, *Food and Natural Resources* (San Diego: Academic Press, 1989), 38; Doyle, 288.

32. Brown et al., *State of the World 1990*, 5, table 1-1.

24. The Sociology of Fat

1. P. J. Brown and M. Konner, "An Anthropological Perspective on Obesity," in Richard J. Wurtman and Judith Wurtman, eds., *Human Obesity, Annals of the New York Academy of Sciences* 499 (1987), 40.

2. Pauline S. Powers, *Obesity: The Regulation of Weight* (Baltimore: William & Wilkins, 1980), 205, 207.

3. Ibid., 206.

4. Ibid., 207.
5. Alan L. Otten, "People Patterns," *Wall Street Journal*, July 14, 1989, B1.
6. George A. Bray, "Overweight Is Risking Fate . . . " in Wurtman and Wurtman, eds., 18.
7. Ibid.
8. Warren E. Leary, "Young Women Are Getting Fatter, Study Finds," *New York Times*, February 23, 1989.
9. Wayne J. Millar and Thomas Stephens, "The Prevalence of Overweight and Obesity in Britain, Canada, and United States," *American Journal of Public Health* (77)1, January 1987, 40–1.
10. Brown and Konner, 39.
11. Esther D. Rothblum, "Women and Weight: Fad and Fiction," *Journal of Psychology* 124 (January 1990), 9.
12. Rita Freedman, *Beauty Bound* (Lexington, Mass.: Lexington Books, 1985), 146–47.
13. Rothblum, 12–13.
14. *MS.* magazine, February 1987; Quoted in Stuart Ewen, *All Consuming Images: The Politics of Style in Contemporary Culture* (New York: Basic Books, 1988), 181.
15. Ewen, 181–82; *Glamour*, February 1984.
16. Quoted in Freedman, 150.
17. Ewen, 173–74.
18. Freedman, 149–50.

25. Marbled Specks of Death

1. M. Hindhede, "The Effect of Food Restriction During War on Mortality in Copenhagen," *Journal of American Medical Association*, February 7, 1920, 381.
2. Gail Vines, "Diet, Drugs and Heart Disease," *New Scientist*, February 25, 1989, 44.
3. Telephone Contact with Barbara Anderson, USDA, Beltsville, Md., 1991, confirming that choice-grade beef has 15% to 19% more fat than select-grade beef.
4. Walter H. Corson, ed., *The Global Ecology Handbook* (Boston: Beacon Press, 1990), 72; Steve Connor, "This Week," *New Scientist*, August 4, 1988, 28; disease death rates from: Bureau of the Census, United States Dept. of Commerce, *Statistical Abstract of the United States, 1990* (Washington D.C.: U.S. Government Printing Office, 1990), Table 115.
5. Connor, ibid.; Corson, 72.
6. U.S. Public Health Service, Office of the Surgeon General, *The Surgeon General's Report on Nutrition and Health* (New York: Warner, 1989).
7. George A. Bray, "Overweight Is Risking Fate . . ." in Richard J. Wurtman and Judith Wurtman, eds., Human Obesity, Annals of the New York Academy of Sciences 490 (1987), 21.
8. Powers, Pauline A., *Obesity*: The Regulation of Weight (Baltimore: William and Wilkins, 1980), 39.
9. Gina Kolata, "Animal Fat Is Tied to Colon Cancer," *New York Times*, December 13, 1990.
10. Quoted in ibid.
11. Walter C. Willet et al., "Relationship of Meat, Fat, and Fiber Intake to the Risk

of Colon Cancer in Prospective Study Among Women," *New England Journal of Medicine*, 333:24 (1990), 1664.

12. J. Raloff, "Breast Cancer Rise: Due to Dietary Fat?" *Science News*, April 21, 1990, 245.

13. *Science News*, Nov. 10, 1990, 302; Geoffrey Howe et al., "A Cohort Study of Fat Intake and Risk of Breast Cancer," *Journal of National Cancer Institute* 85: 5 (March 6, 1991).

14. Micheal Fox and Nancy Wiswall, *The Hidden Costs of Beef* (Washington, D.C.: Humane Society of the United States, 1989), 20.

15. Raloff, 245.

16. Jane E. Brody, "Huge Study of Diet Indicts Fat and Meat," *New York Times*, May 8, 1990, C1.

17. Ibid.

18. Nanci Hellmich, "In Healthful Living, East Beats West," *USA Today*, June 6, 1990.

19. Anne Simon Moffat, "China: A Living Lab for Epidemology," *Science* 248, May 4, 1990, 554.

20. Ibid., 553.

21. Brody, C14.

22. Drew Disilver, "Beefing up Sales; Meat Industry Targets Japan," News Digest, *Vegetarian Times*, February 1988.

23. American Heart Association, *1991 Heart and Stroke Facts* (Dallas: American Heart Association, 1991), 1, 4.

24. National Cancer Institute, *NCI Fact Book* (U.S. Public Health Service, 1989); Fox and Wiswall, 27; $84 billion annual cancer cost figure for 1987 was increased by 5 percent a year to update to 1991.

25. Quoted in Dorothy Mayes, "3 Ounces Per Day," *Beef*, April 1989, 34.

26. Quoted in K. A. Fackelman, "Health Groups Find Consensus on Fat in Diet," *Science News* 137, March 3, 1990, 132.

27. Corson, 72. David Pimentel cites daily U.S. protein consumption as 102 grams per person, including 70 grams of animal protein and 32 grams from plant sources, in Pimentel, "Waste in Agriculture and Food Sectors: Environmental and Social Costs," Draft Commissioned by the Gross National Waste Product Forum, Arlington, Virginia, 1989. 12. The Surgeon General's Report on Nutrition and Health estimates that, in 1985, Americans received much more than the recommended dietary protein allowance.

28. Frances Moore Lappé, *Diet for a Small Planet* (New York: Ballantine Books, 1982), 121–22.

26. Cows Devour People

1. Lester R. Brown, *State of the World 1990*, (Washington, D.C.: Worldwatch Institute; New York: W. W. Norton, 1990), 136.

2. Ibid., 137.

3. Bread for the World, "Hunger 1992: Second Annual Report on the State of World Hunger," Washington, D.C.; and "The Cyprus Initiative," Hunger Project Occasional Papers, 1990, New York.

4. Susan Okie, "Health Crisis Confronts 1.3 Billion," *Washington Post*, September 25, 1989, A1.

5. Ibid.

6. Oxfam-America, "Fact Sheet."

7. Christiane Viedma, "A Health and Nutrition Atlas," *World Health*, May 1988, 11.

8. Saul Balagura, *Hunger: A Biopsychological Analysis* (New York: Basic Books, 1973), 155.

9. Ibid., 158.

10. Viedma.

Part Five. CATTLE AND THE GLOBAL ENVIRONMENTAL CRISIS

27. *Ecological Colonialism*

1. Alfred W. Crosby, *Ecological Imperialism* (New York: Cambridge University Press, 1986), 151.

2. Ibid., 153–54.

3. Ibid., 288.

4. Ibid., 289.

5. Ibid., 158.

6. Ibid., 157.

7. Ibid., 158.

8. Quoted in Robert Schery, "Migration of a Plant," *Natural History* 74, December 1965, 41–49.

9. Crosby, 158–59.

10. Ibid., 164.

11. Ibid., 154–55.

12. Charles Darwin, *Voyage of the Beagle* (Garden City, N.Y.: Doubleday, 1962), 119.

13. Crosby, 160; Darwin, 119–20.

14. Ibid., 161.

15. Ibid., 180.

16. Ibid., 182.

17. Quoted in ibid.

18. Ibid., 162.

19. Quoted in ibid., 289–90.

20. Ibid., 163.

21. Ibid.

28. *Tropical Pastures*

1. Catherine Caulfield, "A Reporter at Large: The Rain Forests," *New Yorker*, January 14, 1985, 79.

2. James Parsons, "Forest to Pasture: Development or Destruction?" *Revista de Biologia Tropical* 24, Supplement 1, 1976, 124.

3. Quoted in James J. Parsons, "The Scourge of Cows," *Whole Earth Review*, Spring 1988, 47; Sandra Kaiser, "Costa Rica: From Banana to Hamburger Republic," *Not Man Apart*, May 1985.

4. Norman Meyers, *The Primary Source* (New York: W. W. Norton, 1983) 133; beef import figures from USDA, Foreign Agricultural Service as summarized

by Scott Lewis, *The Hamburger Connection Revisited: The Status of Tropical Deforestation and Conservation in Central America and Southern Mexico* (San Francisco: Rainforest Action Network, 1991); personal communication with Scott Lewis.

5. Caulfield, 79; Meyers, 134.
6. Meyers, 133; export and production figures from USDA, Foreign Agriculture Service as summarized by Scott Lewis, ibid.
7. Billie R. DeWalt, "The Cattle are Eating the Forest," *Bulletin of the Atomic Scientists*, January 1983, 19; export and production figures from USDA, Foreign Agriculture Service as summarized by Scott Lewis, ibid.
8. Meyers, 133; export figures from USDA, ibid.
9. DeWalt, 19.
10. Quoted in Tom Barry, *Roots of Rebellion* (Boston: South End Press, 1987), 84; quoted in Stephen Downer, "Cattle Ranchers Kill Mexican Rain Forests," *Daily Telegraph*, February 20, 1989.
11. Parsons, "Scourge," 45.
12. Francis Moore Lappé and Joseph Collins, *Food First Beyond the Myth of Scarcity* (New York: Ballantine Books, 1978), 42; Lovell S. Jarvis, *Livestock Development in Latin America* (Washington, D.C.: World Bank, 1986), 157.
13. Andrew Revkin, *The Burning Season* (Boston: Houghton Mifflin, 1990).
14. Caulfield, 49.
15. Julie Denslow and Christine Padoch, *People of the Tropical Rain Forest* (Berkeley: University of California Press, 1988), 168.
16. Meyers, 138.
17. Meyers, 137.
18. Parsons, "Scourge," 44; Caulfield, 49.
19. Jeremy Rifkin, *Biosphere Politics: A New Consciousness for a New Century* (New York: Crown, 1991), 51.
20. Denslow and Padoch, 169.
21. Meyers, 137.
22. Rifkin, 51.
23. Caulfield, 42.
24. Eugene Linden, "Playing with Fire," *Time*, September 18, 1989, 77.
25. Ibid.
26. Meyers, 47.
27. Caulfield, 52.
28. Ibid., 71.
29. Ibid., 53.
30. Caulfield, 54.
31. Ibid.
32. Ibid.
33. Ibid.
34. Meyers, 62.
35. Ibid., 65.
36. Ibid., 7.
37. Caulfield, 59–61.
38. Meyers, 8.
39. Lappé and Collins, 48.
40. James D. Nations, *Tropical Rainforests, Endangered Environment* (New York: Franklin Watts, 1988), 98.
41. World Commission on Environment and Development, *Our Common Future*,

The Brundtland Commission Report (Oxford: Oxford University Press, 1987), 151.

42. Denslow and Padoch, 169.
43. Quoted in Parsons, "Scourge," 44.
44. Quoted in Lappé and Collins, 53.

29. Hoofed Locusts

1. Quoted in David Pimentel and Carl W. Hall, *Food and Natural Resources* (San Diego: Academic Press, 1989), 100–1.
2. World Commission on Environment and Development, *Our Common Future*, The Brundtland Commission Report (Oxford: Oxford University Press, 1987), 127.
3. Paul Ehrlich and Anne Ehrlich, *The Population Explosion* (New York: Simon & Schuster, 1990), 127.
4. Corson, ed., 77.
5. Ehrlich and Ehrlich, 127.
6. Corson, ed., 77.
7. Quoted in Jodi L. Jacobson, *Environmental Refugees: A Yardstick of Habitability*, Worldwatch Paper No. 86 (Washington, D.C.: Worldwatch Institute, 1988), 10.
8. Robert Repetto, "Renewable Resources and Population Growth: Past Experiences and Future Prospects," *Population and Environment* 10:4 (Summer 1989), 228–29.
9. Corson, ed., 76.
10. Seifulaziz Milas, "Desert Spread and Population Boom" (United Nations Environment Program, Desertification Control Bulletin, December 1984), 11.
11. Quoted in Lester R. Brown et al., *State of the World 1990* (Washington, D.C.: Worldwatch Institute; New York: W. W. Norton, 1990), 60.
12. Ibid., 61.
13. Sandra Postel, *Water: Rethinking Management in an Age of Scarcity*, Worldwatch Paper No. 62 (Washington, D.C.: Worldwatch Institute, 1984), 25.
14. Michael Fox and Nancy Wiswall, *The Hidden Costs of Beef* (Washington, D.C.: The Humane Society of the United States, 1989), 29; France Moore Lappé, *Diet for a Small Planet* (New York: Ballantine Books, 1982), 80.
15. David Pimentel, "Waste in Agriculture and Food Sectors: Environmental and Social Costs" (draft commissioned by the Gross National Waste Product Forum, Arlington, Va., 1989), 5.
16. Lappé, 80.
17. Ibid.
18. Pimentel, "Waste in Agriculture and Food Sectors," 6.
19. Alan B. Durning, "Cost of Beef for Health and Habitat," *Los Angeles Times*, September 21, 1986, V3.
20. Based on animal unit monthly herbage consumption; Lynn Jacobs, "Amazing Graze: How the Livestock Industry is Ruining the American West," (United Nations Environmental Program, Desertification Control Bulletin 17, 1988), 14; John Lancaster, "Public Land, Private Profit," *Washington Post*, February 17, 1991, A1, A8, A9.
21. Jon Luoma, "Discouraging Words," *Audubon* 88 (September 1986): 104; Lancaster, A1, A8, A9.

22. Lancaster, A1, A8, A9.
23. Fox and Wiswall, 29; Jacobs, 15.
24. Denzel Ferguson and Nancy Ferguson, *Sacred Cows at the Public Trough* (Bend, Ore.: Maverick Publications, 1983), 61; Jacobs, 15.
25. Ferguson and Ferguson, 61.
26. Ibid.
27. Quoted in ibid., 64.
28. Luoma, 92.
29. George Wuerthner, "The Price Is Wrong," *Sierra*, September/October 1990, 40.
30. Quoted in ibid.
31. Ferguson and Ferguson, 74–75.
32. Philip L. Fradkin, "The Eating of the West," *Audubon* 81 (January 1979), 102. Ferguson and Ferguson, 75.
33. Ferguson and Ferguson, 75–77.
34. Ibid., 77.
35. Wuerthner, 41.
36. Ferguson and Ferguson, 94.
37. Ibid., 101–2.
38. Wuerthner, 41–42.
39. Ferguson and Ferguson, 116.
40. Wuerthner, 41–42.
41. Ferguson and Ferguson, 117.
42. Ibid., 135, 136.
43. Ibid., 136
44. Ibid., 136.
45. Keith Schneider, "Mediating the Federal War of the Jungle," *New York Times*, July 9, 1991, 4E.
46. Carol Grunewald, ed., *Animal Activist Alert*, 8:3 (Washington, D.C.: Humane Society of the United States, 1990), 3.
47. Edward Abbey, *One Life at a Time Please* (New York: Henry Holt, 1988), 13–14.
48. Johanna Wald and David Alberswerth, *Our Ailing Public Rangelands: Conditions Report—1989* (Washington, D.C.: National Wildlife Federation, 1989), 3–4.
49. Wuerthner, 39; Myra Klockenbrink, "The New Range War Has the Desert As Foe," *New York Times*, August 20, 1991, G4.
50. Luoma, 92.
51. Klockenbrink, ibid.
52. Quoted in Wuerthner, 39.
53. John McCormick and Bill Turque, "America's Outback," *Newsweek*, October 9, 1989, 78.
54. Ibid., 78.
55. Ibid., 80.
56. Ibid.

30. *Kicking Up Dust*

1. Klaus Meyn, *Beef Production in East Africa* (Munich: Weltforum-Verlag, 1970), 173–74.

2. Frances Moore Lappé and Joseph Collins, *Food First: Beyond the Myth of Scarcity* (New York: Ballantine Books, 1978), 46.

3. Seifulaziz Milas, "Desert Spread and Population Boom," (United Nations Environmental Program, Desertification Control Bulletin, 1984), 11.

4. Food and Agriculture Organization of the United Nations, *Production, 1989 Yearbook*, table 89; World Resources Institute et al., *World Resources 1990–91*, table 18.3, 282.

5. Lester R. Brown et al., *State of the World 1990* (Washington, D.C.: Worldwatch Institute; New York: W. W. Norton, 1990), 6.

6. David Pimentel and Carl W. Hall, *Food and Natural Resources* (San Diego: Academic Press, 1989), 455.

7. Environmental Investigation Agency, *The Death Trap Buffalo Fence* (Washington, D.C.: Environmental Investigation Agency, March 1991).

8. Micheal Fox and Nancy Wiswall, *The Hidden Costs of Beef* (Washington, D.C.: Humane Society of the United States, 1989), 8.

9. Quoted in Jodi Jacobson, *Environmental Refugees: A Yardstick of Habitability* (Washington, D.C.: Worldwatch Institute, 1988), 14.

10. Michael H. Glantz, ed., *Desertification* (Boulder, Colo.: Westview Press, 1977), 165–66.

11. Milas, 11.

12. Jacobson, 11.

13. Ibid.

14. Ibid.

15. Ibid.

16. Ibid., 12.

17. Ibid.

18. Robert Mann, "Development and the Sahel Disaster: The Case at Gambia," *Ecologist*, March/June 1987; see also Brown et al., *State of the World, 1988*, 10.

31. Quenching Thirst

1. Lester R. Brown et al., *State of the World 1990*, Washington, D.C.: Worldwatch, 1990; New York: W. W. Norton), 48.

2. Sandra Postel, *Water: Rethinking Management in an Age of Scarcity*, Worldwatch Paper 62 (1984), 5.

3. David Pimentel and Carl W. Hall, *Food and Natural Resources* (San Diego: Academic Press, Inc., 1989), 41.

4. Walter H. Corson, ed., *Global Ecology Handbook* (Boston: Beacon Press, 1990), 79; Postel, 13.

5. Corson, ed., 77.

6. Postel, 13.

7. Pimentel and Hall, 41.

8. Francis Moore Lappé, *Diet for a Small Planet* (New York: Ballantine Books, 1982), 76–77.

9. Ibid., 78.

10. Postel, 20.

11. Lappé, 78.

12. General Accounting Office, *Groundwater Overdrafting Must be Controlled*, Report to the Congress of the United States by the Comptroller General, CED-80-96, September 12, 1980, 3.

13. Paul Ehrlich and Anna Ehrlich *The Population Explosion* (New York: Simon and Schuster, 1990), 29.
14. Lappé, 79.
15. Ibid., 85.
16. General Accounting Office, *Federal Charges for Irrigation Projects Reviewed Do Not Cover Costs*, Report to the Congress of the United States by the Comptroller General, PAD-81-07, March 3, 1981, 26.
17. David Pimentel, "Waste in Agriculture and Food Sectors: Environmental and Social Costs," paper for Gross National Waste Product, Arlington, Virginia, 1989, 9–10. 8.
18. Lappé, 86; Brown et al., *State of the World 1991*, 16–17.
19. Quoted in John Robbins, *Diet for a New America* (Walpole, N.H.: Stillpoint, 1987), 368.
20. M. E. Ensminger, *Animal Science* (Danville, Ill.: Interstate Publishers, 1991), 187, table 5–10.
21. David Pimentel, "Waste in Agriculture and Food Sectors: Environmental and Social Costs," paper for Gross National Waste Product Forum, Arlington, Va., 1989, 10–11; Lappé, 84.
22. Alan B. Durning, "Cost of Beef for Health and Habitat," *Los Angeles Times*, September 21, 1986, 3.
23. Ensminger, 187, table 5–9.
24. Based on analysis by John Sweeten, Texas A&M for the National Cattlemen's Association, 1990.

32. Warming Up the Planet

1. Irving Mintzer, *A Matter of Degrees: The Potential for Controlling the Greenhouse Effect*, World Resources Institute Research Report No. 5 (Washington, D.C.: World Resource Institute, 1987), i; World Resources Institute et al., *World Resources 1990–91*, table 24.3, 350.
2. A. M. Solomon, "The Global Cycle of Carbon"; R. M. Rotty and C. D. Masters, "Carbon Dioxide from Fossil Fuel Combustion: Trends, Resources, and Technological Implications"; R. A. Houghton, "Carbon Dioxide Exchange Between the Atmosphere and Terrestrial Ecosystems"; cited in John R. Trabalka, "Atmospheric Carbon Dioxide and the Global Carbon Cycle" (Washington, D.C.: U.S. Government Printing Office, 1985).
3. V. R. Ramanathan, "Trace Gas Trends and Their Potential Role in Climate Change," *Journal of Geophysical Research* 90 (1985), 5547–66.
4. World Resources Institute et al., 346, table 24.1, 109.
5. Ibid.
6. Paul Ehrlich and Anne Ehrlich, *The Population Explosion* (New York: Simon & Schuster, 1990), 115.
7. Robert J. Buschbacher, "Tropical Deforestation and Pasture Development," *BioScience* 36, January 1986, 25.
8. Eugene Linden, "Playing with Fire," *Time*, September 18, 1989, 78.
9. World Resources Institute et al., 38, 102, 346, table 24.1. Based on an older continuous estimate series. The new LANDSAT series does not extend back to 1987—telephone contact with Eric Rodenburg, WRI (measurement in tons of carbon).
10. Ibid., 348, table 24.2, 15, table 2.2.

11. David Pimentel, "Waste in Agriculture and Food Sectors: Environmental and Social Costs," paper for Gross National Waste Product, Arlington, Virginia, 1989, 9–10; Pimentel concludes that substituting a grass-feeding livestock system for the present grain and grass system would reduce energy inputs about 60 percent.

12. Alan B. Durning, "Cost of Beef for Health and Habitat," *Los Angeles Times*, 21 September 1986, p. 3.

13. Based on 65 pounds of beef consumed per person per year. The auto CO_2 emissions comparisons come from Andrew Kimbrell, "On the Road," in Jeremy Rifkin, ed., *The Green Lifestyle Handbook* (New York: Owl Book, 1990).

14. Lester R. Brown et al., *State of the World 1990* (Washington, D.C.: Worldwatch Institute; New York: W.W. Norton, 1990), 67.

15. Fred Pearce, "Methane: The Hidden Greenhouse Gas," *New Scientist*, May 6, 1990, 38.

16. Ibid.

17. Ibid., 37.

18. Ibid.

19. Ibid.

20. Methane emissions from livestock from World Resources Institute et al., 1990–91, 346, Table 24.1; cattle emissions as a percent of livestock emissions from Michael Gibbs and Kathleen Hogan, "Methane," *EPA Journal* (March/April 1990)

21. Pearce, 38; estimates of biomass and termite sources from World Resource Institute et al., 354.

22. Ibid.

23. Andrew Revkin, "Endless Summer," *Discover* 9, October 1988, 50.

24. Ibid.

25. James Hansen, NASA Goddard Institute for Space Studies, quoted in Revkin, 20.

26. Revkin, 18–19.

27. W. R. Rangley, "Irrigation and Drainage in the World," paper delivered at the International Conference on Food and Water, Texas A&M University, College Station, Texas, May 26–30, 1985.

28. Ibid.

29. Richard Akers, "Report Urges Greenhouse Action Now," *Science*, July 1988, 23.

30. Quoted in Jill Jaeger, "Developing Policies for Responding to Climate Change" (The Bellagio Report), Stockholm, Sweden: Beijer Institute's World Climate Programme—Impact Studies, April 1988, 1–2.

31. Quoted in Anthony Ramirez, "A Warming World," *Fortune*, July 4, 1988, 104.

Part Six. THE CONSCIOUSNESS OF BEEF-EATING CULTURES

33. The Psychology of Beef

1. Quoted in Theodor Adorno, *Minima Moralia: Reflections from Damaged Life* (London: NLB, 1978), 78.
2. Yi-fu Tuan, *Dominance and Affection: The Making of Pets* (New Haven: Yale University Press, 1984), 9.
3. Anne Murcott, "You Are What You Eat: Anthropological Factors Influencing Food Choice," in C. Ritson et al., eds., *The Food Consumer* (New York: Wiley, 1986), 110.
4. Quoted in Pauline S. Powers, *Obesity: The Regulation of Weight* (Baltimore: William & Wilkins, 1980), 224.
5. Roland Barthes, "Towards a Psychosociology of Contemporary Food," in Robert Forster and Orest Ranum, eds., *Food and Drink in History* (Baltimore: Johns Hopkins University Press, 1979), 168; Leslie Gofton, "The Rules of the Table: Sociological Factors Influencing Food Choice," in C. Ritson et al., 145–46.
6. Barthes, 167.

34. Meat and Gender Hierarchies

1. Carol J. Adams, *The Sexual Politics of Meat* (New York: Continuum, 1990), 189; Joseph Campbell, *The Masks of God: Primitive Mythology*, Vol. 1 (New York: Penguin, 1959, 1978), 129, 137.
2. Campbell, 129.
3. Claude Lévi-Strauss, *The Origin of Table Manners* (New York: Harper & Row, 1978), 478–79.
4. Ibid., 489.
5. Ibid., 484.
6. Quoted in Anne Murcott, "You Are What You Eat: Anthropological Factors Influencing Food Choice," in C. Ritson, et al., eds., *The Food Consumer* (New York: Wiley, 1986), 109.
7. Julia Twigg, "Vegetarianism and the Meanings of Meat," in Anne Murcott, ed., *The Sociology of Food and Eating* (Croft, Aldershot, England: Gower, 1983), 21–22; Julia Twigg, "Food for Thought: Purity and Vegetarianism," *Religion* 9, Spring 1979, 17; Murcott, "You Are What You Eat," 111.
8. Twigg, "Vegetarianism," 22.
9. Ibid., 23.
10. Murcott, "You Are What You Eat," 111–12.
11. Twigg, "Vegetarianism," 24.
12. Murcott, "You Are What You Eat," 111–12; Twigg, "Food for Thought," 20.
13. Twigg, "Vegetarianism," 24.
14. Ibid., 25.
15. Ibid.
16. Adams, 35.
17. Ibid.
18. From Hegel's *Philosophy of Right*, para. 166, 263, quoted in Nancy Tuana, "The

Misbegotten Man: Scientific, Religious, and Philosophical Images of Women," unpublished manuscript.

19. Adams, 36.
20. Joanne Finklestein, *Dining Out* (New York: New York University Press, 1989), 48.
21. Pierre Bourdieu, *Distinction: A Social Critique of the Judgment of Taste*, trans., R. Nice (Cambridge, Mass.: Harvard University Press, 1984), 190, 192.
22. Ibid., 192.
23. Frederick J. Simoons, *Eat Not This Flesh: Food Avoidances in the Old World* (Madison: University of Wisconsin Press, 1961, 1967), 12.
24. Laura Oren, "The Welfare of Women in Laboring Families: England, 1860–1950," *Feminist Studies* 1: 3–4 (Winter-Spring 1973), 110, quoting B. S. Rowntree and May Kendall, *How the Labourer Lives: A Study of the Rural Labor Problem* (London: Thomas Nelson & Sons, 1913).
25. Adams, 29.
26. Ibid., 28.
27. Marion Kerr and Nicola Charles, "Servers and Providers: The Distribution of Food Within the Family," *Sociological Review* 34:1 (February 1986), 140.
28. Ibid., 155.
29. Ibid.
30. Adams, 28.
31. Quoted in "Red Meat: American Man's Last Symbol of Machismo," *National Observer* 10, July 1976, 13.
32. R. Emerson Dobash and Russell Dobash, *Violence Against Wives: A Case Against the Patriarchy* (New York: Free Press, 1979), 100.
33. Erin Pizzey, *Scream Quietly or the Neighbors Will Hear* (Hamondsworth, England: Penguin, 1974), 35.

35. Beef, Class, and Nationalism

1. Leslie Gofton, "The Rules of the Table: Sociological Factors Influencing Food Choice," in C. Ritson et al., eds., *The Food Consumer* (New York: Wiley, 1986), 141.
2. Carson I. A. Ritchie, *Food in Civilization* (New York: Beaufort Books, 1981), 184.
3. Ibid.
4. Kathryn Grover, ed., *Dining in America, 1850–1900* (Amherst: University of Massachusetts Press, 1987), 172.
5. Quoted in Richard J. Hooker, *Food and Drink in America* (Indianapolis: Bobbs-Merrill, Inc., 1981), 313–14.
6. Roland Barthes, *Mythologies* (New York: Hill & Wang, 1971), 62.
7. Ibid., 62–63.
8. Ibid., 63.
9. Quoted in Adams, *The Sexual Politics of Meat* (New York: Continuum, 1990), 30.
10. From George M. Beard, M.D., *Sexual Neurasthenia*, quoted in ibid.
11. Ibid.
12. Ibid.
13. Quoted in Keith Thomas, *Man and the Natural World* (New York: Pantheon Books, 1983), 298.

14. Quoted in ibid., 299.
15. Adams, 32.
16. Russell Baker, "Red Meat Decadence," *New York Times*, April 3, 1973, 43.

36. Cattle and the Frontier Mentality

1. Quoted in Roderick Nash, *Wilderness and the American Mind* (New Haven: Yale University Press, 1982), 32.
2. Ibid., 24–25.
3. James Serpell, *In the Company of Animals* (New York: Basil Blackwell, 1988), 122.
4. From Book of Genesis, quoted in ibid.
5. Quoted in Keith Thomas, *Man and the Natural World* (New York: Pantheon Books, 1983), 18.
6. Quoted in John Herman Randall, *The Making of the Modern Mind* (Cambridge, Mass.: Houghton Mifflin, 1940), 224.
7. Bacon, "Novum Organum," *The Works of Francis Bacon*, Vol. 4, 246.
8. Quoted in Thomas, 27.
9. Quoted in ibid., 29.
10. Serpell, 124.
11. P. Singer, *Animal Liberation* (Wellingborough, England: Northants, Thorsons, 1983), 217–23.
12. Quoted in ibid., 219.
13. John Locke, *Two Treatises of Government*, ed. Peter Laslett (Cambridge, England: Cambridge University Press, 1967), 315.
14. Quoted in Leo Strauss, *Natural Rights and History* (Chicago: University of Chicago Press, 1953), 258.
15. Marquis de Condorcet, "Outline of an Historical View of the Progress of the Human Mind," quoted in John Hallowell, *Main Currents in Modern Political Thought* (New York: Holt, Rinehart & Winston, 1950), 132.
16. Frederick J. Turner, *The Significance of the Frontier in American History* (Ann Arbor, Mich.: University Microfilms, 1966), Foreword, 199.
17. Ibid., 199, 227.
18. Ibid., 200.
19. Ibid.
20. Ibid., 226–27.

37. The Hamburger and the Highway Culture

1. Curt Suplee, "Slave of the Lawn," *Washington Post Magazine*, April 30, 1989, 20.
2. Bureau of the Census, *Statistical Abstract 1990* , table 25.
3. Mark Edelman, "From Costa Rican Pasture to North American Hamburger," in Marvin Harris and Eric B. Ross, eds., *Food and Evolution* (Philadelphia: Temple University Press, 1987), 3.
4. Rose Dosti, "Whatever Happened to the Hamburger," *Los Angeles Times*, September 14, 1989, 8BB.
5. Max Boas and Steve Chain, *Big Mac—McDonald's* (New York: Dutton, 1976), 194; Richard D. Hooker, *Food and Drink in America* (Indianapolis: Bobbs Merrill, 1981), 329.

6. Boas and Chain, 47; Harris, *The Sacred Cow and the Abominable Pig* (New York: Touchstone/Simon & Schuster; 1987), 121; Hooker, 329.

7. Kenneth T. Jackson, *Crabgrass Frontier* (New York: Oxford University Press, 1985), 170–71.

8. Ibid., 161–62.

9. Ibid., 249.

10. Harris, *Sacred Cow*, 122.

11. Hooker, 327.

12. Ibid., 328.

13. Kenneth T. Jackson, 162.

14. Hooker, 325.

15. Harris, *Sacred Cow*, 120.

16. Ibid.

17. Ibid., 121.

18. Ibid., 124.

19. Ibid.

20. Ibid., 125–26.

21. Ibid., 126.

22. Eric B. Ross, *Beyond the Myths of Culture* (New York: Academic Press, 1980), 213–15.

23. Ibid., 214–15.

24. Alden C. Manchester, "Food Marketing Industry," USDA *Marketing, U.S. Agriculture 1988 Yearbook of Agriculture* (Washington, D.C.: U.S. Government Printing Office, 1988) 7.

25. Ibid., 8.

26. Steven D. Mayer, "W. S. Foodservice Industry," in ibid., 86.

27. Ibid.

28. Debi Sue Edmund, "The Secret Behind the Big Mac? It's Simple!" *Management Review* 79 (May 1990), 32–33.

29. Joanne Finkelstein, *Dining Out: A Sociology of Modern Manners* (New York: New York University Press, 1989), 46.

30. Boas and Chain, 36.

31. Conrad Kottak, "Rituals at McDonald's," in Marshall W. Fishwick, ed., *Ronald Revisited: The World of Ronald McDonald* (Bowling Green, Ohio: Bowling Green University Popular Press, 1983), 55.

32. Quoted in Margaret King, "Empires of Popular Culture," in Fishwick, ed., 118.

33. Kottak, in Fishwick, ed., 55.

34. Michael Steele, "What Can We Learn . . ." in Fishwick, ed., 127.

35. Boas and Chain, 53.

36. Ibid., 26.

37. Ray Kroc, *Grinding It Out: The Making of McDonald's* (Chicago: Regnery, 1977), 96.

38. Boas and Chain, 48.

39. Quoted in ibid., 50–51.

40. Ibid., 26.

41. Quoted in Sam Riley, "You Are What You Speak," in Fishwick, ed., 41.

42. Quoted in Boas and Chain, 177.

38. The Deconstruction of Modern Meat

1. Wolfgang Schad, *Man and Mammals* (Garden City, NY: Waldorf Press, 1977), 97.
2. Richard L. Kohls and Joseph N. Uhl, *Marketing of Agricultural Products* (New York: Macmillan, 1990), 391.
3. Douglas M. Considine and Glenn D. Considine, eds., *Foods and Food Production Encyclopedia* (New York: Van Nostrand Reinhold, 1982), 1170.
4. Ibid.
5. P. Thomas Zeigler, *The Meat We Eat* (Danville, Ill.: Interstate Publishers, 1966), 10; Travers Moncure Evans and David Greene, *The Meat Book* (New York: Charles Scribner's Sons), 107.
6. Considine and Considine, eds., 1164.
7. Ibid., 1165.
8. Ibid., 1199.
9. Elmer L. Cooper, *Agriscience, Fundamentals & Applications* (Albany: Delmar Publishers, 1990), fig. 30–6, 401.
10. James Serpell, *In the Company of Animals* (New York: Basil Blackwell, 1988), 144–45.
11. Ibid., 166–67.
12. Walter Burkert, *Homo Necans*, trans. P. Bing (Berkeley: University of California Press, 1983), 3–12.
13. Ibid.
14. Serpell, 168.
15. Ibid., 163–64.
16. Keith Thomas, *Man and the Natural World* (New York: Pantheon, 1983) 294; Serpell, 165.
17. Thomas, 295; Serpell, 165.
18. Quoted in Thomas, 294; Serpell, 165.
19. Quoted in Ronald Pearshall, *The Worm in the Bud: The World of Victorian Sexuality* (Toronto: Macmillan, 1969), 313.
20. Alain Corbin, *The Foul and the Fragrant: Odor and The French Social Imagination* (Cambridge, Mass.: Harvard University Press, 1986), 31.
21. Serpell, 155.
22. Quotations from the slaughterhouse tour episode found in Upton Sinclair, *The Jungle* (Urbana: University of Illinois Press, 1988), 36.
23. Adams, *The Sexual Politics of Meat* (New York: Continuum, 1990), 67; Serpell, 159.
24. "Doublespeak Awards Don't Mince Words," *Dallas Morning News*, November 20, 1988, 4A.
25. Serpell, 158.
26. William Hazlitt, "The Plain Speaker," quoted in Thomas, 300.

SELECTED BIBLIOGRAPHY

Abbey, Edward. *One Life at a Time, Please.* New York: Henry Holt, 1988.

Adams, Carol J. *The Sexual Politics of Meat.* New York: Continuum, 1990.

Akers, Richard. "Report Urges Greenhouse Action Now." *Science*, July 1988.

Alisky, Marvin. *Uruguay.* New York: Praeger, 1969.

Alston, Julian M., et al., "A Choices Debate on Japanese Beef Trade Liberalization." *Choices*, Fourth Quarter 1989.

American Heart Association. *1991 Heart and Stroke Facts.* Dallas: Texas: American Heart Association, 1991.

American National Cattle Women, Inc. *When Is a Cow More Than a Cow?* Pamphlet. Englewood, Colorado.

Baker, Russell. "Red Meat Decadence." *New York Times*, April 3, 1973, 43.

Balagura, Saul. *Hunger: A Biospsychological Analysis.* New York: Basic Books, 1973.

Barloy, J. J. *Man and Animals.* London: Gordon & Cremonesi, 1974.

Barrett, James R. *Work and Community in the Jungle: Chicago's Packinghouse Workers.* Urbana: University of Illinois Press, 1987.

Barry, Tom. *Roots of Rebellion.* Boston: South End Press, 1987.

Barthes, Roland. *Mythologies.* New York: Hill & Wang, 1972.

———. "Towards a Psychosociology of Contemporary Food." In Robert Forster, and Orest Ranum, eds. *Food and Drink in History.* Baltimore: Johns Hopkins University Press, 1979.

Batra, S. M. *Cows and Cow Slaughter in India*. The Hague: Institute of Social Studies Occasional Papers, 1981.

Beard, George M. *Sexual Neurasthenia (Nervous Exhaustion) Its Hygiene, Causes, Symptoms and Treatment*. New York: E.B. Treat, 1898; New York: Arno Press, 1972.

"Beef Consumption Is Down." *Agricultural Outlook*. June 1990, 16.

Berkes, F., et al. "The Benefits of the Commons." *Nature* 340, July 13, 1989.

Billington, Ray Allen. *The Frontier Thesis*. New York: Holt, Rinehart & Winston, 1966.

———. *Land of Savagery, Land of Promise*. New York: W. W. Norton, 1981.

Birchall, Annabelle. "The Rough Road to Slaughter." *New Scientist*, November 24, 1990, 33–38.

Blumenthal, Dale. "Making Sense of the Cholesterol Controversy." *FDA Consumer*, June 1990.

Boas, Max, and Steve Chain. *Big Mac: The Unauthorized Story of McDonald's*. New York: Dutton, 1976.

Boffey, Philip M., "Spread of Deserts Seen as a Catastrophe Underlying Famine." *The New York Times*. Science Section, January 8, 1985, C2.

Bolton, Herbert E. *Fray Juan Crespi: Missionary Explorer on the Pacific Coast, 1769–1774*. Berkeley: University of California Press, 1927.

Bolton, Herbert E. *The Padre on Horseback*. San Francisco: Sonora Press, 1932.

Boorstin, Daniel J. *The Americans: The Democratic Experience*. New York: Vintage Books, Random House, 1974.

Booth, William. "Nitrogen Fertilizers May Be Adding to 'Greenhouse Effect.' " *Washington Post*, September 23, 1989.

Bourdieu, Pierre. *Distinction: A Social Critique of the Judgment of Taste*. Trans. R. Nice. Cambridge, Mass.: Harvard University Press, 1984.

Braudel, Fernand. *Capitalism and Material Life, 1400–1800*. Glasgow: Fontana/William Collins, 1975.

Braunstein, Mark Matthew. "How Your Food Choices Affect Wild Animals." *East West*, February 1990.

Bray, George A. "Overweight is Risking Fate . . ." In Richard J. Wurtman and Judith Wurtman, eds., *Human Obesity, Annals of the New York Academy of Sciences* 499 (1987), 18.

Brisbane, Arthur S. "World's Grain Reserves Called Dangerously Low." *Washington Post*, September 26, 1989.

Brody, Jane E. "Huge Study of Diet Indicts Fat and Meat." *New York Times*, May 8, 1990, C1.

Brown, Mark H., and W. R. Felton, *Before Barbed Wire*. New York: Henry Holt, 1956.

Brown, P. J., and M. Konner. "An Anthropological Perspective on Obesity." In Richard J. Wurtman and Judith Wurtman, eds., *Human Obesity, Annals of the New York Academy of Sciences*, 499 (1987).

Brown, Lester, et al. *State of the World 1989*. Worldwatch Institute, New York: W. W. Norton, 1989.

———. *State of the World 1990*. Washington, D.C.: Worldwatch Institute; New York: W. W. Norton, 1990.

Burkert, Walter. *Homo Necans*. Trans. P. Bing. Berkeley: University of California Press, 1983.

Buschbacher, Robert J. "Tropical Deforestation and Pasture Development." *Bioscience* 36, January 1986.

Carlson, Peter. "Who Put the Sunshine in the Sunshine State?" *Washington Post Magazine*, December 16, 1990.

"Cattle Feeding Concentrates in Fewer, Larger Lots," *Farmline*, June 1990, 2–5.

Caulfield, Catherine. "The Rain Forests." *New Yorker*. January 14, 1985, 41.

Coats, C. David. *Old MacDonald's Factory Farm*. New York: Continuum, 1989.

Cody, William F. *The Life of Hon. William F. Cody: An Autobiography*. Lincoln: University of Nebraska Press, 1978.

Commons, John R., ed. "Labor Conditions in Slaughtering and Meat Packings," *Trade Unionism and Labor Problems*, Boston: Ginn and Co., 1905.

"ConAgra Ousts IBP as Nation's Largest Packer." *Beef*, September 1988.

Conrad, Jack Randolph. *The Horn and the Sword*. Westport, Conn.: Greenwood Press, 1973.

Considine, Douglas M., and Glenn D. Considine, eds. *Foods and Food Production Encyclopedia*. New York: Van Nostrand Reinhold, 1982.

"Cooking Up Colon Cancer." *Science News*, November 10, 1990, 302.

Cooper, Elmer L. *Agriscience, Fundamentals and Applications*. Albany: Delmar Publishers, 1990.

Corbin, Alain. *The Foul and the Fragrant: Odor and the French Social Imagination*. Cambridge, Mass.: Harvard University Press, 1986.

Corson, Walter H., ed. *The Global Ecology Handbook*. Boston: Beacon Press, 1990.

Cowen, Robert C., "Rapid Rise in Methane Gas May Speed Worldwide Climatic Changes." *Christian Science Monitor*, March 15, 1988.

"Concentration in Meat Packing." *CRA Newsletter*. Walthill, Nebraska: Center for Rural Affairs, August 1987.

Crosby, Alfred W. *Ecological Imperialism*. New York: Cambridge University Press, 1986.

Cummings, Richard Osborn. *The American and His Food*. Chicago: University of Chicago Press, 1940.

Dale, Edward Everett. *Cow Country*. Norman: University of Oklahoma Press, 1943.

Dary, David. *Cowboy Culture*. New York: Knopf, 1981.

Denslow, Julie, and Christine Padoch. *People of the Tropical Rain Forest*. Berkeley: University of California Press, 1988.

DeWalt, Billie R. "The Cattle Are Eating The Forest." *Bulletin of the Atomic Scientists*. January 1983.

Diamond, Jared. "War Babies." *Discover*, December 1990.

Dobash Emerson, R., and Russell Dobash. *Violence Against Wives: A Case Against the Patriarchy*. New York: The Free Press, 1979.

Dobie, J. Frank. *The Longhorns*. New York: Grosset & Dunlap, 1941.

Dosti, Rose. "Whatever Happened to the Hamburger." *Los Angeles Times*, Sept. 14, 1989.

Downer, Stephen. "Cattle Ranchers Kill Mexican Rain Forests." *Daily Telegraph*, Feb 20, 1989.

Doyle, Jack. *Altered Harvest*. New York: Viking Penguin, 1985.

Drew, Christopher. "Meatpackers Pay the Price." *Chicago Tribune*, Sunday, October 23, 1988, Sec. I.

Drinnon, Richard. *Facing West: The Metaphysics of Indian-Hating and Empire Building*. Minneapolis: University of Minnesota Press, 1980.

Durning, Alan B. "Cost of Beef for Health and Habitat." *Los Angeles Times*, September 21, 1986, V3.

Egan, Timothy. "In West, a Showdown over Rules on Grazing." *New York Times*, August 19, 1990.

Ehrlich, Paul R., et al. *Ecoscience: Population, Resources, Environment*. San Francisco: W. H. Freeman, 1977.

Ehrlich, Paul R., and Anne H. Ehrlich. *The Population Explosion*. New York: Simon & Schuster, 1990.

Eisler, Riane. *The Chalice and The Blade*. San Francisco: Harper & Row, 1987.

Eller, James M. "Cattle Genetics Made to Order." *Beef*, September 1989.

Ensminger, M. E. *Animal Science*. Danville, Ill.: Interstate Publishers, 1991.

Environmental Investigation Agency. *The Death Trap Buffalo Fence*. Washington, D.C.: Environmental Investigation Agency, March 1991.

Epstein, H. "Domestication Features in Animals as Functions of Human Society." In Philip L. Wagner and Marvin W. Mikesell, *Readings in Cultural Geography*. Chicago: University of Chicago Press, 1962.

Eriksen, P. J. *Slaughterhouse and Slaughterslab Design and Construction*. Rome: Food and Agriculture Organization of the United Nations, 1978.

Ernst, Margaret, and James Thurber. *In a World*. New York: Harper & Row, 1960.

Ewen, Stuart. *All Consuming Images: The Politics of Style in Contemporary Culture*. New York: Basic Books, 1988.

Ewer, T. K. *Humane Killing and Slaughterhouse Techniques.* Herfordshire, England: Universities Federation for Animal Welfare, 1971.

Ferguson, Denzel, and Nancy Ferguson. *Sacred Cows at the Public Trough.* Bend, Ore.: Maverick Publications, 1983.

Finkelstein, Joanne. *Dining Out.* New York: New York University Press, 1989.

Fishwick, Marshall W. "The Cowboy: America's Contribution to the World's Mythology." *Western Folklore* 11:2 (April 1952).

Fishwick, Marshall, ed. *Ronald Revisited: The World of Ronald McDonald.* Bowling Green, Ohio: Bowling Green University Popular Press, 1983.

Food and Agriculture Organization of the United Nations. *Production, Producción, 1989 Yearbook.* Vol. 43. Rome, Italy: FAO, 1990.

———. *Report on Natural Resources for Food and Agriculture in the Asia and Pacific Region.* FAO Environment and Energy Paper 7. Rome, Italy: FAO, 1986.

———. *Trade, Commerce, Commercio.* Vol. 43. Rome, Italy: FAO, 1989.

"Food Consumption." *National Food Review*, April-June, 1989, p.1.

"Foodservice Trends." *National Food Review* 37, c. 1986.

Foreman, Carol, Commentary to Linda Carey, May 15 1989. United States Department of Agriculture. Food Safety and Inspection Service. Public Docket No. 83-008P, 53 *Federal Register* 48262, November 30, 1988. "Public Comments on Food Safety and Inspection Service Proposed Rule on Streamlined Inspection System for Meat Safety."

Foundation on Economic Trends. Jeremy Rifkin, Petition to USDA, Center for Disease Control, and NIH on Bovine Immunodeficiency Virus. August 3, 1987; James Wyngaarden, B(NIH) and Bert Hawkins (USDA). Letter to Jeremy Rifkin, Foundation on Economic Trends, Washington, D.C., September 23, 1987.

Foundation on Economic Trends. Petition to Dr. Bernadine Healy, NIH, Edward Madigan, USDA, and James Glosser, APHIS, USDA, on BIV, BLV and Retroviruses of American Cattle. Washington, D.C.: Foundation on Economic Trends, September, 23 1987.

Fox, Michael, and Nancy Wiswall. *The Hidden Costs of Beef.* Washington, D.C.: Humane Society of the United States, 1989.

Fradkin, Philip L. "The Eating of the West." *Audubon* 81, January 1979.

Frazier, Ian. *Great Plains.* New York: Farrar, Straus & Giroux, 1989.

Free Our Public Lands. *Public Lands Ranching Statistics.* Tucson, Ariz.: c. 1989.

Freedman, Rita. *Beauty Bound.* Lexington, Mass.: Lexington Books, 1985.

Friend, Tim. "Colon Cancer Linked to Red Meat." *USA Today*, December 13, 1990.

Frink, Maurice, et al. *When Grass Was King.* Boulder: University of Colorado Press, 1956.

Galway, Katrina, et al. *Child Survival: Risks and Road to Health.* Columbia, Md.: Institute for Resource Development, March 1987.

Gard, Wayne. *The Great Buffalo Hunt.* New York: Knopf, 1959.

General Accounting Office. *Federal Charges for Irrigation Projects Reviewed Do Not Cover Costs.* Report to the Congress of the United States by the Comptroller General, PAD-81-07, March 3, 1981.

————. *Groundwater Overdrafting Must Be Controlled.* Report to the Congress of the United States by the Comptroller General, CED-80-96, September 12, 1980.

Gibbs, Michael, and Kathleen Hogan. "Methane." *EPA Journal*, March/April 1990.

Giedion, Siegfried. *Mechanization Takes Command: A Contribution to Anonymous History.* New York: W. W. Norton, 1969.

Gilbertson, G. B., et al. *Controlling Runoff for Livestock Feedlots.* Agricultural Research Service, Bulletin No. 441. Washington, D.C.: USDA, October 1981.

Gimbutas, Marija. "Old Europe, 7000–3300 BC: The Earliest European Civilization Before the Infiltration of the Indo-European Peoples." *Journal of Indo-European Studies* 1, Spring 1973.

————. "The First Wave of Eurasian Steppe Pastoralists into Copper Age Europe." *Journal of Indo-European Studies* 5, Winter 1977, 277–338.

Glantz, Michael H., ed. *Desertification.* Boulder, Colo.: Westview Press, 1977.

Glanz, Dawn. "The American West as Millennial Kingdom." In Lois Parkinson Zamora, ed., *The Apocalyptic Vision in America: Interdisciplinary Essays on Myth and Culture.* Bowling Green, Ohio: Bowling Green University Popular Press, 1982.

Glew, George. "Catering-Food Service Outside the Home." In C. Ritson, et al., eds., *The Food Consumer.* New York: Wiley, 1986.

Gofton, Leslie. "The Rules of the Table: Sociological Factors Influencing Food Choice." In C. Ritson, et al, eds., *The Food Consumer.* New York: Wiley, 1986.

Gold, Mark. "On the Meat-hook." *New Internationalist.* January 1991.

Goldblatt, Philip B., et al. "Social Factors in Obesity." *Journal of American Medical Association* 192:12 (June 21, 1965).

Goldemberg, Jose, et al. *Energy for Development.* Washington, D.C.: World Resources Institute, c. 1987.

Goldschmidt, Walter. "Theory and Strategy in the Study of Cultural Adaptability." *American Anthropologist* 67, 1965.

Goodenough, Ward. "The Evolution of Pastoralism and Indo-European Origins." In George Cardona, et al., eds., *Indo-European and Indo-Europeans.* Philadelphia: University of Pennsylvania Press, 1970.

Goody, Jack. *Cooking, Cuisine, and Class*. Cambridge, England: Cambridge University Press, 1982.

Government Accountability Project. Summary of 1990 Whistleblowing Disclosures on USDA's Proposed Streamlined Inspection System-Cattle. Washington, D.C.: GAP, 1990.

Griffin, Susan. *Woman and Nature*. New York: Harper & Row, 1980.

Grover, Kathryn, ed. *Dining in America, 1850–1900*. Amherst: University of Massachusetts Press, 1987.

Grunewald, Carol, ed. *Animal Activist Alert* 8:3. Washington, D.C.: The Humane Society of the United States, September, 1990.

Hackett, Charles, ed. *Historical Documents Relating to New Mexico, Nueva Vizcaya, and Approaches Thereto, to 1773*. Vol. 1. Washington, D.C.: Carnegie Institution, 1923.

Hallberg, George R. "From Hoes to Herbicides, Agriculture and Ground-water Quality." *Journal of Soil and Water Conservation*, November-December 1986.

Halliday, John M. *Convenancing Law and Practice in Scotland*. Vol. 2. Edinburgh: W. Green, 1986.

Hansen, Art, and Della E. McMillan. *Food in Sub-Saharan Africa*. Boulder, Colo.: Lynne Rienner Publishers, 1986.

Harris, Marvin. *Cannibals and Kings*. New York: Random House, 1977.

———. *Cows Pigs Wars and Witches*. New York: Vintage/Random House, 1974.

———. *The Sacred Cow and The Abominable Pig*. New York: Touchstone/Simon & Schuster, 1987.

———. "The Revolutionary Hamburger." *Psychology Today*, October 1983.

Harris, Marvin, and Eric B. Ross. "How Beef Became King." *Psychology Today*, October 1978.

———. *Food and Evolution*. Philadelphia: Temple University Press, 1987.

"Health Groups Find Consensus on Fat in Diet." *Science News* 137, March 3, 1990, 132.

Hersey, Robert D. "Meatpacker Fined a Record Amount on Plant Injuries." *New York Times*, October 29, 1988.

Hess, John L., and Karen Hess. *The Taste of America*. New York: Penguin, 1977.

Hindhede, M. "The Effect of Food Restriction During War on Mortality in Copenhagen." *Journal of the American Medical Association*, February 7, 1920, 381.

Hinman, Robert B., et al. *The Story of Meat*. Chicago: Swift, 1939.

Hodgson, Harlow J. "Forages, Ruminant Livestock, and Food." *BioScience* 26:10 (1976), 625–630.

Hooker, Richard J. *Food and Drink in America*. Indianapolis: Bobbs-Merrill, 1981.

Hough, Emerson. *The Passing of the Frontier*. New Haven: Yale University Press, 1920.

Howe, Geoffrey, et al. "A Cohort Study of Fat Intake and the Risk of Breast Cancer." *Journal of National Cancer Institute* 85:5 (March 1991).

International Institute for Environment and Development and World Resources Institute. *World Resources, 1987*. Rangeland Conditions. New York: Basic Books, c. 1987.

"The Irrational Connection Between Diet and Demeanor." *Psychology Today*, October 1989, 14.

Ingersol, Bruce. "Worker Injuries Highest in Meat Packing." *Los Angeles Times*, October 18, 1978.

Isaac, Erich. "On the Domestication of Cattle," *Science* (137), July 20, 1962, 195–204.

Ivanovich, David. "Texas Research Team Produces Genetically Engineered Calves." *Houston Chronicle*, June 8, 1990.

Jackson, Jack. *Los Mestenos: Spanish Ranching in Texas, 1721–1821*. College Station: Texas A&M University Press, 1986.

Jackson, Kenneth T. *Crabgrass Frontier*. New York: Oxford University Press, 1985.

Jacobs, Lynn. "Amazing Graze: How the Livestock Industry is Ruining the American West." In *Desertification Control Bulletin* No. 17. Nairobi, Kenya: United Nations Environmental Program, 1988.

Jacobson, Jodi. *Environmental Refugees: A Yardstick of Habitability*. Worldwatch Paper No. 86. Washington D.C.: Worldwatch Institute, 1988.

"Japanese Investing in Beef Plants." *Beef*, September 1988.

Jarvis, Lovell S. *Livestock Development in Latin America*. Washington, D.C.: World Bank, 1986.

Jensen, Rue, and Donald R. Mackey. *Diseases of Feedlot Cattle*. Philadelphia: Lea & Febiger, 1965.

Kenney, Jeannine, and Dick Fallert. "Livestock Hormones in the United States." *National Food Review*, July–September 1989, 21.

Kerr, Marion, and Nicola Charles, "Servers and providers: the distribution of food within the family." *The Sociological Review* 34:1 (February 1986).

Kester, Warren. "A Biotech Marvel." *Beef*, February 1990.

Kohls, Richard L., and Joseph N. Uhl. *Marketing of Agricultural Products*. New York: Macmillan, 1990.

Kolata, Gina. "Animal Fat Is Tied to Colon Cancer." *New York Times*, December 13, 1990.

Kosambi, Damodar. *An Introduction to the Study of Indian History*. Bombay: Popular Prakshan, 1975.

Krebs, A. V. *Heading Towards the Last Roundup: The Big Three's Prime Cut*. Des Moines: Prairie Fire Rural Action, June 1990.

Kroc, Ray. *Grinding It Out: The Making of McDonald's.* Chicago: Henry Regnery, 1977.

Kwitny, Jonathan. *Vicious Cycles: The Mafia in the Marketplace,* New York: W. W. Norton, 1979.

Lancaster, John. "Public Land, Private Profit." *Washington Post,* February 17, 1991.

Lappé, Frances Moore. *Diet for a Small Planet.* New York: Ballantine Books, 1982.

Lappé, Frances Moore, and Joseph Collins. *Food First: Beyond the Myth of Scarcity.* New York: Ballantine Books, 1978.

———. *World Hunger: Twelve Myths.* New York: Grove Press, 1986.

Lawrence, Elizabeth Atwood. *Rodeo.* Knoxville: The University of Tennessee Press, 1982.

Leary, Warren. "Young Women Are Getting Fatter Study Finds." *New York Times,* February 23, 1989.

Leeds, Anthony and Andrew P. Vayda. *Man, Culture, and Animals.* Washington, D.C.: American Association for the Advancement of Science, 1965.

Lévi-Strauss, Claude. *The Origin of Table Manners.* New York: Harper & Row, 1978.

Lincoln, Bruce. *Priests, Warriors, and Cattle.* Berkeley: University of California Press, 1981.

Linden, Eugene. "Playing With Fire." *Time,* September 18, 1989.

Locke, John. *Two Treatises of Government,* ed. Peter Laslett. Cambridge, England: Cambridge University Press, 1967.

Lofchie, Michael F. "The External Determinants of Africa's Agrarian Crisis." In W. Ladd Hollist and F. LaMont Tullis, *Pursuing Food Security.* Boulder, Colo.: Lynne Rienner, 1987.

Lonsdale, Steven. *Animals and the Origins of Dance.* London: Thames & Hudson, 1982.

Lundholm, B. "Domestic Animals in Arid Systems." *Ecol. Bull., Stockholm* 24, 1976, 29.

Luoma, Jon R. "Discouraging Words." *Audubon* 88, September 1986.

Madison, Robert J., and Jilann O. Brunett. "Overview of the Occurence of Nitrate in Ground Water in the United States." Water-Supply Paper 2275. In United States Geological Survey, *National Water Summary, 1984.* Washington, D.C.: U.S. Government Printing Office, 1985.

Mahar, Dennis J. *Government Policies and Deforestation in Brazil's Amazon Region.* Washington, D.C.: World Bank, 1989.

Malone, Michael P., ed. *Historians and the American West.* Lincoln: University of Nebraska Press, 1983.

Malthus, Thomas Robert. *Population: The First Essay.* Ann Arbor: Ann Arbor Paperbacks/University of Michigan Press, 1959.

Mann, Robert. "Development and the Sahel Disaster: The Case at Gambia." *The Ecologist*, March/June 1987.

Marston, Ruth M., and Susan O. Welsh. "Nutrient Content of the U.S. Food Supply, 1982." *National Food Review*, NFR-25, c. 1982.

Mason, Jim. "Taking Stock: From Farm to Slaughter." *Animals' Agenda*, April 1991, 16–23.

Mason, Jim, and Peter Singer. *Animal Factories*. New York: Harmony Books, 1990.

McCaull, Julian, and Janice Crossland. *Water Pollution*. New York: Harcourt Brace Jovanovich, 1974.

McCormick, John, and Bill Turque. "America's Outback." *Newsweek*, October 9, 1989.

McDonald, Archie P., ed. *Shooting Stars*. Bloomington: Indiana University Press, 1987.

McHugh, Tom. *The Time of the Buffalo*. New York: Knopf, 1972.

McNair, Joel. "Bypass Protein Still Safe." Wisconsin State Journal, Madison: July 21, 1991.

McWilliams, Carey. *Factories in the Field*. Santa Barbara, Calif.: Peregrine, 1971.

Meek, Theophile. *Hebrew Origins*. New York: Harper & Brothers, 1950.

Mercatante, Anthony S. *Zoo of the Gods*. New York: Harper & Row, 1974.

Mettlin, Curtis J., and M. Steven Piver. "A Case-Control Study of Milk Drinking and Ovarian Cancer Risk." *American Journal of Epidemiology* 132:5 (1990), 871.

Meyers, Norman. *The Primary Source*. New York: Norton, 1983.

Meyn, Klaus. *Beef Production in East Africa*. Munich: Weltforum-Verlag, 1970.

Milas, Seifulaziz. "Desert Spread and Population Boom." United Nations Environment Program, Desertification Control Bulletin, December 1984.

Mintzer, Irvin. *A Matter of Degrees: The Potential for Controlling the Greenhouse Effect*. World Reources Institute Research Report No. 5. Washington, D.C.: World Resources Institute, 1987.

Moffat, Anne Simon. "China: A Living Lab For Epidemiology." *Science* 248, May 4, 1990.

Monastersky, Richard. "The Fall of the Forest." *Science News* 138, July 21, 1990.

Moran, Victoria. "They Used to Call them Slaughterhouses." *Animals' Agenda*, April 1991, 40–45.

Mtetwa, Jonathan. *Man and Cattle in Africa*. Fort Lauderdale: Verlag Breitenbach, 1982.

Nash, Roderick. *Wilderness and the American Mind.* New Haven: Yale University Press, 1982.

National Association of Federal Veterinarians, Edward L. Menning. "Statement Present to the National Academy of Sciences Committee on Evaluation of the U.S. Department of Agriculture's Inspection System for Cattle." Washington, D.C., January 23, 1990.

National Cancer Institute. *Fact Book 1989.* Bethesda, Md.: National Cancer Institute, 1989.

National Cattlemen's Foundation. "Public Concerns About Animal Care Are Limited." Press Release. Denver, December 19, 1989.

National Research Council, Board on Agriculture. *Alternative Agriculture.* Washington, D.C.: National Academy Press, 1989.

Nations, James D. *Tropical Rainforests, Endangered Environment.* New York: Franklin Watts, 1988.

Nevins, Allan. *Ford: The Times, The Man, The Company.* New York: Scribners, 1954.

Newkirk, Ingrid. *Save the Animals.* New York: Warner, c. 1990.

Nyberg, Bartell. "ConAgra Exercising Option to Buy SIPCO," *Denver Post,* July 25, 1989.

Oddy, Derek, and Derke Miller. *The Making of the Modern British Diet.* Totowa, N.J.: Rowman & Littlefield, 1976.

Office of Technology Assessment, U.S. Congress. *Technologies to Sustain Tropical Forest Resources.* OTA-F-214. Washington, D.C.: Office of Technology Assessment, March 1984.

Okie, Susan. "Health Crisis Confronts 1.3 Billion." *The Washington Post,* September 25, 1989.

Olsen, Jack. *Slaughter the Animals, Poison the Earth.* New York: Simon & Schuster, 1971.

Ostendorf, David L. "The Social Costs of Meatpacking Industry." *Des Moines Register,* June 28, 1990.

Pain, Stephanie. "Mad Cows and Ministers Lose Their Head." *New Scientist,* August 11, 1968.

Parsons, James J. "The Scourge of Cows." *Whole Earth Review,* Spring 1988.

Partridge, Eric. *Origins: A Short Etymological Dictionary of Modern English.* New York: Greenwich House, 1983.

Patterson, Mrs. Edna B. "Early Cattle in Elko County." *Nevada Historical Society Quarterly* 30:2 (Summer 1987).

Pearce, Fred. "Methane: The Hidden Greenhouse Gas." *New Scientist,* May 6, 1989, 37–41.

———. "Felled Trees Deal Double Blow to Global Warming." *New Scientist,* September 16, 1989.

Pendle, George. *Uruguay.* London: Oxford University Press, 1963.

Perlez, Jane. "Dinkaland, Where Cattle Are Treated Like Equals." *New York Times*, July 18, 1990, A4.

Pimentel, David. *Food, Energy, and the Future of Society*. Boulder: Colo. Associated University Press, 1980.

————. "Waste in Agriculture and Food Sectors: Environmental and Social Costs." Draft Commissioned by the Gross National Waste Product Forum, Arlington, Virginia, 1989.

Pimentel, David, and Carl W. Hall. *Food and Natural Resources*. San Diego: Academic Press, 1989.

Pimentel, David, and Marcia Pimentel. *Food, Energy and Society*. New York: Wiley, 1979.

Pimentel, David, et al. "Energy and Land Constraints in Food Protein Production." *Science* 190.

Pirke, Karl M., and Detlev Ploog. "Biology of Human Starvation." In Pierre J. V. Beaumont, et al., eds., *Eating Disorders*. Part I. New York: Elsevier Publishers B.V., 1987.

Pizzey, Erin. *Scream Quietly or the Neighbors Will Hear*. Harmondsworth, England: Penguin, 1974.

Postel, Sandra. *Water: Rethinking Management in an Age of Scarcity*. Washington, D.C.: Worldwatch Institute, 1984.

Powers, Pauline S. *Obesity: The Regulation of Weight*. Baltimore, Md.: Wilkins & Wilkins, 1980.

Putnam, Judith Jones. "Food Consumption." *National Food Review* 13:3 (November 20, 1990).

Pye, Veronica I., et al. *Groundwater Contamination in the United States*. Philadelphia: University of Pennsylvania Press, 1983.

Ramanthan, V. R. "Trace Gas Trends and Their Potential Role in Climate Change." *Journal of Geophysical Research* 90 (1985), 5547–66.

Ramirez, Nora E. "The Vaquero and Ranching in the Southwestern United States, 1600–1970." Ph.D. diss., Indiana University, 1979.

Rand, Colleen S. W., and John M. Kuldau. "The Epidemiology of Obesity and Self-Defined Weight Problem in the General Population." *International Journal of Eating Disorders* 9:3 (1990), 329–43.

Randall, John Herman. *The Making of the Modern Mind*. Cambridge, Mass: Houghton Mifflin, 1940.

Rangley, W. R. "Irrigation and Drainage in the World." Paper delivered at the International Conference on Food and Water, College Station, Texas A&M University, May 26–30, 1985.

Reader, John. "Human Ecology: How Land Shapes Society." *New Scientist*, September 8, 1988.

Regenstein, L. *How to Survive in America the Poisoned*. Herndon, Va.: Acropolis, 1982.

Reisner, Marc. *Cadillac Desert*. New York: Penguin, 1986.

Repetto, Robert. "Renewable Resources and Population Growth: Past Experiences and Future Prospects." *Population and Environment* 10:3 (Summer 1989).

Repetto, Robert C. *The Forest for the Trees?* Washington, D.C.: World Resources Institute, c. 1988.

Revel, Jacques. "A Capital City's Privileges: Food Supplies in Early-Modern Rome." In Robert Forster, and Oreste Ranum, eds., *Food and Drink in History*. Baltimore: Johns Hopkins University Press, 1979.

Revkin, Andrew. *The Burning Season*. Boston: Houghton Mifflin, 1990.

———. "Endless Summer." *Discover* 9, October 1988.

Richter, Jay. "Washington Report." *Beef*, July 1989.

Rifkin, Jeremy. *Biosphere Politics: A New Consciousness for a New Century*. New York: Crown, 1991.

Rifkin, Jeremy, ed. *The Green Lifestyle Handbook*. New York: Owl Book, 1990.

Rifkin, Jeremy, and Ted Howard. *Entropy: Into the Greenhouse World*. New York: Bantam, 1989.

Ritchie, Carson I. A. *Food in Civilization: How History Has Been Affected by Human Tastes*. New York: Beaufort, 1981.

Ritson, Christopher, Leslie Gofton, and John McKenzie, eds. *The Food Consumer*. New York: John Wiley, 1986.

Ritvo, Harriet. *The Animal Estate*. Cambridge, Mass.: Harvard University Press, 1987.

Robbins, John. *Diet for a New America*. Walpole, N.H.: Stillpoint, 1987.

Ross, Eric B. *Beyond the Myths of Culture*. New York: Academic Press, 1980.

Rothblum, Esther D. "Women and Weight: Fad and Fiction," *Journal of Psychology* 124, January 1990.

Royte, Elizabeth. "Showdown in Cattle Country." *New York Times Magazine*, December 16, 1990.

Rule, Sheila. "Fatal Illness in Cows Leads to British Inquiry." *New York Times*, May 20, 1990.

Sahlins, Marshall. *Culture and Practical Reason*. Chicago: University of Chicago Press, 1976.

Salisbury, David F. "When Cattle Encroach on the Jungle." *Christian Science Monitor*, May 14, 1980.

Savage, William W., Jr. *The Cowboy Hero*. Norman: University of Oklahoma Press, 1979.

Sayce, A. H. "Bull (*Semitic*)." *Encyclopedia of Religion and Ethics*. Vol. 2. New York: Scribners, 1911, 888.

Schein, Harry. "The Olympian Cowboy." *The American Scholar*, Summer 1955.

Schery, Robert. "Migration of a Plant." *Natural History* 74, December 1965.

Schneider, Keith. "AIDS-like Cow Virus Found at Unexpectedly High Rate." *New York Times*, June 1, 1991.

———. "Mediating the Federal War of the Jungle." *New York Times*, July 9, 1991, 4E.

———. "Texas Researchers Develop 4 Gene-Altered Calves." *New York Times*, June 8, 1990.

Scobie, James R. *Argentina: A City and a Nation*. New York: Oxford University Press, 1971.

Secretariat of the United Nations Conference on Desertification. *Desertification: Its Causes and Consequences*. New York: Pergamon Press, 1977.

Selzer, Richard. *Taking the World In for Repairs*. New York: Morrow, 1986.

Serpell, James. *In the Company of Animals*. New York: Basil Blackwell, 1988.

Shabecoff, Philip. "Loss of Tropical Forests Is Found Much Worse Than Was Thought." *New York Times*, June 8, 1990.

Shagam, Shayle, and Linda Bailey. "World Meat Consumption and Trade Patterns." *National Food Review*, January–March 1989.

Shannon, Fred A. *The Farmer's Last Frontier Agriculture, 1860–1897*. Armonk, N.Y.: M. E. Sharpe, 1973.

Shepperson, Wilbur S. "The Maverick and the Cowboy." *Nevada Historical Society Quarterly* 30:2 (Summer 1987).

Shoumotoff, Alex. "Murder in the Rain Forest." *Vanity Fair*, April 1989.

Silver, Timothy. *A New Face on the Countryside*. Cambridge, England: Cambridge University Press, 1990.

Simons, Marlise. "Global Warming Tied to Fires Set in Amazon." *New York Times*, August 12, 1988.

Simoons, Frederick J. *Eat Not This Flesh: Food Avoidances in the Old World*. Madison: University of Wisconsin Press, 1961.

Simoons, Frederick J., and Elizabeth S. Simoons. *A Ceremonial Ox of India*. Madison: University of Wisconsin Press, 1968.

Sinclair, Upton. *The Jungle*. With an Introduction and Notes By James R. Barrett. Urbana: University of Illinois Press, 1988.

Singer, Peter. *Animal Liberation*. Willingborough, England: Northants, Thorsons, 1983.

Singh, Shamsher. *Sub-Saharan Agriculture*. Washington, D.C.: World Bank, 1983.

Skaggs, Jimmy M. *Prime Cut*. College Station: Texas A & M University Press, 1986.

Slater, Gilbert. *The English Peasantry and the Enclosure of Common Fields*. New York: Augustus M. Kelley, 1968.

Slatta, Richard W. *Cowboys of the Americas*. New Haven: Yale University Press, 1990.

Smith, Richard A., and Richard B. Alexander. "Trends in Concentration of Dissolved Solids, Suspended Sediments, Phosphorous, and Inorganic Nitrogen . . ." In United States Geological Survey, *National Water Summary, 1984*. Water-Supply Paper 2275. Washington, D.C.: U.S. Government Printing Office, 1985.

Smith, Henry Nash. *Virgin Land*. Cambridge, Mass.: Harvard University Press, 1950.

Soler, Jean. "The Semiotics of Food in the Bible." In Robert Forster and Oreste Ranum, eds. *Food and Drink in History*. Baltimore: Johns Hopkins University Press, 1979.

Sorre, Max. "The Geography of Diet." In Philip L. Wagner and Marvin W. Mikesell, *Readings in Cultural Geography*. Chicago: University of Chicago Press, 1962.

Stone, Roger D. *Dreams of Amazonia*. New York: Penguin, 1986.

"A Story of Success." *Beef*, July 1990.

Sugarman, Carole. "Lower-Fat Fast Food." *Washington Post*, Health section, July 31, 1990.

Super, John C., and Thomas C. Wright. *Food, Politics, and Society in Latin America*. Lincoln: University of Nebraska Press, 1985.

Suplee, Curt. "Slave of the Lawn." *Washington Post Magazine*, April 30, 1989.

"Surgeon General Tells America to Stop Chewing the Fat." *New Scientist*, August 4, 1988.

Swanson, Wayne, and George Schultz. *Prime Rip*. Englewood Cliffs, N.J.: Prentice-Hall, 1982.

Tannahill, Reay. *Food in History*. New York: Stein and Day, 1973.

"Task Force Charges Beef Packer Monopoly." *Beef*, June 1990.

Taylor, Lonn, and Ingrid Maar. *The American Cowboy*. Washington, D.C.: Library of Congress, 1983.

Thomas, Verl M. *Beef Cattle Production*. Philadelphia: Lea & Febiger, 1986.

Thomas, Keith. *Man And The Natural World*. New York: Pantheon Books, 1983.

Tuan, Yi-fu. *Dominance and Affection: The Making of Pets*. New Haven: Yale University Press, c. 1984.

Tullis, F. LaMond, and W. Ladd Hollist, eds. *Food, the State, and International Political Economy*. Lincoln: University of Nebraska Press, 1986.

Turner, Frederick J. *The Significance of the Frontier in American History*. Ann Arbor, Mich.: University Microfilms, Inc., 1894.

Twigg, Julia. "Food For Thought: Purity and Vegetarianism." *Religion* 9, Spring 1979.

———. "Vegetarianism and the Meanings of Meat." In Anne Murcott, ed., *The Sociology of Food and Eating*. Croft, Aldershot, England: Gower Publishing Company Ltd., 1983.

United Nations Environment Programme. *Desertification Control Bulletin.* Nairobi, Kenya: UNEP, No. 15, 1987.

U.S. Department of Agriculture. *Economic Research Service, World Agricultural Supply and Demand Estiimates.* Washington, D.C.: USDA, July 1991, WASDE-256.

———. Food Safety and Inspection Service. Public Docket No. 83-008P, 53 *Federal Register* 48262, November 30, 1988. Public Comments on Food Safety and Inspection Service Proposed Rule on Streamlined Inspection System for Meat Safety; comments of the Public Accountability Project, May 15, 1989.

———. *Marketing, U.S. Agriculture: 1988 Yearbook of Agriculture.* Washington, D.C.: U.S. Government Printing Office, 1988.

———. *1982 Yearbook of Agriculture.* Washington, D.C.: U.S. Government Printing Office, 1982.

U.S. Department of Commerce. Bureau of the Census, *Statistical Abstract of the United States 1990.*

U.S. Department of Health and Human Services. Public Health Service, Centers for Disease Control, National Center for Health Statistics. Thomas Stephens, *The Prevalence of Overweight and Obesity in Britain, Canada, and the United States.* Washington, D.C.: U.S. Government Printing Office.

U.S. Forest Service. USDA. *An Assessment of the Forest and Range Land Situation in the United States.* Washington, D.C.: Government Printing Office, 1988.

U.S. Public Health Service. Office of the Surgeon General. *The Surgeon General's Report on Nutrition & Health.* New York: Warner, c. 1989.

Vansickle, Joe. "Grazing's in Their Sights." *Beef*, November 1988.

———. "Mad Cow Disease Baffles British." *Beef*, August 1990.

———. "A Tripling by Century's End." *Beef*, August 1990.

Viedma, Christiane. "A Health Nutrition Atlas." *World Health*, May 1988.

Vines, Gail. "Diet, Drugs, and Heart Disease." *New Scientist*, February 25, 1989.

Viola, Herman J. *After Columbus: The Smithsonian Chronicle of the North American Indian.* New York: Orion Books, 1990.

Vocke, Gary. "The Changing Nature of World Agriculture." *National Food Review*, April-June 1990.

Wald, Johanna, and David Albersworth. *Our Ailing Public Rangelands: Conditions Report–1989.* Washington, D.C.: National Wildlife Federation, October 1989.

Ward, G. M., et al. "Beef Production Options and Requirements for Fossil Fuel." *Science* 198 (1977), 265–71.

Webb, Walter Prescott. *The Great Plains.* Boston: Ginn, 1931.

"What Do You Get If You Cross . . ?" *The Economist*, August 15, 1987, 67–69.

Whitehead, Toby Larry. "Sociocultural Dynamics and Food Habits in a Southern Community." In Mary Douglas, ed., *Food in the Social Order*. New York: Russell Sage Foundation, 1984.

Wildavsky, Ben. "McJobs, Inside America's Largest Youth Training Program." *Policy Review* (49), Summer 1989.

Willett, Walter C., et al. "Relationship of Meat, Fat, and Fiber Intake to the Risk of Colon Cancer in a Prospective Study Among Women." *The New England Journal of Medicine*. 323:24 (1990), 1664–72.

Williams, Gavin. "Introduction: Farmers, Herders and the State." *Rural Africana* 25–26 (Spring-Fall 1986).

Willis, Roy. *Man and Beast*. New York: Basic Books, 1974.

Wilson, C. Anne. *Food and Drink in Britain*. London: Constable, 1973.

World Bank. *Poverty and Hunger*. Washington, D.C.: World Bank, 1986.

World Commission on Environment and Development. *Our Common Future: The Bruntland Commission Report*. Oxford: Oxford University Press, 1987.

World Resources Institute and International Institute for Environment and Development. *World Resources, 1986*. New York: Basic Books, 1986.

———. *World Resources, 1988–89*. New York: Basic Books, 1988.

———. *World Resources 1990–91*. New York: Oxford University Press, 1990.

Wright, Quincy. *A Study of War*. Chicago: University of Chicago Press, 1942.

Wuerthner, George. "The Price Is Wrong." *Sierra*, September/October 1990.

Wurtmann, Richard J., and Judith Wurtman, eds. "Human Obesity." *Annals of the New York Academy of Sciences* 499. New York: New York Academy of Sciences, 1987.

Ziegler, P. Thomas. *The Meat We Eat*. Danville, Ill.: Interstate Publishers, 1966.

Zuckerman, Edward. "How Now to Sell a Cow?" *New York Times Magazine*, November 29, 1987.

INDEX

TIMELY ADVICE

(0452)

☐ **HOW TO GAIN AN EXTRA HOUR EVERY DAY by Ray Josephs.** This is the book that can give you the extra hour you *wish* you had. Acclaimed as the bible of effective time-management in Japan, this completely updated edition presents over 1,000 tips for eliminating routine tasks and distractions in every part of your life. (267838—$11.00)

☐ **THE 90-MINUTE HOUR *Using Time Extension to Get the Most Out of Every Hour* by Jay Conrad Levinson.** Here is the first time-management book to combine technology with the latest psychological research in order to reduce the stress level of a heavy work load. This revolutionary approach demonstrates the difference between working hard and working smart. (265967—$9.00)

☐ **HOW TO GET A BETTER JOB IN THIS CRAZY WORLD by Robert Half.** In this important and insightful book, America's #1 authority on job placement guides you to landing the job you want in the challenging, fiercely competitive business environment of the 1990s. (265975—$8.95)

☐ **THE GREAT MARKETING TURNAROUND *The Age of the Individual—and How to Profit from It* by Stan Rapp and Tom Collins.** Filled with case histories and dollars-and-sense inspiration, this new triumph will show business readers how to cast off outmoded marketing strategies and begin to implement the great marketing turnaround in their own organizations. (267498—$12.00)

Prices slightly higher in Canada.

Buy them at your local bookstore or use this convenient coupon for ordering.

PENGUIN USA
P.O. Box 999, Dept. #17109
Bergenfield, New Jersey 07621

Please send me the books I have checked above.
I am enclosing $_____ (please add $2.00 to cover postage and handling). Send check or money order (no cash or C.O.D.'s) or charge by Mastercard or VISA (with a $15.00 minimum). Prices and numbers are subject to change without notice.

Card # _____ Exp. Date _____
Signature _____
Name _____
Address _____
City _____ State _____ Zip Code _____

For faster service when ordering by credit card call **1-800-253-6476**

Allow a minimum of 4-6 weeks for delivery. This offer is subject to change without notice